Notable British Trials Series No. 85

TRIAL OF

# LOUISE MASSET

EDITED BY

Kate Clarke

LONDON
MANGO BOOKS

First edition published 2018 (Hardcover)
This edition 2019 (Softcover)

Copyright © Kate Clarke, 2018, 2019

The right of Kate Clarke to be identified as the author of this work has been asserted in accordance with the Copyright, Designs & Patents Act 1988.

All rights reserved. No part of this book may be reprinted or reproduced or utilised in any form or by any electronic, mechanical or other means, now known or hereafter invented, including photocopying and recording, or in any information storage or retrieval system, without the prior permission in writing of the publishers.

ISBN: 978-1-911273-27-1 (hardcover)
ISBN: 978-1-911273-59-2 (softcover)
ISBN: 978-1-911273-28-8 (ebook)

Notable British Trials imprint ©William Hodge & Company (Holdings) Ltd
Used with kind permission.

Cover illustration of Louise Masset at her trial by William Hartley
Courtesy of the Mayor's Office of Policing and Crime.

General Editors:
David Green - M.W. Oldridge - Adam Wood

Published by Mango Books
www.mangobooks.co.uk
18 Soho Square
London W1D 3QL

Notable British Trials Series No. 85

# TRIAL OF
# LOUISE MASSET

EDITED BY

Kate Clarke

Louise Masset sketched by court artist William Hartley
*Courtesy of the Mayor's Office of Policing and Crime*

# CONTENTS.

Introduction .................................................... 1
Leading Dates................................................... 61

THE TRIAL —

### FIRST DAY — WEDNESDAY 13th DECEMBER 1899.

Opening Speech for the Prosecution................................ 69

| | | | |
|---|---|---|---|
| Frederick Humphreys.............. | 72 | Ernest Mooney..................... | 80 |
| Eleanor Gentle .................. | 72 | Thomas Bonner .................... | 81 |
| Léonie Cadisch................... | 77 | Georgina Worley................... | 81 |
| Maud Clifford.................... | 79 | Kate Swaker....................... | 82 |

### SECOND DAY — THURSDAY 14th DECEMBER 1899.

| | | | |
|---|---|---|---|
| Ellen Reece...................... | 83 | Alice Riall ...................... | 105 |
| Clara Haas ...................... | 99 | John Findlay...................... | 106 |
| Mary Teahan...................... | 99 | Ann Skeet......................... | 106 |
| Margaret Biggs................... | 100 | Henry Court....................... | 106 |
| Thomas Hall...................... | 100 | William Brown..................... | 106 |
| Joseph Standing ................. | 100 | Richard Nursey.................... | 106 |
| David Bunday..................... | 101 | Richard Cadisch .................. | 108 |
| James Patmore ................... | 102 | Alice Sonnenthal ................. | 108 |
| Eudore Lucas .................... | 102 | | |

### THIRD DAY — FRIDAY 15th DECEMBER 1899.

| | | | |
|---|---|---|---|
| George Simes..................... | 109 | Marion Fitzgerald................. | 114 |
| William Burch.................... | 111 | James Fennell..................... | 114 |
| Henry Willis..................... | 112 | Charles Jackman................... | 116 |
| William Bowers................... | 112 | Thomas Bond....................... | 117 |
| John Whittle..................... | 112 | Frederick Forth [recalled]........ | 117 |
| Frederick Forth.................. | 112 | James Fennell [recalled].......... | 117 |
| Horace Baker .................... | 113 | Louise Masset..................... | 118 |

Masset.

### FOURTH DAY — SATURDAY 16th DECEMBER 1899.

Louise Masset. . . . . . . . . . . . . . . . . . . . . . . . 133    Eleanor Gentle [recalled] . . . . . . . . . . . . . . 185

### FIFTH DAY — MONDAY 18th DECEMBER 1899.

Closing Speech for the Prosecution . . . . . . . . . . . . . . . . . . . . . . . . . . . . . . . . . . . . . . . 187
Speech for the Defence. . . . . . . . . . . . . . . . . . . . . . . . . . . . . . . . . . . . . . . . . . . . . . . . 188
Judge's Summing Up . . . . . . . . . . . . . . . . . . . . . . . . . . . . . . . . . . . . . . . . . . . . . . . . . 190
The Verdict. . . . . . . . . . . . . . . . . . . . . . . . . . . . . . . . . . . . . . . . . . . . . . . . . . . . . . . . . 206

Appendices. . . . . . . . . . . . . . . . . . . . . . . . . . . . . . . . . . . . . . . . . . . . . . . . . . . . . . . . . 209
Index. . . . . . . . . . . . . . . . . . . . . . . . . . . . . . . . . . . . . . . . . . . . . . . . . . . . . . . . . . . . . . 253
Notable British Trials Series. . . . . . . . . . . . . . . . . . . . . . . . . . . . . . . . . . . . . . . . . . . . 259

# LIST OF ILLUSTRATIONS.

Louise Masset at her trial . . . . . . . . . . . . . . . . . . . . . . . . . . . . . . . . . . . . . . . . . *Frontispiece*
Dalston Junction Railway Station . . . . . . . . . . . . . . . . . . . . . . . . . . . . . *facing page* . . . . . . . 4
Manfred Masset's jacket and the shawl found over his body. . . . . . . . . . . . . . . " . . . . . . . . . 4
The body of Manfred Masset as photographed in the morgue. . . . . . . . . . . . . " . . . . . . . . . 4
Manfred Masset. . . . . . . . . . . . . . . . . . . . . . . . . . . . . . . . . . . . . . . . . . . . . . . " . . . . . . . . 14
The clinker brick found at the murder scene . . . . . . . . . . . . . . . . . . . . . . . . . " . . . . . . . . 72
Mr Charles Mathews QC . . . . . . . . . . . . . . . . . . . . . . . . . . . . . . . . . . . . . . . " . . . . . . . . 72
Lord Coleridge QC . . . . . . . . . . . . . . . . . . . . . . . . . . . . . . . . . . . . . . . . . . . " . . . . . . . . 88
London Railways Schematic . . . . . . . . . . . . . . . . . . . . . . . . . . . . . . . . . . . . " . . . . . . . 108
Diagram of London Bridge Railway Station . . . . . . . . . . . . . . . . . . . . . . . . . " . . . . . . . 132
Mr Justice Bruce . . . . . . . . . . . . . . . . . . . . . . . . . . . . . . . . . . . . . . . . . . . . . " . . . . . . . 192

# LOUISE MASSET.

## INTRODUCTION.

### I.

There is no human creature in this country, or in any other, so defenceless as an illegitimate child, for the simple reason that, while it is to nobody's material advantage to keep it alive, there are obvious reasons why its death would be welcome. Deprived, in almost every case, of a father's protection, and a cause of disgrace to relatives who might otherwise have taken an affectionate interest in it, the poor thing has but one refuge – its mother's love.[1]

The setting for the shocking murder of three year old Manfred Louis Masset was London, 1899, towards the end of Queen Victoria's reign, an era of great industry and innovation despite the gloomy spectre of the Widow of Windsor. A familiar figure, seemingly weighed down with impenetrable sorrow and swathes of black bombazine, she had remained monumentally morose, apparently surrendering herself (at least in public) to an all-consuming grief for the loss of Prince Albert.

During her reign, the London district of Stoke Newington had spawned numerous schools and academies, exclusively for young ladies.[2] The murdered boy's mother, a thirty-six year old Anglo-French woman called Louise Josephine Jemima Masset, worked as a governess offering lessons in French and music. On 24 April 1896, at 17 Highgate Hill, Holloway,[3] Louise gave birth to an illegitimate son, Manfred Louis. His French father – supposedly named Maurice Mason, but conspicuous by his absence on Manfred's birth certificate – returned to France in August 1898, but (according to Louise) he continued to pay maintenance for the child. That same year, Louise moved in with her married sister, Léonie Ernestine Mary Anne Cadisch, and her husband, Richard, a Swiss commission merchant, at 29 Bethune Road, Stoke Newington. Her mother, Elizabeth Armstrong, lived next door.[4] In August 1898 – at or around the time

---

1 *Pall Mall Gazette*, 19 December 1899.
2 In 1875, directly after Edwin Bartlett married his young wife, Adelaide, he sent her to one of these establishments for two years to complete her education. See editor's book, *In the Interests of Science: Adelaide Bartlett and the Pimlico Poisoning*.
3 This was the home of Mrs Eliza Ballard, a certified midwife, who was probably running a bona fide lying-in establishment catering for the birth of illegitimate babies. Such establishments were often used as cover for nefarious baby-farming activities.
4 Elizabeth Rebecca Reffell, Louise Masset's mother, married Ernest Etienne Masset, who died in 1877, aged 43. He was described as a foreign correspondent. In 1883, she married Peter William Armstrong, who died on 27 September 1899. Louise Masset formally witnessed her mother's remarriage, as she had her sister Léonie's marriage in 1882.

# Masset.

of the shadowy Mason's departure for the continent – Mrs Armstrong took in a lodger, a French trainee correspondence clerk of approximately eighteen years of age called Eudore Lucas.[5] Probably because of their French connections, he became friendly with the occupants of number 29.

Louise's baby was not welcomed by members of her family – indeed, she had always refused to divulge the father's name – and so, at three weeks old, he was placed in the care of a children's nurse called Eleanor Eliza Gentle, known as Nellie, a single woman living at 210 Clyde Road, South Tottenham, with her mother, Sarah, who had remarried and was now Mrs Norris. Though Manfred was a nurse-child, Nellie was genuinely fond of him and cared for him very well. She had previously been employed by a clergyman and his family, but, when her mother's health deteriorated, she wished to remain at home, and so she advertised for a nurse-child to look after. Louise Masset responded to Nellie's advertisement, and an agreement was reached. The monthly fee of £1 17s was paid by the child's father, with Léonie Cadisch acting as guarantor. Louise seemed fond of the child and at first visited him every couple of weeks; after he reached the age of two, she would endeavour to see him every Wednesday and, if the weather was fine, take him for walks on Tottenham Green, which was only ten minutes away from Nellie Gentle's home.

On the morning of 16 October 1899, Nellie's mother, Mrs Norris, received a letter from Louise informing her that Manfred's father wanted him to live in France. The letter read:

> Dear Mrs Norris,
>
> I thought I should be able to see Manfred last Friday, but was obliged to meet his father who came over quite unexpectedly.
>
> Since I have seen him, I must let you know that Manfred will soon be taken from your care, as his father considers him a big boy now & quite old enough to make a change. He wishes him to be brought up in a cousin's family so that he can have him under his personal supervision, & he must also start the French language which at his age can be picked up very quickly.
>
> I am very sorry to remove him from your loving care, but if I raise any objection I shall simply be interfering with his future welfare & prospects.
>
> Shall be over on Wednesday & will talk matters over with you again, but thought it wise to give you as long a notice as I possibly could.
>
> Was glad after all we had had the Dr. as I was satisfied that the little chap was not in for worse than an indigestion & was able to tell his father so.

---

5   He was no more than eighteen in August 1898, when he and Louise moved to neighbouring properties on Bethune Road.

# Introduction.

Love & kisses for him, & kindest regards to you & daughter.
Yours truly,
Louise Masset.

There followed a postscript:

Will bring over the shoes he tried on lately for the house as his clothing will be seen to in his new home & there is no need for him to carry over too much luggage.[6]

Louise subsequently visited as usual on Wednesday 18 October and arranged to collect the child on Friday 27 October, saying she would take him to London Bridge Station; from there, she would travel by rail to Newhaven, and then catch the ferry to France where she would hand him over to his father's cousin.

Though saddened to part with him, Nellie Gentle did as she was asked, dressing little Manfred in a blue serge frock and cloth coat, and tucking his 'baby curls' under a jaunty red sailor's hat with *HMS Raven* on the front.[7] She also packed two brown paper parcels, one containing a bundle of spare clothes, and the other the boy's new favourite toy – a set of miniature scales on which he liked to weigh small objects, and which had been gifted to him by his mother on 25 October – to amuse him on his journey. The arranged meeting point was a public house called the Birdcage, half a mile away on Stamford Hill – a short tram ride. Nellie and Manfred were early. Louise arrived at about 12.45 pm, still draped in the black mourning attire she'd worn since her stepfather's death a few weeks before; she was also carrying a Gladstone bag, borrowed from her brother-in-law. After some tearful farewells, Nellie placed the child on a seat in a horse-drawn omnibus, and, at 12.48 pm, watched as the bus drew the fretful child and his mother on their way to London Bridge Railway Station.

However, Louise had, in fact, secretly made quite a different arrangement for that weekend, and, as she made her way to London Bridge that morning, she had no intention of catching the ferry. For some time she had been concealing an amorous attachment to her neighbour, young Eudore Lucas. When they met at Liverpool Street Station on Wednesday 25 October, they arranged to spend the following weekend together in Brighton; they would book separate rooms, numbers 10 and 11, as brother and sister, in the name of Brooks, at Mr Findlay's

---

[6] TNA:PRO CRIM 1/58/5. The doctor had been called to attend Manfred on 11 and 12 October after he had developed sickness and a rash.
[7] Although dressing infant boys and girls in similar clothing had largely gone out of vogue by the 1930s, the cutting of a boy's 'baby curls' at about three years old was considered a milestone in his development and a ritual visit to the barber was still celebrated as late as the 1950s.

# Masset.

Hotel at 36 Queens Road.[8] As Lucas was unable to leave work until Saturday, she would meet his train from London at Brighton Station at about 3.00 pm. Her movements after she and little Manfred arrived at London Bridge Station will emerge as the story unfolds during the subsequent trial.

## II.

At 6.19 pm that Friday evening, two young students, Mary Teahan and her friend, Margaret Ellen Biggs, alighted from their train at Dalston Junction Station. They were on their way to a French lecture at a school in Tottenham Road; the train had run fourteen minutes late, and they hurried to the ladies' waiting room on platform 3 so that Mary Teahan could use the lavatory. She attempted to enter one of the two cubicles, but noticed 'a dark object on the floor, lying at right angles to the door when it was closed'. Stooping in the darkness, she made out a face. Margaret alerted a porter, Joseph Standing, saying that, 'there was someone ill in the waiting room'; Standing, after inspecting the scene for himself, called for assistance from the station inspector, David Bunday, and he fetched a lamp to illuminate the shocking discovery – the lifeless body of a small child, naked except for a shawl laid across his middle. He had been battered about the face and head, presumably by the decorative clinker brick – broken in two – which was found nearby. The police were called, and Dr James Patrick Fennell, who had a surgery in nearby Dalston Lane, was sent for and arrived shortly before 7.00 pm, examining the body before ordering its removal to the mortuary. A description of the murdered child was issued to the press; several newspapers printed it in their Saturday editions. At this point, nobody knew who he was, or had been.

In the meantime, Louise, presumably unaware of the gruesome discovery, went unaffectedly about her weekend by the seaside. She returned home from Brighton on Sunday evening and, not surprisingly after a passionate weekend with her young lover, was so tired that she went straight to bed. Her demeanour the next day seemed perfectly normal, and she left the house at 1.30 pm to carry out her usual round of afternoon and evening teaching appointments in North London.

Nellie Gentle, by comparison, had been unable to enjoy the blithe pleasures of a normal life. At breakfast on Monday morning, she was shocked by the lurid headlines in her newspaper, describing the discovery of a child's body at Dalston Junction on Friday evening:

---

8   In 1935, Alma Rattenbury and George Stoner engaged in a similar deception when they stayed at the Royal Palace Hotel in Kensington (see NBT 64).

Dalston Junction Railway Station
*Author's Collection*

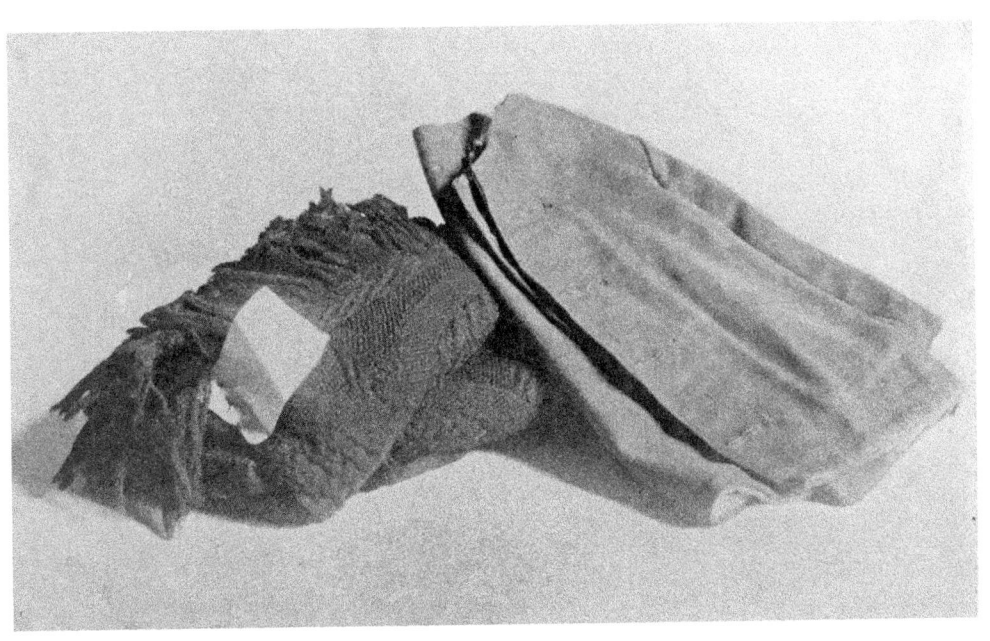

Manfred Masset's jacket and the shawl found over his body

*from The Police Encyclopedia, Vol II (1914)*

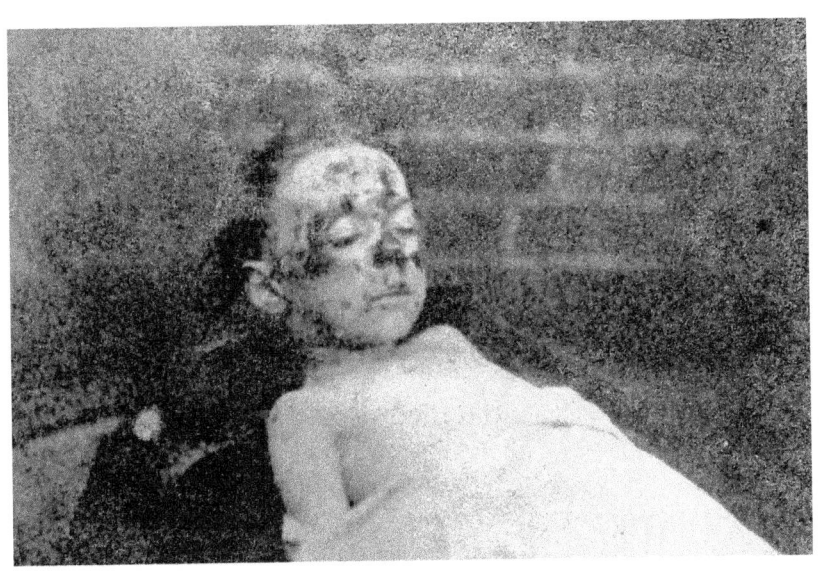

The body of Manfred Masset as photographed in the morgue
*Author's collection*

# Introduction.

### DALSTON MYSTERY.
### No Glimmer of Light on the Crime.

At a late hour last night there had been no identification of the little boy's body which was found in the ladies' waiting room at Dalston Junction on Friday evening under circumstances which predicated a foul and mysterious murder.

Until the identity of the dead child is revealed, the detectives cannot obviously get a fair start at the commencement of the trail of the crime; and the criminal who committed the deed is not yet even suspected or guessed at.

The unusual delay which is occurring in obtaining identification may have its significance. The dead child must have been missed by its mother or the person in charge of it by this time, for two days' absence in the case of a child of such tender age must be highly abnormal. Why has not that person been to the police to say that her child, or her charge, as the case may be, is missing – a course which would have led to immediate identification? An explanation may be forthcoming hereafter; but at present the silence of those in whose abode the seat of the little fellow has been vacant for more than two days is, to say the least, astonishing, if it be not.

### THE SILENCE OF GUILT.

If, indeed, the murder has been done by some relative or custodian of the little boy, who cannot be expected to come forward, the identification may be rendered very difficult to obtain. Detective Inspector Forth, who is in charge of the case, assisted by Detective Sergeant W. Burch – two thoroughly capable officers – has therefore promptly circulated a description of the body. It is that of a boy between five and six, 3 ft. 6 in. high, with wavy, light-brown hair and light blue eyes. The child was well nourished and well cared for, the finger nails, for instance, being clean and neatly cut; and he was in all probability of Jewish parentage.[9]

There was more – journalistic speculation about the mysteries of the case – but this alone would have been enough to convince Nellie that the article described Manfred. She consulted with her doctor, and then went with a neighbour to the mortuary at Hackney, where she was, between sobs, able to confirm that the victim was, indeed, Manfred Masset.[10] (Compounding this traumatic ordeal, Nellie returned home later the same day to find that two letters from Louise had arrived in the post: one contained a character reference, and the other reassured her, quite falsely, that little Manfred, though he was missing her and had been unwell on the ferry crossing to France, was now settled and doing well.)

---

9   *Daily Mail*, 30 October 1899. Manfred was not of Jewish parentage, but he had been circumcised, apparently at Louise's behest. Nellie thought that Manfred had 'never seemed quite so well' since that time.

10  TNA:PRO CRIM 1/58/5.

# Masset.

Once she had recovered her composure, Nellie was also able to describe the clothes the little boy had been wearing – a navy blue serge frock trimmed with white braid on the cuffs and round the collar, and with a braided band round the waist. Underneath this the boy was dressed in two petticoats – one of white flannelette, and one of grey striped flannel, the latter of which was tacked on to red stays; a pair of white flannelette drawers with lace at the bottom; and a white cotton shirt with lace round the neck and sleeves. On his legs, a pair of long, buttoned gaiters that came above the knee; a pair of brown socks (much darned); and a pair of brown strap shoes. The outfit was topped with a blue cloth coat with two brass anchor buttons, two fawn capes edged in blue, a white serge lining and gauntlet cuffs; and a white satin ribbon tie. On his head was the round cap made of red cloth with the words *HMS Raven* on the front.[11]

Nellie also gave the police a list of the spare clothes she had packed in a brown paper parcel and given to Louise Masset for the journey. The parcel contained a white flannel undervest bound with red; a short sleeved shirt with lace around the neck and sleeves; a grey striped flannelette petticoat; a white petticoat; a pair of white flannelette drawers with white lace; a white serge dress trimmed with lace; two overalls – one striped in blue and white, and one with a red pattern; one pair of black socks; a pair of black patent shoes; a white nightdress; and a pair of white leggings.[12]

A brown paper parcel containing two of these items – curiously, two which Manfred had been wearing when he left Stamford Hill, rather than two which had been parcelled up at that time – had been found by Ann Skeet, a waiting room attendant at Brighton Railway Station, at 3.30 pm on Saturday 28 October. It had been secreted in one of Mrs Skeet's cap boxes, which she kept in a room adjoining the ladies' lavatory. (Louise, of course, had been at the station that afternoon to meet Eudore Lucas's train from London, and the train had chuffed to a stop at about 3.20 pm; Mrs Skeet said that she was 'sure' that the package had not been there before.) When the parcel remained unclaimed, it was sent to London Bridge and, on 1 November, opened by Detective Sergeant Richard Nursey. It contained Manfred's blue serge frock, with the braid torn from the collar and cuffs, and from the belt around the waist; and his blue cloth coat, with the buttons, the capes, the collar and the cuffs removed. In addition, the edge of the brown paper was found to match the original, larger piece from which it had been cut by Nellie Gentle. They could be fitted back together, proving their common origin. The printed name of the shop from which Nellie had obtained it was divided by the cut – E. Shaw, a draper of Tottenham, with the 'E. S' on

---

11    TNA:PRO CRIM 1/58/5.
12    Ibid.

# Introduction.

one part, and 'haw' on the other.

Naturally, with the body identified and clues beginning to emerge, the police were anxious to interview Louise Masset as soon as possible, and a posse of officers, including Detective Sergeant William Burch, Detective Sergeant Richard Nursey, Detective Inspector Frederick Forth and Detective Constable Frederick Allen, were assigned to watch the house in Bethune Road for her return from her Monday evening lessons.

As it happened, the carefree disposition which Louise had exhibited earlier on Monday had long since evaporated. While out with one of her students in Baker Street at about 4.00 pm, Louise saw a newspaper – 'several' newspapers, she said – which announced the finding of the child's body at Dalston Junction, and described the victim. By her own account, she had a feeling that the description could have been Manfred's, but she completed her lesson with her student, went on to another house, taught there, and then, shortly before 7.00 pm, made her way to Loudoun Road Station for her usual journey home. By this time, the newspapers had learned about Nellie Gentle's identification of the body. Louise saw the placard – 'Dalston Tragedy: Child Identified'; she bought a copy of the *Evening News*. She panicked. Instead of returning home as she usually did at about 8.00 pm, she made her way to the home of her younger sister, Mathilde, who lived with her auctioneer husband, George Richard Simes, in Stretton Road, Croydon, arriving there at 11.00 pm.

The police were still watching for her return to 29 Bethune Road when, in the early hours of the following day, Tuesday 31 October, they saw George Simes arrive at the house. There was stillness overnight, and then, at about 8.00 am, Simes and Richard Cadisch left the house together. Burch and Allen followed the pair as they walked to London Bridge to catch the train to Croydon. The *Evening Standard* printed an account of the pursuit, headed:

THE MURDER OF A BOY AT DALSTON.
Arrest of the Mother.

While the pursuers and pursued were waiting for the train one of the gentlemen suddenly wheeled round and, boldly confronted the officers, said, 'You are watching me.' 'Quite true,' replied one of them, 'we are, and we must follow you until we are satisfied.' Then the gentleman, the brother-in-law of the accused, is said to have told the officers that no trouble would be given, and that Miss Masset was at the house in Croydon. Thither the officers proceeded and the lady was arrested and conveyed to Dalston Police Station.[13]

---

13   *London Evening Standard*, 1 November 1899.

# Masset.

When the officers questioned George Simes, he told them that Louise had knocked on his door at about 11.00 pm the night before. She had been in a very distressed state, saying that she was being 'hunted for murder'. She said that she felt that the body was Manfred's, but denied having anything to do with her son's death, and launched into a long story about meeting two women by arrangement at London Bridge station on Friday afternoon, and handing Manfred to them. That, she said, was the last she saw of him.

When the police reached Stretton Road, Louise, still very distressed, repeated the story of the mysterious women. Burch took down her statement.

> I last saw my child, Manfred Louis Masset, age three and a half, on Friday at London Bridge Railway Station, in the waiting room. I gave it to two women who gave me their address at 45 King's Road, Chelsea, with £12, mostly gold, to take care of it for a whole twelve months.
>
> I had seen them at Tottenham Green four Wednesdays back. I had the child with me then. They first spoke to me and by their conversation with me they found out it was a nurse-child. They said they were setting up a home and would I mind letting them have mine for £12 a year.
>
> At first I didn't agree with it. I met them there again the next Wednesday. I had the child with me then. I decided then to leave it with them for that sum. I then arranged to meet with them at London Bridge at 2.00 pm Friday last, in the waiting room, London-Brighton – where the refreshment room is on the left.
>
> I met them there but before going there I went into another waiting room, the one near where the parcels come out. There was a woman attendant there, had a cap on, and another one came to relieve her while I was there. They [the ladies from Tottenham Green] left to go to the refreshment room and took the boy with them as they asked him if he would like a cake.
>
> They were to come back and bring me a receipt for the money. I waited there two or three minutes but they never came back. I have not seen my child since.[14]

She 'did not give me any names,' recalled Burch; 'I did not ask for them. I only let her say what she liked, and I took a careful note of it.'[15] The urgency of finding the ladies to whom Louise had entrusted Manfred – she had provided their stated address, but not their names, although it would later be urged on her behalf that she had indeed mentioned their names to Simes – had apparently not occurred to her. Clearly unconvinced by the story, the police arrested her and took her to Dalston Police Station under suspicion of murder. 'I'll go there

---

14   TNA:PRO CRIM 1/58/5.
15   Ibid.

# Introduction.

willingly,' said Louise.[16]

### III.

In the interests of brevity – for there is much else to discuss in this case – we must pass over the judicial proceedings which preceded the trial. There were five magistrates' hearings at the North London Police Court, with the final sitting on 1 December; and there were three hearings before the coroner, the last of these being on 16 November. Both processes warranted Louise for trial at the Old Bailey on the charge of murdering her son, and much evidence – as we will see – was obtained to compete with her description of what had happened to Manfred. There were a few highlights along the way, one or two of which are worth mentioning here, simply for the insights they provide into the emotional landscapes and mentalities of some of those caught up in the matter: the request of George Simes to the magistrate, for example, praying that he would ensure that the press should refrain from publishing names and addresses when reporting on the case. The magistrate, Mr Edward Fordham, replied, 'I have no control over the press. All that happens here is in open court, and the press is such a mighty organ that I should not attempt to interfere with it. Of course the members of the press will use their own discretion as to what they print of the case.'[17] Later on, Léonie Cadisch would say that the family had 'forgiven' Louise for giving birth to an illegitimate child, but even this comment suggested some residual shame and embarrassment. The reader may wish to observe this dynamic as we progress.

Likewise, the crushing effect which Manfred's murder had had on Nellie Gentle was brought increasingly into focus. She was often a good witness, but she was always a reluctant one, insisting that Louise was a 'good' and 'kind' mother to little Manfred, and saying that he 'wanted for nothing on the part of the mother, and the poor little fellow used to look forward to her weekly visit with great pleasure'. After one hearing at the coroner's court, Nellie, 'who was greatly affected, warmly shook hands' with Louise.[18] She had found no way to adapt to the horror of what had come to pass, and, perhaps worse, her survivor's guilt seemed to be mixed up with experiences which (retrospectively) looked like supernatural precognitions:

> The love of Miss Gentle for the child, which she had brought up, was as strong as that which is often found in the fondest of mothers. It was reciprocated by the

---

16 TNA:PRO CRIM 1/58/5.
17 *Pall Mall Gazette*, 2 November 1899.
18 *London Evening Standard*, 3 November 1899.

child so much that there was a mysterious magnetic current between them. The mother had often been to see it and tried to get the child to accompany her but it seemed repelled by its mother's overtures and screamed terribly when she tried to get it away. Miss Gentle had no power to resist the mother, but she tells of her fearful suspicions which she had in a warning vision. She says that one evening, while mending stockings, the door of her room opened and she saw the figure of the little child quite plainly walking towards her.[19]

The intensity of the public's fascination with the case was evident. One report described the coroner's court, at Hackney, as 'crowded to the doorway'. Louise was constantly scrutinised by reporters who hoped that clues to her personality would be visible in her behaviour. Frequently, however, the evidence in this regard cut both ways: if she was upset, then perhaps this was an indication of guilt – or perhaps merely the sorrow of the grieving mother, falsely accused; but if she was not upset (and often she was not), then perhaps she was cruel and amoral – or perhaps she was simply lifted in her spirits because she knew that she was not guilty. This account, full of hints so ambiguous to be useless and typical of countless others, derived from an inquest hearing:

[T]hroughout the investigation her demeanour was characterised by wonderful composure. At times she whispered to her female companion, and smiled when she replied. Now and again she beckoned her solicitor (Mr Newton) to come across the room to speak to her, the conversation being carried on in French.[20]

On one occasion, before the magistrates, Detective Inspector Forth recounted going with her to the mortuary to see Manfred's remains:

The body was in a large shell. She leaned over the side, placed her hand to the head of the deceased and said, 'Oh, my child, my poor boy'.[21]

Here, then, was a different Louise, and perhaps a less sanguine Louise. The *Morning Post* took the opportunity to glance again at the prisoner, hoping for the mask to slip:

Miss Masset was dressed in black, and her demeanour in the dock was cool and collected, except when allusions were made by medical witnesses to the appearance of her child after death, and by Inspector Forth to the incidents connected with her own viewing of the body.[22]

19  *Lloyd's Weekly Newspaper*, 12 November 1899.
20  Ibid.
21  *Bristol Mercury*, 2 December 1899.
22  *Morning Post*, 2 December 1899.

# Introduction.

The court was informed by Arthur Newton that Louise Masset would not attend the last day of the inquest on account of the 'filthy, vile, disgusting abuse' she suffered from the public at her last appearance.[23]

The *amuse-bouches* of the inquest and the committal proceedings were over. The trial would be held – and completed – before Christmas.

## IV.

The trial of Louise Masset was opened on Wednesday 13 December 1899 at the Central Criminal Court of the Old Bailey, before Mr Justice Bruce.[24] Mr Charles Mathews[25] and Mr Richard Muir[26] appeared for the prosecution with Lord Coleridge, Q.C.,[27] Mr Arthur Hutton[28] and Mr Bovill William Smith[29] for the defence.

According to the *Evening Standard*, in its edition of the following day:

> There was great public interest taken in the trial, but only a limited number of people were admitted to the court. The prisoner was dressed in black, and wore no hat. She showed much emotion when asked to plead, replying to the charge whether she was guilty of the murder, 'No, sir'. She was accommodated with a seat in the dock.[30]

The *Western Mail* reporter, however, saw no such signs of distress:

> Prisoner is a Frenchwoman, thirty-six years of age, and of attractive appearance. At no time during the proceedings did she display the least nervous apprehension. She sat calmly listening to the whole of the evidence, only now and then

---

23  *London Standard*, 17 November 1899.
24  Sir Gainsford Bruce, Q.C., M.P. (1835-1912). His obituary described him as 'one of the most conscientious and hard-working of our judges, slow to master evidence, but rarely wrong in his judgement' (*Yorkshire Evening Post*, 27 February 1912).
25  Charles Willie Mathews (1850-1920), later Sir Charles. Senior Counsel to the Treasury, and, from 1908, Director of Public Prosecutions, he appeared in several other cases covered in this series: see, for example, *Trial of the Stauntons* [NBT 11], *Trial of Adelaide Bartlett* [NBT 41] and *The Baccarat Case* [NBT 56].
26  Richard David Muir (1857-1924), later Sir David. Counsel to the Treasury, and the meticulous, driven representative of the Crown's case at the trials – among others – of Hawley Harvey Crippen [NBT 24], Steinie Morrison [NBT 28] and Ronald True [NBT 36].
27  Bernard John Seymour Coleridge (1851-1927), Q.C., M.P. Second Baron Coleridge, son of Baron John Coleridge (1820-1894). See also *Trial of Thomas Neill Cream* [NBT 31].
28  A barrister whose appearances at the Old Bailey were frequent, if not always notable. He defended in the cases of Mary Pearcey and George Chapman (on the latter, see NBT 50).
29  Bovill William Smith, a longstanding associate of Lord Coleridge whose work was normally confined to the Western Circuit.
30  *Evening Standard*, 14 December 1899.

# Masset.

conversing with her solicitor.[31]

Charles Mathews opened the proceedings by regaling the court with the salient points of the case against Louise Masset, the details of which were already familiar to those who had avidly read the newspaper accounts of the proceedings at both the magistrates' hearings and the coroner's inquest. He also referred to the prisoner's relationship with her lover, Eudore Lucas. This had flourished after Louise had joined Lucas and two friends for a few days in Brighton during the previous Whitsun holiday; they had stayed at Mr Findlay's Hotel, but sexual intercourse did not, on that occasion, take place. Once the couple had started courting, Louise had told him that she had an illegitimate child – but he considered it of no consequence, as marriage between them was never an option. The lovers exchanged letters and enjoyed numerous trysts whilst ensuring that Louise's sister and other family members remained unaware of the affair.

At about 12.45 pm on the fateful Friday, Charles Mathews reminded the court, Louise met Nellie Gentle and little Manfred at the Birdcage public house on Stamford Hill. The boy was dressed in his distinctive, rather nautical fashion. Referring to the parcel of spare clothes which Nellie Gentle handed to Louise, Charles Mathews emphasised the importance of the brown paper wrapping.

The court then learned that Mr Findlay, the proprietor of the Brighton hotel, had found Manfred's favourite toy – a pair of miniature scales – in a drawer in room 11 and that they had been forwarded to the police. The toy was also identified by Nellie Gentle as the one she had given Manfred when she handed him over to his mother.

Charles Mathews proceeded to list all the known facts about the movements of Louise Masset from the time she arrived, with the child, at London Bridge Station. He also emphasised that Louise Masset passed through Dalston Junction several times a week travelling to and from various pupils' homes in North London, and often met Lucas there on her way home in the evenings. She was, therefore, familiar with the station and could have known that, unlike the facilities at London Bridge, there was no attendant on duty in the ladies' waiting room on platform 3 at Dalston Junction.

After speaking for more than two hours, Charles Mathews called the first prosecution witness – the nurse, Nellie Gentle, described as 'middle-aged and respectably dressed' (in fact, she was thirty years old – hardly middle-aged). Although she was as reluctant a witness as she had been before, she repeated her testimony concerning her care of Manfred since he was a baby, her parting

---

31 *Western Mail*, 15 December 1899.

# Introduction.

with the child, and her subsequent identification of his body. Cross-examined by Lord Coleridge, Nurse Gentle reiterated her previous evidence, stating that Louise Masset was an affectionate and caring mother.

The next witness to be called was Mrs Léonie Cadisch, Louise Masset's sister. She, too, had identified Manfred's body at the mortuary. She said that her sister had lived with her family at 29 Bethune Road since 1898. In answer to questions about Louise's relationship with Manfred, Mrs Cadisch said that she was 'very fond of her child' and spoke of him in 'terms of affection'. The *Evening Standard*, summarising the testimony, reported that, at the beginning of 1899, Louise had mentioned to Léonie that she was considering placing Manfred with people who were 'more educated' than Nellie Gentle and her family.[32]

Lord Coleridge, for the defence, rose to question Mrs Cadisch, and established the brick believed to have been used to stun the child was similar to bricks used in her garden both in the rockery and as a path edging; however, as far as she could tell, the only missing bricks were those taken away by the police during their investigations. Similar bricks were used in most of the gardens, sometimes in grottoes, in the neighbourhood.

Maud Clifford, the assistant in McIlroy's draper's shop at 161 High Street, Stoke Newington, testified that the shawl found over the child's body was similar to the one she had sold to a woman resembling Louise Masset on Tuesday 24 October, three days before the murder. Lord Coleridge, pointed out that, at the magistrates' hearing and the inquest, Miss Clifford had been unable to swear that Louise had been the purchaser; however, as the prosecution showed, she had managed to pick her out of a line-up.

The drapery shop's manager, Ernest Hopkins Mooney, was also cautious in his commitments. He had stocked three identical black woollen shawls and Maud Clifford had sold one – the shawl found on the child's body was identical to the two that remained in stock. Before ordering them, he had been unfamiliar with the design of the shawls, which perhaps suggested that they were unusual and distinctive; but he reasoned that the same item could be available in other shops.

A critical witness to Louise's movements on Friday 27 October was Mrs Georgina Worley. She worked as an attendant in the first and second class waiting room of the London, Brighton and South Coast Railway at London Bridge, and was on duty (wearing a white cap) from 7.30 am to 2.30 pm. She first noticed a woman and a little boy there at about 1.45 pm:

> I saw a little boy in the waiting room. … He had a little blue serge dress and

32  *London Evening Standard*, 14 December 1899.

a little blue serge coat. I do not remember what kind of a cap he had on. The coat had one or two bright brass buttons, and a little collar round the neck, of either red or brown. This is the frock [produced]. This is the coat, only there was something round the neck.

A lady was with the boy; she was dressed in black – a black round hat.

She recognised the photograph she was shown of the boy, but could not positively identify the prisoner as the woman she had seen with him. She said that the child 'kept running up and down the settee. It appeared quite happy.' The woman had told Mrs Worley that she was not going to catch a train, but was waiting 'for someone to come'. Mrs Worley left the room at about 2.30 pm, returning ten minutes later, by which time both the woman and the child had gone.

## V.

The second day of the trial, Thursday 14 December, was fully reported in the *Telegraph*:

> Fortunately for the comfort of those professionally concerned, the under-sheriffs had considerately taken precautions to prevent overcrowding, although from the structural conditions of the court those present could hardly escape from breathing an atmosphere that was far from pleasant as the afternoon wore on.
>
> Dressed in black, the prisoner sat quietly in the dock during the whole proceedings, displaying no signs of emotion until the part of the evidence was reached which had reference to the finding of the child's body in the Dalston waiting room [lavatory]. She then became much affected, quietly shed tears for a time and used her pocket handkerchief constantly. Any signs, however, of breaking down were quickly dispelled. She soon resumed her normal quiet interest in the tragedy which was being slowly unfolded before her and occasionally gave instructions to her solicitor, leaning for that purpose over the dock and emphasising her conversation with a quick movement of her hands, on which she wore kid gloves.
>
> Justice as administered in English courts is never hasty or hysterical. The case against the prisoner, accordingly, proceeded slowly and quietly for hours, at a rate, indeed, which must almost have sorely taxed the characteristic patience of his lordship.[33]

First to be called to give evidence was Mrs Ellen Reece, the attendant in the first class waiting room at the main line station at London Bridge. On Friday 27 October, she had been on duty from 2.30 pm to midnight, and began her

---

33   *Daily Telegraph*, 15 December 1899.

Manfred Masset

*Author's collection*

# Introduction.

evidence by testifying that she saw Louise Masset and little Manfred at 2.40 pm, ten minutes into her shift. She took particular notice because the child was 'grizzling'; she spoke briefly to Louise Masset, and, at about five or ten minutes past three, saw the woman and child go in the direction of the refreshment bar. She said that the photograph of Manfred which was shown to her in court depicted the child she had seen in the waiting room, but that, on that day, he had been wearing 'a little red hat'.

The next time she saw her, Louise was in the lavatory at – she estimated – 6.54 pm, washing her hands.[34] She asked Mrs Reece for a towel and the use of a clothes brush. Mrs Reece offered to brush her down but she declined. She was alone. There was no sign of the child. She asked the time of the next train to Brighton and, when told it was due to leave from the station at 7.20 pm, she grabbed a brown paper parcel and her gloves and hurried off to catch it.

It was nearly a month later that Ellen Reece went to the police and picked out Louise Masset from among a group of women as the person she had seen at the railway station. When it was suggested by Lord Coleridge in his cross-examination that she might have been 'assisted' by Detective Inspector Frederick Forth in identifying Louise Masset, she vehemently denied it. She did admit, however, that prior to the identification parade, she had read accounts of the case in the newspapers, and had seen a picture of Louise Masset in circumstances over which counsel for the defence seemed to wish to draw a veil.

> LORD COLERIDGE: Now, you saw a picture of the prisoner? — I saw a picture, but that was after I had said that it was –
> Never mind – you are so anxious in this case. — I am not anxious at all.

Still, Mrs Reece had recognised Miss Masset immediately at the identification parade, and had pointed at her with her umbrella; Inspector Forth, who had been standing behind her, told her she must place her hand on the woman's shoulder, which she did.

Mrs Clara Haas confirmed that Louise Masset had been a daily governess to her daughter for a period of four years – except for an interval of five months in 1896, presumably at the time of Manfred's birth – and her days for giving lessons were Mondays and Thursdays. She had arrived for her usual lesson on Monday 30 October, reaching the house at 5.15 pm, leaving an hour and a half later, and appearing cheerful and untroubled the whole while.

---

34   In her statement to the police, Mrs Reece said she 'fixed' the second time she saw Louise as she was finishing off a piece of crochet work and remembered that she hadn't had her tea. She looked at the clock and saw it was 6.50 pm and she was putting on the kettle when Louise came in. Neither woman referred to their earlier conversation or the whereabouts of the child.

# Masset.

Next came Mary Teahan, who repeated the evidence she had given at the inquest; she recalled finding the body of Manfred at about 6.20 pm and alerting the station staff. After attending her lecture, she and her friend, Margaret Biggs had returned home, but, on reading a report of the murder in the Sunday newspapers, they went to the police to make statements.

The spectators must have been especially eager to scrutinise the face of another witness summoned to the court, as illustrated by the following account in the *Telegraph*:

> It was well on in the afternoon when a large sprinkling of ladies of various ages found themselves within good view of the prisoner, and in good time to hear the evidence of her lover – a quiet, unpretentious young Frenchman named Eudore Lucas – about whom many stories more or less interesting had been floating about in the precincts of the court. He gave an interesting little story about his ripening friendship with Miss Masset, and as he spoke uncommonly good English he was well understood by all present. More or less habitually speaking in a low voice he was several times requested by Mr. Justice Bruce to speak up.[35]

Eudore Lucas, as depicted in a drawing in the press, was a dapper, handsome young man of nineteen who, having removed his top hat, balanced it on the ledge of the witness box. He confirmed that he had once been a neighbour of Louise Masset, but had recently moved to 23 Mildmay Grove, Islington.[36] He told the court that he sometimes met Louise after classes in the evenings and travelled with her to Dalston Junction, where they would board a tram back to Bethune Road. He and Louise exchanged letters which he had subsequently destroyed. He denied that they were love letters, referring to them as 'letters of appointment or friendship', but admitted that he had told the magistrate that 'there were loving terms in them'. He was somewhat out of his depth, and fell back upon his cultural misapprehensions: 'Love is not the same thing in France as it is in England. I do not think they would be called love letters in England. I think you cannot call them loving terms in English.'

He freely admitted that he and Louise Masset had spent the weekend together in Brighton and that sexual intercourse had taken place. When she met him at Brighton Station on the Saturday afternoon she seemed perfectly normal – not in the least agitated or upset, but 'calm and quiet'. She did not mention Manfred at all during the weekend, and they returned to London late on Sunday evening. He stopped at the junction of St Kilda's Road and Bethune Road, while Louise

---

35  *Daily Telegraph*, 15 December 1899.
36  On 9 November, at the inquest, Richard Cadisch said: 'I know Lucas, and that he knew her [Louise]. He has lived next door to us until last night.' (TNA:PRO CRIM 1/58/5.)

# Introduction.

went ahead. Except for her waterproof, she was only carrying the Gladstone bag – there was no brown paper parcel.

When questioned by Lord Coleridge for the defence, Lucas said that Louise had told him that she had a child but it made no difference to him: his salary as a clerk was only £3 a month, so marriage was out of the question. They had never discussed the age difference between them, but he testified that he thought she was thirty-four years old (in fact, she had turned thirty-six in June 1899, about three weeks after their chaste Whitsun sojourn to Brighton).

The *Telegraph* reporter noted that:

> The young Frenchman's evidence was sufficiently incidental and interesting to satisfy a court full of eager listeners. Most of the ladies departed when he stood down, and on an intimation from the judge before the clock struck four that he should not sit beyond another hour there was a very material exodus from the court, only those professionally interested, together with those who can never hear too much of a murder trial – jaded though they must have been – remaining to hear the closing evidence for the day which referred to the finding of the murdered boy's clothes in the waiting-room at Brighton Railway Station, and to the affectionate consideration the accused had invariably exhibited towards children.[37]

## VI.

The third day of the trial, Friday 15 December, proved to be even more fascinating for the crowds desperately seeking entry to the courtroom.

Three medical practitioners were questioned. Dr James Patrick Fennell, of 20 Dalston Lane, testified that when he was called to attend to the body of the child at Dalston Junction he found that the trunk was still warm, although the arms, legs and feet were cold. It was lying on the floor of the cubicle with the head facing towards the passage and the feet facing the water closet. The body was naked, except for the shawl covering its middle part. The left leg was slightly bent with the foot resting under the right thigh; the right leg was extended in a natural position.

The next day, Saturday 28 October, at ten o'clock in the evening, Dr Fennell, assisted by a police surgeon, Mr Charles Howard Jackman, carried out a post mortem examination and found the body to be 'clean and well-nourished'. There was no sign of disease in any of the boy's internal organs although the brain was congested, a condition which could indicate suffocation. It was noted

---

37  *Daily Telegraph*, 15 December 1899.

that the child had been circumcised. The bruises and lacerations to the face were extensive and, in the doctors' opinion, the wounds to the forehead were caused by brutal blows and the weapon used was undoubtedly the clinker brick on which were found a small stain of what may have been blood and two hairs corresponding to those on Manfred's eyebrows. The lips were blue and the tongue was protruding between the teeth – these signs pointed to suffocation. The upper lip and the tip of the nose were badly bruised which, Dr Fennell concluded, was probably due to 'pressure over the nose'. In his opinion, therefore, Manfred had been first stunned, and then suffocated.

It was impossible, the doctor said, to specify an actual time of death, but it was probably 'about an hour' before he was called; since he had been called shortly before 7.00 pm, this put the time of death shortly before 6.00 pm. He considered it possible, but less likely, that Manfred had been dead for a longer period.

The police surgeon, Charles Howard Jackman, from Stoke Newington, 'wish[ed] to differ' from Dr Fennell over the question of the time of death. He believed that death had occurred a little earlier – at the police court, he had suggested that at least two hours had elapsed before the discovery of the body – but he had been at a disadvantage, since he had not seen the body until the post mortem, which had been held at 10.00 pm that night.[38] His opinion relied on the clinical observations which Dr Fennell had made at the scene of the body's discovery, and there was some disagreement between witnesses about the accuracy and utility of these: one point about which consensus could not be achieved was whether the station lavatories were 'draughty', which could affect the rate at which heat left the body – Fennell thought that they were, but Detective Inspector Forth, who had 'made experiments with matches and so on', thought not. Nonetheless, Jackman agreed that the time of death was difficult to fix with certainty; heat, he said, could 'remain in the body for eight or sixteen hours if you wrap it up; under the conditions in which this body was found, it might be from eight to four hours'. This observation was reiterated by the next witness, Dr Thomas Bond, of 7, The Sanctuary, Westminster. He was a consulting surgeon at Westminster Hospital and had lectured on forensic medicine for many years. He agreed that to ascertain more accurately the time of death, one must take into consideration how long a body had lain between death and discovery and the temperature of its surroundings, and these were questions to which he had given 'special attention'. The best estimate was 'between one hour and four'.[39]

---

38  TNA:PRO CRIM 1/58/5.
39  At the police court, Bond had been a little more positive, stating that 'the most probable time of death is

# Introduction.

The appearance of Louise Masset in the witness box must have caused quite a stir amongst those spectators gathered on the public benches, engendering a great many surreptitious nudges and whispers. Not only was the woman before them charged with brutally murdering her own child, but her affair with a man not much more than half her age was considered scandalous.

Once again, the *Telegraph* offered its readers a glimpse of the atmosphere at the Old Bailey that day:

> Somebody has given the 'Newgate Calendar' a very bad name. It is said to vie with the 'Biography of Authors' in being the most sickening chapter in the history of man. If this be true, not even the hoary antiquity of the Central Criminal Court can save it from a like condemnation. There was nothing in the climatic conditions yesterday to give it any attraction except to those elements which are professional and morbid. Every endeavour was made to cheer it up with its gas lights as some set off to the terrors of the thick December fog which hung over the City like a sepulchral pall.
>
> Well-dressed ladies, accompanied in some cases by well-dressed gentlemen, were there in varied raiment, and helped to give the place a brightness which it much wanted. Long before Mr Justice Bruce arrived from Bromley they had, in fact, taken their seats and settled down comfortably. Several of them have indicated every day since the trial commenced an interest in the prisoner intelligent enough to produce little quiet discussions until the sharp-eyed janitors have cried out 'Silence!'
>
> Sensation is a term of elastic import, but if the statement made by the prisoner late in the sitting may be regarded in the light of something unusual, it might well come under that denomination. At three o'clock the case for the prosecution had finished, after a large show of incidents not very freshening. The court was jaded, or very nearly so, when suddenly Lord Coleridge called upon the prisoner to give evidence. The prisoner tripped quickly from the dock to the witness box, looked pleased with the change, clasped her hands, and leaned over the rail ready to begin. She had taken off her gloves and stood, dressed in deep black, and without a hat. As her statement proceeded she constantly shifted her position, but always without the least sign of nervousness, spoke excellent English, and generally indicated a tone of educated refinement. Many of the spectators were plainly astonished at her general bearing and the nature of her evidence. She remained in the witness box for about an hour.[40]

Drawings of Miss Masset in the press showed a rather gaunt woman wearing

---

about two hours before Dr Fennell saw it'. This tended to reinforce Jackman's estimate of the time of death, rather than Fennell's, but Bond added the significant qualifier: 'There can be no certainty – absolutely none'. (TNA:PRO CRIM 1/58/5.)

[40] *Daily Telegraph*, 16 December 1899.

# Masset.

fashionable clothes and with her hair swept up into an elegant chignon. She insisted on sticking to her original story about the two mysterious women. She began by describing the regular visits she made to Manfred while he was with Nurse Nellie Gentle. She usually collected him each Wednesday and together they would go for walks in the park at Tottenham Green, sometimes accompanied by Nellie. On Wednesday 4 October, Manfred was playing with a little girl called Millie, who seemed to belong to the younger of two women sitting on a bench nearby. Louise fell into conversation with them and was told that their names were Browning – the elder of the two was a widow and the younger was her sister-in-law. (This was an unexpected novelty, since the names of the women had not been given in any previous evidence; Louise stubbornly testified to mentioning their names to her solicitor, Mr Newton, 'long ago', and it would later be said, without proof, that she had also given the names to George Simes.) The talk naturally turned to childcare and early learning, and Louise expressed some concern about her son's need for a good education. She was particularly concerned by the fact that he was using the expression 'ain't', and pointing to objects with the words, 'Look at them things'. It was at this point that the older of the two women suggested that she hand over little Manfred and, in return for a fee, he would be given full board and education for a year by the younger Browning woman. They had just started 'a kind of kindergarten', she said, and gave the address as 45 King's Road, Chelsea.

Louise told the court that she had, for some time, thought that the boy would be better placed in a more stimulating environment than that provided by Nellie Gentle, so she made up the story of taking the child to live with his father's family in France to avoid hurting Nellie's feelings. Having thought about the Brownings' suggestion, Louise met them again in the park on 11 October and told them of her decision; terms were agreed between her and the two women, and it was arranged that Louise would bring Manfred to them at London Bridge Station on Friday 27 October.

As the judge was obliged to keep another important engagement the court proceedings were adjourned until the following day.

## VII.

It was nearly eleven o'clock on Saturday 16 December by the time Mr Justice Bruce took his seat in court on the fourth day of the trial. His railway journey had been delayed by the dense winter fog that hung over the city.

Louise Masset was brought back into the witness box to continue her story of the arrangement to hand over Manfred to the two Browning women at London

# Introduction.

Bridge station. She told the court that she waited for some time for the women to appear and when they eventually arrived, she said, 'Well, you have come at last. I have waited long enough.' To this, the older Mrs Browning replied, 'I am very sorry, but it has taken us one and a half hours to get here'. They went to sit in the general waiting room, right at the back. It had been Louise's intention to go with them to see the school in Chelsea but, as she had waited so long, she was afraid she might miss the 4.00 pm train to Brighton. Mrs Browning said, 'Well, you know he will be all right. You could trust him to us.'

She had given the woman a £12 deposit, in gold, on the total of £18 for the year, which would include ten shillings a month for his education. When she asked for a receipt, Mrs Browning said she would go to the refreshment bar to see 'if they had pen and ink, and [would] make me one out'. She left the waiting room, and the younger Browning and Manfred went with them. Louise watched them go, but then she turned back to fetch her Gladstone bag, 'to bring it nearer to the window'. By the time this had been accomplished, the mysterious ladies were no longer in sight, and nor was Manfred. Louise waited for a few minutes, and then looked around the station for any sign of them, but there was none. They had vanished.

Asked if she felt any concern that the women and her child had disappeared, Louise said she did not: she had the women's names and address and, moreover, they had promised to write to her on the following Monday. She then proceeded to travel in a first class compartment on the 4.00 pm train to Brighton.

When she arrived in Brighton, she told the court, she walked down to the seafront and, at 6.15 or 6.20 pm, she went into a café – Mutton's Restaurant and Hotel – for some refreshments. After this, she walked to West Brighton, window shopping until shortly after 9.00 pm – she remembered seeing the time on the Jubilee clock in Queens Road. She then returned to the railway station to collect her Gladstone bag – which she had deposited in the cloakroom – and from there to the hotel where, at 9.45 pm, she was checked into Room 11 by the chambermaid, Alice Riall. In evidence, Alice had recalled that Louise was carrying a Gladstone bag and a small hold-all, bound up with leather straps. When questioned about the toy scales which would later be found in the room, Louise said that she was going to return them to Manfred 'the following Wednesday, when I was to go down and see him'.

Louise admitted that she and Eudore Lucas enjoyed an illicit two days in Brighton, returning to Stoke Newington on Sunday evening. She told the court that, on 8 October, Lucas had thrown a romantic poem over the wall of her sister's house in Bethune Road. When they met at Liverpool Street Station on Wednesday 25 October, she expressed a wish to return to Brighton at the weekend, and he readily agreed to join her there.

There had been 'not the slightest talk' of marriage with Lucas, Louise told the court. The idea 'would have been absurd'. By the law of his country Lucas could not marry before he had served in the army. He was only nineteen years old, and would not begin his military service until he was twenty-one. She admitted that her relatives were unaware of her affair with Lucas. The story about the trip to France was a ruse, concealing the truth of her weekend's absence.

Asked by Lord Coleridge if there was any truth in the suggestion that she had murdered her child, Louise said, 'No'.

In cross-examination by Charles Mathews, Louise swore that she had never been in the ladies' lavatory at Dalston Junction, not even when meeting Lucas in the evenings.

A child called Winnie Allam was brought into court and Louise was asked if this was the same little girl, supposedly belonging to the younger Browning woman, with whom, she said, Manfred had played at Tottenham Green. She was unable to swear that it was.

Charles Mathews continued to interrogate Louise 'at very great length' but, in the view of *Lloyd's Weekly Newspaper*, he 'was unable to shake her evidence on any material point'.[41] A member of the jury asked if she had told the Browning women that she was going to Brighton on the 4.00 pm train; to this, she replied that she had, and that this was the reason that she did not have time to go with them to the address in Chelsea. The *Telegraph* described Louise as 'an uncommonly good witness'.[42] It is certainly true to say – as this example shows – that her memory and her perspicacity stood up well to her ordeal. She clung to the disparate threads of her story as tightly as she could, protecting the internal consistency of her narrative against the forces which threatened to tear it apart.

By the time the court was adjourned that day, Louise Masset had been in the witness box for hours, and, as she stepped down to return to her place in the dock, she looked exhausted and 'for some minutes covered her face with her hands and sobbed'.[43] Before the court rose, some discussion took place with regard to the accommodation of the jury, who had been locked up nightly and had hoped to be relieved of their duties that day. Brushing aside their complaints, Mr Justice Bruce intimated that recreation would be provided, suggesting that some chaperoned open-air walks in Temple Gardens on Sunday might suffice.[44]

To this, a juror rose to address the judge: 'We are getting rather tired; can we

---

41  *Lloyd's Weekly Newspaper*, 17 December 1899.
42  *Daily Telegraph*, 18 December 1899.
43  *Lloyd's Weekly Newspaper*, 17 December 1899.
44  *Daily Telegraph*, 18 December 1899.

go to a place of amusement tonight?'
'I think not,' came the stern reply.⁴⁵

## VIII.

On Monday 18 December, the last day of the trial, Louise Masset was brought back into court and Charles Mathews rose to sum up the case for the prosecution. The case, extensively reported in the press, had sparked nationwide interest. On 22 December, the *Lincolnshire Chronicle* noted Mathews's damning rhetoric:

> Admitting that the prisoner possessed great intelligence and ability, he mingled his admiration with regret that much of the quick talent of a southern race, with which she was connected, should be used to defeat the ends of justice. If it were true that she was a woman of resource, and would invest statements with circumstantiality, it was obvious that to an iron nerve that was necessary to commit this crime must be added the tongue of the serpent.⁴⁶

The same article went on to describe the closing acts of the drama:

> At two o'clock Lord Coleridge commenced his address for the prisoner. In asking the jury to believe the prisoner's story, he would point out two grave inherent improbabilities in the case for the prosecution. If she committed the crime she was a monster, inhuman, not only cruel, but pitiless. Was that her true character? Those who know her united in testifying that she was kind, sympathetic and affectionate, attached to children, and beloved by them, and that the attachment was demonstrated in the case of her own child. Many women desired to know no more about their illegitimate children. But that was not the wish of the prisoner. They knew that she visited her child with increasing frequency – visits which it was not incumbent on her to pay, and which could only have been prompted by maternal affection.
>
> The second grave improbability was the absence of motive. There might be motives which induced women to destroy their offspring. The desire arose sometimes with the object of concealing their shame. There was no such motive in this case.
>
> It has been suggested that the prisoner might have done it with a desire to marry the Frenchman, Lucas. There was no evidence of it.
>
> Another motive was said to be money. But money came regularly from the child's father. As to the woman [sic – women] who took the child, there existed baby-

---

45   *Lloyd's Weekly Newspaper*, 17 December 1899.
46   *Lincolnshire Chronicle*, 22 December 1899.

## Masset.

farmers in the metropolis to whom in their innocence mothers handed over their children.[47] The story was not incredible, because experience told them it was true. The question of morality had nothing to do with the issue. That was not a court of morals, but a court of justice. ... He protested against every bit of evidence – whether good, bad or indifferent – being regarded as conclusive evidence in the circumstantial story which the prosecution had tried to make out. ... As to the evidence of identification by Mrs Rees [sic – Reece], who was in charge of the waiting room at London Bridge Station, and who said she saw the prisoner there in the evening[, t]housands of persons frequented this waiting room, a fact which made identification improbable. If the prisoner travelled to Brighton by the four o'clock train she could not have committed the murder. No-one connected with the railway had been called to show that she travelled by the 7.30 train [sic – 7.20 train]. If she had wished it she could have left the country to evade arrest but she told her brother-in-law everything and the police everything and again and again asked to see the body of her little boy. This was not the action of a guilty person. Not a single inaccuracy, not a single error, not a single slip had the prisoner made in her statement, notwithstanding all the arts and crafts that Mr Mathews could employ to detect faults in it. He did not ask for mercy. If she were the author of the crime she deserved no mercy. He asked them, however, not to act upon surmise, but only upon proof, upon that only which dictated their sober judgement and enabled them with confidence in themselves to find a verdict.[48]

The *Northampton Mercury*, on Friday 22 December, described the closing scenes on the last day of the trial, by which time the public benches were, once again, crowded:

When placed in the dock the prisoner appeared composed and calm, and she listened with [sic – without] apparent emotion to the lengthy speeches which occupied the day. It was only towards the end that she broke down. Mr Mathews's reply on behalf of the Crown occupied exactly three hours. It was not of a vindictive character. It was strikingly effective in its quiet but scathing criticism of the 'strange story' which had been told by 'this loving and affectionate mother'. What human eye, asked Mr Mathews, had ever seen the two mysterious ladies or the little girl of whom the accused had spoken? The evidence of the principal witnesses for the prosecution had been corroborated by what he termed the coincidence of facts in connection with the prisoner's story. Had a single witness been called in confirmation of that story? However painful their duty might be, it was for the jury to say whether or not this child had been destroyed

---

47   The vile crime of baby-farming was still practised at the time, and a number of sensational court cases had occurred. Only three years before, in 1896, the despicable Amelia Dyer, thought to have killed many of the babies in her charge, was hanged at Newgate.
48   *Lincolnshire Chronicle*, 22 December 1899.

# Introduction.

in order that the mother might obtain the object of her ambition.

Lord Coleridge, on behalf of the prisoner, said the address of his learned friend was an appeal to passion characterised by a vindictive spirit. He (Lord Coleridge) would make no appeal to their passions; he would strain no point in favour of the woman he represented, but would appeal to the sober sense of the jury and ask them to believe the story which she had told in the box.

The Crown had endeavoured to show that the prisoner was a monster in human form, but after the evidence which had been given was that a true characterisation of the accused? In his closing sentences Mr. Mathews had endeavoured to show a motive, but would any woman get up in a public court and admit that intercourse with Eudore Lucas unless her story was true? With that relationship they had nothing to do; it was not a court of morals, but one of justice.

Dealing with the evidence as laid before the court, Lord Coleridge pointed out that if Miss Masset knew Dalston Junction well she must have been well known there, but not a tittle of evidence had been adduced to show that she had travelled from London Bridge to Dalston Junction and back between the hours of six and seven on the evening of 27 October.

Was it likely, he asked, that this 'cunning and clever woman', with her hands reeking with the blood of her child, would go back to the very waiting room in which she had been seen earlier with the child, thus courting identification? He contended that all the prisoner's actions after 27 October were consistent with her innocence. Human judgement is frail and fallible, but it is upon human judgement that you have to rely. I ask you not to act upon surmising but only upon proof.

Mr Justice Bruce, in summing up, said they (the jury) were the judges of fact, his duty being only to decide on questions of law. What, his lordship asked later on, would have been the action of an innocent woman when she saw the child had been identified? Her first impulses would have been to apply to the police and tell the story, but instead of that she went to her brother in Croydon, where she said, 'I am being hunted for murder, but I have not done it'. One would have thought she would ask that the women should be searched for by the police at once.

Towards the end of his lordship's address the prisoner (who had interrupted once or twice) broke down, and sat with her face in her hands, sobbing and rocking herself to and fro in the dock.[49]

The judge's feelings about the case were suggested at the beginning of this report in the *Worcestershire Chronicle*, on 23 December:

Mr Justice Bruce, in his summing up, was careful to point out that the case was of great importance to the general public. 'There can be little doubt,' said His Lordship, 'that the little boy was brutally and cruelly murdered, and that its

---

49  *Northampton Mercury*, 22 December 1899.

clothes were stripped from its body to destroy identification; but hard as must have been the heart of the murderer there was one touch of human feeling, and so a shawl was thrown over the body.'[50]

And the report of the fifth and final day of the trial carried by *Lloyd's Weekly Newspaper* went straight to the crux of the matter:

> The court was again densely crowded, especially in the afternoon, when the speeches of counsel were finished. Replying for the Crown, Mr Mathews said that the whole case rested on one question. Did Miss Masset travel from London Bridge to Brighton on the afternoon of 27 October by the 4.00 pm train? If, as she had sworn, she did, then she was falsely accused. If she did not, and the evidence of the Crown was true that she was at London Bridge that evening at seven o'clock, and travelled by the 7.22 pm train to Brighton, where subsequently the clothes of the murdered child were found, what inference could the jury draw as to her innocence or guilt?
>
> No human being ever set eyes on the two strange women but the accused. There was no corroboration of her story. It had been fabricated for the purpose of meeting the exigencies of the case. To the nerve of iron she had added a tongue of deceit. She had lied to get possession of the child, and practised deception on her friends, and for what object, if her story was a true one?
>
> If it was true that Miss Masset, though she denied it, had formed a very strong attachment for Lucas, and found the child an obstacle in the path of her ambitions, might it not be that she conceived and carried out a determination to get rid of it?
>
> Lord Coleridge, addressing the jury in defence, said the prisoner had shown always the greatest affection for her child, and there was not the slightest evidence of any motive she could have to get rid of it. Further, what proof was there that the accused was ever seen with the shawl which covered the dead body, or that she was ever at Dalston Station on the afternoon of the murder? He urged that a reasonable doubt existed as to the guilt of the accused, and that, therefore, she was entitled to an acquittal.
>
> Mr Justice Bruce, in summing up, observed that the jurymen were the judges of the facts, and with them alone rested the responsibility for their verdict. The finding of the clinker brick, the purchase of the shawl, and the discovery of some of the murdered child's clothes at Brighton, where Miss Masset went, were circumstances which called for the most careful attention.
>
> If Mrs Rees [sic – Reece], the attendant at London Bridge station, was not mistaken, it showed that Miss Masset was in London after the murder took place, and did not go to Brighton by the 4.00 pm train. Referring to her conduct after the discovery of the murder, his lordship said that undoubtedly she had told falsehoods

---

50  *Worcestershire Chronicle*, 23 December 1899.

# Introduction.

about the taking of the child to France. She had given an explanation as to why she made those statements, but was it merely to account for the disappearance of the child in order that no inquiry would be made?

The prisoner: 'The father in France would have asked questions about the child, and it would have been found out that way.'

Mr Justice Bruce, continuing, pointed out that no motive had been shown for the crime, but the jury had to judge the conduct of the accused after the discovery of the murder and the identification of the body. One would have thought that, if innocent, the first thing she would have done would have been to go to the police and say she had handed the child over to the women in order that the police might be put on their track.

It was the duty of the Crown to establish the prisoner's guilt, not for her to prove her innocence. If as men of the world, the jury came to the conclusion that the accused was guilty, they would say so by their verdict; but if they were satisfied that there existed a reasonable doubt the prisoner was entitled to an acquittal.

A juror asked if Miss Masset could say why she had not called any evidence bearing on her visit to Brighton by the 4.00 pm train on the day of the murder and the visit to a restaurant there.

Mr. Justice Bruce did not think the question could be asked. He preferred that the jury should return their verdict on the evidence as it stood.

Another juror asked if there was any mark – a ticket or label – on the Gladstone bag belonging to the prisoner to show when it was deposited in the cloakroom at Brighton station.

The Judge: 'You should see the bag for yourselves, gentlemen.'

The jury retired to consider their verdict at ten minutes to five o'clock, and, after a deliberation of half an hour, returned into court with a verdict of 'Guilty'.

The prisoner, on hearing the verdict, was so overcome with emotion that she sank down in the chair in the dock. She rallied, however, in a moment, and, rising, said in a broken voice, in reply to the usual question why sentence of death should not be passed, 'I am quite innocent of the charge, sir'.

In passing sentence the judge said:

Louise Masset – After a most careful trial, the jury have found you guilty of the crime with which you are charged. I will not harrow your feelings by making any observations on that verdict, but will content myself with passing on you the sentence of the law." The sentence was then pronounced in the usual formula.

The prisoner the while closed her eyes and sank back fainting, being supported on her seat by two wardresses. There was a brief pause, after which the prisoner was asked if she had anything to urge in stay of the execution of her sentence. She was now in a state of collapse, and seemed not to realise the nature of the query. It was repeated in plainer phraseology by one of the wardresses supporting her.

# Masset.

Eventually, still with her eyes closed and still receiving support from the gaol attendants, she was apparently aroused and brought to understand that a reply was expected from her, whereupon she shook her head slowly, with an agonised weariness, from side to side. She was then supported from the dock, retiring by the steps leading to Newgate Prison.

The jury were excused from further attendance upon juries for six years. The foreman expressed the obligations of himself and his colleagues to the under-sheriffs for the excellent arrangements which had been made for their comfort. The judge said he was glad to hear the statement, as the sheriffs were known for the liberal treatment which extended to jurors.

The execution has been fixed for 9 January.

After the sentence the prisoner was so ill as a result of the long strain of the trial, that it was considered inadvisable to inform her of the date fixed for the execution. It has transpired since the trial that the prisoner had not been helped of late, at any rate, by the mysterious father of the child, and was in arrears with her payments for its keep.[51]

## IX.

Press coverage in the aftermath of the trial was extensive. The following article in the *Evening Standard* summed up the whole case:

The Dalston murder trial ended last night in the verdict of Guilty against Louise Masset. The offence for which she has been sentenced to suffer the last penalty of the law was a peculiarly cruel one. Many women have murdered young children who were an encumbrance on their means, injured their reputation, or stood in the way of their ambition. But in the Dalston case it was never suggested that the prisoner was in any financial straits or embarrassments. Her associate in the liaison in which she involved herself was aware of the existence of the child, and was much her junior in years, nor had any question of marriage ever arisen between them. She was apparently attached to her victim. What, then, was the cause of her crime? But for recent legislation[52] which has made prisoners competent, although not compellable, witnesses on their own behalf, the answer would not be easy or conclusive. It is simple enough, no doubt, to say that in the administration of the criminal law account has to be taken of acts and not motives, no motive being sufficient reason for murder; and, therefore, that no presumption of innocence can be drawn from the inadequacy of an alleged motive, as judged by an evenly-balanced intellect and a normal character. But, however, cogent such considerations might be, viewed from the logical and metaphysical standpoint,

---

51  *Lloyd's Weekly Newspaper*, 24 December 1899.
52  Criminal Evidence Act 1898.

# Introduction.

the absence of reasonable cause has all along been a favourite, and frequently a successful, argument with Counsel for the Defence.

How largely its effect has been weakened by the Act which enables prisoners to go into the witness box and give their story on oath, the Dalston case very clearly illustrates. If Louise Masset had been tried under the old law, the eloquent Counsel who defended her would have driven home into the minds of the jury all the improbabilities and gaps in the case for the prosecution; and then lamented the fact that his client's mouth was closed and prevented from clearing up the mystery by the act of the law itself. Now that the legal disability has been removed, this special line of defence to which we have referred is greatly impaired. If the prisoner declines to give evidence, an inference is drawn which no statutory or judicial disapprobation can repress. If the evidence is given, either the real motive is discovered or an utterly unconvincing explanation of adverse circumstances is put forward.

The examination and cross-examination of Louise Masset had left her motives still a matter of speculation. But the account which she gave of her movements on that day when her child was admittedly murdered, and the entire narrative which she asked the jury to believe, confirmed, by their inherent weakness, the very positive case put forward against her by the Crown. To take a single crucial point – she surrenders the care of her child to strangers of whom she knows nothing, and whose place of residence she does not think it worthwhile to visit beforehand. It is not likely that a woman really devoted to her child would act in this manner. In addition to this piece of negative evidence, we have a tissue of other improbabilities – the sudden appearance of the unknown baby-farmers, their equally prompt disappearance after the tragedy, not the faintest sign of their presence in the waiting room or the apartment where the poor child was done to death, and the time said to have been spent by the prisoner in wandering about Brighton, without managing to leave such traces of her roamings as would enable their genuineness to be ascertained. Against this strange texture of improbable circumstances the jury had to set a formidable body of facts. It was undoubted that the prisoner was herself the last person in whose care the child had been seen. She secured possession of the child by falsehood. Some of the clothes that he had worn before his murder were found in her hands. The brick with which the deed was done resembled in shape and general appearance bricks to which she had access in the home of a friend [referring to Léonie Cadisch's house] and it could easily have been carried in the bag which she had with her on the day of the murder. All that could be said to weaken these considerations was that no human being could be so callous as to make a murder the preliminary act in an intrigue. But, unhappily, the history of crime shows how untrustworthy are deductions of this sort.[53]

---

53  *London Evening Standard*, 19 December 1899.

# Masset.

On the same day *The Globe* ran this article on the case:

The crime for which Louise Masset was convicted yesterday is so peculiarly horrible and inhuman that it is only natural to feel the greatest reluctance to believe in her guilt, in spite of almost any evidence. Unhappily, the evidence in this case, and more particularly that which was supplied by the prisoner herself, leaves very little room for doubt. By the body of the murdered child was found a brick similar to those which are admitted to be in the garden of the prisoner's residence, and upon the body lay a shawl resembling one which had been sold to her by a draper's assistant, who picked her out among fourteen women. In the waiting room at Brighton railway station a brown paper parcel containing some of the child's clothing was left about the time that the prisoner was known to have been there, and an attempt had been made, by mutilating the various articles, to prevent them from being identified.

On the other hand, is it possible to believe her story of the two women to whom she says she entrusted the child? No one ever saw her during these alleged interviews; she made no arrangements to see the home to which her child was going; and she did not ask the two women for references, as she had done in the case of the Gentles to whom he was first consigned. Then, when she saw in a newspaper an account of the discovery of the body, she appears at once to have jumped to the conclusion that it was that of her child. Why should she have thought so if she had not the best of reasons for knowing that it was? As the judge pointed out in his summing-up, the natural thing for an innocent person who entertained such a suspicion would be to go at once to the police, but Louise Masset went to her brother-in-law and said, 'I am being hunted for murder, but I have not done it,' before she even told him of the child's death at all. Is any theory of her innocence consistent with such behaviour as this?[54]

*The Times* added this comment to an account of the case:

In the first agony of shame and apprehension women frequently kill a newborn infant, and probably persuade themselves that killing a thing barely alive is no murder. Most men, we imagine, feel more compassion than indignation when a woman so sore beset and probably scarcely responsible for her actions falls into crime. But there are no mitigating circumstances of that kind in this case. It was a very deliberate, callous, and cold-blooded murder, although carried out with the extreme clumsiness which we are accustomed to find in similar cases. The woman met her lover unperturbed, and returned to her duties on Monday without betraying the smallest concern. It was only when she found that the body had been identified that she fell into hysterical agitation, and went to her brother-in-

---

54 *The Globe*, 19 December 1899.

# Introduction.

law with her exceedingly weak and improbable story.[55]

An article in the *Pall Mall Gazette* was equally stern in tone:

The case of Louise Masset is one of those in which the law must reach out an unflinching hand to protect a class of society which is peculiarly unable to protect itself. There is no human creature in this country, or in any other, so defenceless as an illegitimate child, for the simple reason that, while it is to nobody's material advantage to keep it alive, there are obvious reasons why its death would be welcome. Deprived, in almost every case, of a father's protection, and a cause of disgrace to relatives who might otherwise have taken an affectionate interest in it, the poor thing has but one refuge – its mother's love. Rarely, except in the first almost irresponsible burst of shame and despair at its birth – to the consequences of which the law is rightly lenient – does the great maternal instinct fail. But if that makes default, all is, indeed, lost for the child. For the unnatural mother who beat in her little boy's forehead with a brick, strangled and stripped him, and went her way all unmoved to meet her paramour at Brighton, the law will have no mercy. Hanging is almost too good for such a murderous monster as Louise Masset.

The other noteworthy feature, besides the peculiarly cold-blooded nature of the crime, is the exceptional completeness of the chain of circumstantial evidence – for it was purely circumstantial – which the successive actions of the murderess had involuntarily forged. Bold and unflinching in her terrible determination though the woman was, she had, nevertheless, a double dose of that strange stupidity in her composition which so often makes the murderer himself the most damning witness for the Crown. Had she not chosen to do the deed at a station with which she was familiar, and with a clinker brick taken from a heap of clinker bricks in the garden of the house she lived in; had she not taken the murdered child's clothes and toy to Brighton with her; had she not, when she returned to London Bridge Station after the murder, spoken to the only witness who had seen her there with him, counsel might have instilled the saving doubt in the minds of the jury. But, in spite of the instinctive dislike of juries to convict on purely circumstantial evidence (though that, in this case, is often entirely worthy of credence), there was no doubt of which the prisoner could get the benefit. Never was the case for the prosecution more complete, or that of the defence more hopeless.[56]

On 19 December, the *Daily Chronicle* wrote:

A more heartless murder it would be difficult to conceive. The prisoner was a

---

55　*The Times*, 19 December 1899.
56　*Pall Mall Gazette*, 19 December 1899.

single woman, and the victim of what we may call her insane frenzy was her natural son. ... The case is not one which can be called, in the ordinary sense of the term, a case of merely circumstantial evidence. On the one side there are many converging facts; on the other side, it is impossible to find corroboration for the prisoner's story. Painful as it is to come to a conclusion which involves the extreme penalty of the law for this unhappy woman, we fear that no question can be raised as to the justice of yesterday's verdict and sentence.[57]

The *Daily News* also took the view that the death sentence was just, but it attempted to fathom the motive behind the murder:

There is no element of romance in the crime for which Louise Masset was yesterday convicted and sentenced to death. It was the cruel murder of a boy by his own mother, who was perfectly sane, and influenced by motives of the basest self-interest. ... At the same time, it must be admitted that the story is an odd one. The prisoner had always been good to the child. The murder was a most cruel and savage one. The risk of detection was enormous, and, indeed, the prisoner made no attempt to escape. The motive is difficult even to conjecture, and a very strong motive is required for so atrocious a deed. Probably the solution lies in some unknown part of the prisoner's life, which may or may not have been connected with the boy's father. There was some evidence that she corresponded with him, and he may have stopped his supplies. This, however, is mere conjecture. If the prisoner had told a credible story in the witness box, the result might have been different. It might have been different if her mouth had been closed. The cross-examination of a woman on trial for her life is not a pleasant thing, but it undoubtedly assists the ends of justice.[58]

According to a notice in *The Times* on 26 December 1899, Madame Tussaud's Wax Museum was already exhibiting a portrait model of Louise Masset, dubbed the Dalston Murderer, in its Chamber of Horrors – a Boxing Day treat for those determined to see out the 1800s in a certain style.

On 3 January 1900, a sad little story played itself out in the North London Police Court. Nellie Gentle appeared before Mr Fordham asking for advice on what she should do about Manfred's toy mail cart and a few articles of his clothing still in her possession. The Masset family wanted them back, but Nellie was unsure if it would be right to give them up. Mr Fordham suggested she might return the items to the family in a fortnight's time. Nellie then revealed to the court how devastated she had been by the murder: she had been under constant medical treatment ever since and had had to sell her piano to pay the

---

57  *Daily Chronicle*, 19 December 1899.
58  *London Daily News*, 19 December 1899.

# Introduction.

doctor's bill. Moreover, Miss Masset's allegations against her in the witness box – that she did not take proper care of Manfred, that she was uneducated and unfit to be in charge of children – had ruined her reputation as a nurse. Sobbing, and in great distress, she told the court that since those slurs had been published she had not been able to get another nurse child. Mr Fordham sympathised, and remarked that if the jury did not believe Louise Masset then he was sure nobody else would.[59] (Nellie's fears were unfounded, for, by the spring of 1901, she was once more caring for a nurse-child: Percival James Mansfield, the illegitimate child of Alice Maria Mansfield.)

Though the overwhelming consensus of opinion in the press was that Louise Masset was guilty, her solicitor, a dubious character by the name of Arthur Newton, fought hard to save her from the gallows, or to inflate his reputation, whichever came first. Members of her family – George and Mathilde Simes, Richard and Léonie Cadisch, and Louise's mother, Elizabeth – presented a petition pleading for a reprieve, as one Home Office official put it, 'on the double lines of belief in her innocence and insanity in the family if she did commit the crime'.[60] This was rejected by the Home Office (just as a more conventional petition – presented by Newton on 30 December 1899 – had been), but its details cannot fail to intrigue.[61]

The petition listed cases of insanity in the family and included a letter sent by a relative, Mr Albert H. G. Burchatt, stating that his father and Louise's maternal grandmother were brother and sister and listing the following family members known to have suffered from, if not certifiable insanity, at least some form of mental instability: Aunt Maria, who committed suicide; Aunt Susan, who was an authenticated case of insanity; Aunt Charlotte, who was a rumoured suicide; Uncle Thomas, who also attempted suicide and was undoubtedly insane; Uncle Edward, who committed suicide; Cousin Alfred Houghton, who suffered from permanent insanity, as did cousin Mary Ann Burchatt; Maria Burchatt, who committed suicide by drinking poison; Mary Ann's sister, Elizabeth Wyeth, who was temporarily insane and detained in an asylum; and her son, Daniel, who was clinically classified as an 'idiot', and was unable to speak or control the use of his limbs.

As for Louise Masset, he had this to say:

---

59   *Daily Chronicle*, 4 January 1900 (see Appendix III).
60   TNA:PRO HO 144/1540/A61535/80 (see Appendix VI).
61   A similar petition had been compiled by members of Christiana Edmunds's family in 1871, in a poison case also centred in Brighton. However, she had the backing of the celebrated diagnostician, Sir William Gull, was reprieved on the grounds of insanity, and spent the rest of her life in Broadmoor. See editor's book, *Fatal Affairs*.

# Masset.

Louise Masset ... is of good physique, with strong and little-controlled passions, a quick but most short-sighted intelligence and a rudimentary or non-existent moral sense so abnormal as to permit of her committing the cruel and unnatural act of which she has been pronounced guilty, without altering her equanimity or disturbing her in the slightest degree in the pursuit either of her pleasures or her ordinary avocations; and in my humble opinion the soundness of her mental condition is, to say the least, so doubtful that she ought not to be subjected to the extreme penalty of the law.[62]

Also included were typed copies of two letters, originally in French, which Louise had apparently sent to Maurice, the father of Manfred, shortly before the murder. They had not been produced by her defence counsel, Lord Coleridge, at the murder trial:

Saturday Morning,<br>30th September, 1899

My dear little Husband,

I am really astonished not to have received any news from you. For mercy's sake write to me!!! you know how unhappy I am and unhappily placed for the present you would help me for I know your heart. I can only suppose that you are not receiving my letters or that you are travelling and that thus you do not know how unhappy I am, but however you had promised me to let me know the result of the revision. Were you taken – yes or no? Will you help me – yes or no?

They are wondering in the family that I do not buy black things and I answer that I will think of it during the week. What will they say when they see me one day come back with Manfred – Or rather I do not think I shall ever have courage to bring the child to the house, then we will have to stop without shelter that is all, for I have promised not to speak about you and if I bring back the child they will force me to say your name I was not thinking a year ago, that I should be so frightfully unhappy, I had faith in your heart and love for us and when I read over again your lust letter it shows that you still love us; then why this complete silence? If your father interferes let me at least know it, do not leave me in my frightful despair for I am at the last extremity.

Your little Loulou – who beseeches you to help her.

The second letter, supposedly written on 6 October, read as follows:

---

[62] TNA:PRO HO 144/1540/A61535/80 (see Appendix VI).

# Introduction.

219 Clyde Road,
South Tottenham,
Middlesex,
October 6th 1899.

My dear Maurice,

In receiving the few lines you sent me on Wednesday I felt as if stunned, the shock was too great especially after your last letter still full of love. But to-day I am awake and I accept for me the fate destined to me. I do not find you a coward to have loved another but a coward to leave me just at the time of my greatest misery for you know as well as I that your son will never be received in my family. They have told me often enough. I ask nothing for myself, it was your kisses I wanted, because I loved you and will always love you but having had advice outside the family I tell you that your son cannot and must not be thoroughly as dirty linen. I ask you then to assure him a shelter to send him an annual sum of 12 pounds, it is very little for a father who comes from a wealthy family. In that case I <u>swear</u> that you will never be bothered in any way. At the age of 15, that is in 12 years time, the annual sum can cease as Manfred, your flesh, will have then I hope a fairly good education and health to work himself – Answer me on that subject and all correspondence will end between us but do not let me wait long for your answer. Your heart is your master but remember my own is a mother's heart and it also speaks.

Your well-wisher,
Louise.
Mrs Mason.[63]

Let us pause here to consider the authenticity of these letters, and the origins of the idea that Louise may have murdered Manfred because she feared that she could no longer afford to pay for him. It is proper to say that the offer which she had supposedly received from the Brownings – total cost, £18 per annum – was lower than the amount she was paying to Nellie Gentle (£22 4s per annum). This saving of four guineas a year might have been tempting, especially since the Brownings, whom Louise considered to be women of good breeding, would probably not mangle Manfred's vocabulary – no 'ain't', no 'them things'. Indeed, we might even say that the offer of a better standard of education in a more salubrious part of the city, all for a substantial discount, was too good to be true. Perhaps Louise was seeking to reduce her costs. But Léonie Cadisch, who had guaranteed Manfred's expenses, had never been

---

[63] TNA:PRO HO 144/1540/A61535/80 (see Appendix VI).

## Masset.

asked to step in, which showed that Louise was managing her commitments. Indeed, sometimes she paid Nellie Gentle in advance. Maintenance payments from Manfred's father may well have made a big difference here, but Louise was apparently only working two, three or four afternoons a week, and Mrs Sonnenthal, whose daughter she taught, considered that Louise gave 'every satisfaction'. Other commissions would surely have been possible, since Mrs Sonnenthal had already recommended Louise to Mrs Haas; she could easily have obtained extremely helpful references. Léonie, besides, was determined that Louise was not to be financially overburdened. 'My husband is well-to-do,' she told the inquest. Louise paid no rent on her accommodation, and was 'kept … free of expense'.[64]

There is little, therefore, to tell us that Louise was imminently at risk of economic meltdown. Nor is there anything to indicate that the aforementioned maintenance payments were due to come to an end. Louise testified in court that Manfred's father had always met his financial commitments, 'and would now', if only circumstances were different. However, after the trial, suggestions of exactly this sort began to emerge. Lord Coleridge wrote to the Home Secretary, Matthew White Ridley, from Devon on 29 December 1899:

> I see that a movement is on foot for a reprieve in this case, and, as I was counsel for the accused, I think I ought to communicate the fact that the prisoner had reason to think that she was abandoned by the father of the child, & I believe did think so.
>
> This ~~fact~~ state of things naturally I suppressed, as to disclose it would have been to supply a motive for the crime, & I argued that no sufficient motive was disclosed by the prosecution.
>
> I think that you, sir, should know this, before arriving at a final decision in the case.[65]

This letter posed more questions than it resolved. How had Lord Coleridge come to know that Louise feared financial ruin? What evidence had been available to him before the trial to suggest it? Had he seen the letters quoted above – ideally, the originals, not manuscript copies or transcripts? Did he even know of them? Nothing in his letter reveals the source of his information.

At the Home Office, much discussion followed. 'This letter,' wrote Charles Murdoch, the assistant undersecretary, annotating the correspondence, 'supplies the missing link of motive'.

---

64   TNA: PRO CRIM 1/58/5.
65   TNA:PRO HO 144/1540/A61535/23.

# Introduction.

Desertion by the father whereby the burthen of maintenance of the child is thrown wholly upon the mother is, of course, always taken into account in the infanticide and child murder cases which come before the Home Office. This feature was brought prominently forward in the last case of infanticide before [the] S[ecretary of] S[tate] (see case of Lucy Gould ...).

But in Lucy Gould's case, and the general run of cases, desertion by the father means destitution to the mother.

But in Masset's case, this is not so. ...

I fear that Lord Coleridge's case letter, while tending to clinch the prisoner's guilt by supplying the motive, does not go further in favour of the prisoner than to show that she might possibly be subjected to inconvenience by reason of the burthen – but not to any such distress as might fairly be considered as a mitigating circumstance.[66]

In a note to the Home Secretary himself, Murdoch observed, 'Lord Coleridge's letter seems to destroy any weight the sol[icito]rs petition might possibly have had beforehand, for he abandons the first line of defence and appears, somewhat doubtfully, to put in a plea ad misericordiam'.[67]

Only after this letter did Arthur Newton press the idea that his client was facing some form of financial incapacity. Until this time, at the trial and even in the first petition against the sentence, the defence had kept to its position, which was, as Newton wrote in the petition, that Louise 'always had plenty of money in her possession and at her disposal'.[68] But the futility of this line of defence must have become increasingly obvious, especially once the first petition had been unfavourably received.

Instead, the opposite angle was tried, and the next petition, submitted to the Home Office on 8 January 1900 emphasised Louise's alarm at her financial

---

66 TNA:PRO HO 144/1540/A61535/23. Lucy Gould's case was described in a Home Office memo in the following terms: 'Lucy Gould (21), Essex, 11 November 1899. Domestic servant. Murdered her illegitimate child of a fortnight old, by drowning. Prisoner was seduced by her master (a married man with children), who sent her over from Hamburg to Dovercourt for her confinement. He sent her over £4 at first, but subsequently cut off all supplies. Strongly recommended to mercy by the jury; judge heartily concurring. ... Lucy Gould was no doubt cruelly deceived, and basely deserted. She was only twenty or twenty-one, a most affectionate mother, had provided baby clothes and paid her way as long as she could, and when arrested had only a penny farthing in her pocket ... It seems to me that the features in the case to be chiefly considered are her great depression, her sufferings from lactation, and her weakness at the time when the murder was committed.' (TNA:PRO HO 144/1540/A61535/7.) In the editor's *Deadly Dilemmas*, several similarly desperate cases are recounted. The 1856 case of Celestina Sommer, who killed her ten year old, 'inconvenient' daughter (like Manfred, a nurse-child since birth) bears some points of resemblance with Louise Masset's case: both were middle-class, educated women unable to attribute their actions to poverty.
67 TNA:PRO HO 144/1540/A61535/23.
68 TNA:PRO HO 144/1540/A61535/44 (see Appendix II).

abandonment. Her letters were meant to prove the fact of Manfred's father's new love, and his intention to cease his maintenance payments. But they are hardly persuasive – much more persuasive would have been a letter from Manfred's father himself. Newton was said to have 'been to France' to see the elusive Maurice (whom Louise said was serving in the French army at the time), and the solicitor was said to have 'the whole of these original letters in his possession'.[69] But where we would expect to see something saying, 'I have found someone to whom I wish to be married, and I shall therefore be unable to continue paying for Manfred's upkeep', we see, transcribed, rather than in manuscript, two letters apparently from, rather than to, Louise, both of which very probably derived not from the condemned woman, but from the creative typewriter of Arthur Newton himself.

If this seems like a serious charge to make against a legal professional, then Newton's subsequent history needs to be taken into account. In other cases in which he acted – those of Hawley Harvey Crippen and Samuel Herbert Dougal, both covered in this series (NBT 24 and NBT 44 respectively) – he was shown to be quite mischievous, if one may put it euphemistically; or operating outside the law, if one may not. He and his clerk, Frederick Taylorson, had both been tried in 1890 for conspiring to defeat the ends of justice (Newton pleaded guilty to the sixth of six charges; the charges against Taylorson were not proceeded with). His work in other cases – particularly those of Marie Herman, Robert Wood (NBT 65) and John Tyrwhitt (with a possible link to A. J. Monson – NBT 7) – need further examination, but space forbids it here. He was certainly not beyond fabricating evidence, and Louise Masset's 'letters' can be considered in this context.

Beyond Newton's curious efforts, other petitions had done the rounds. One had been compiled by Madame Andrée Téry, the editor of an all-female Parisian publication, *La Fronde*, and it arrived at the Home Office together with Newton's covering letter:

> Re: Louise Masset
>
> Now a Prisoner under sentence of death at H. M. Prison Newgate.
>
> We have the honour to present to you a Petition to Her Most Gracious Majesty The Queen, which has been prepared at the instance of "La Fronde" Newspaper, which as you no doubt know is a paper owned by, edited by, and written by women alone.
>
> The Petition in question is signed by over 1,000 French ladies, many of whom are French Governesses and who all feel that the extreme sentence of the Law should

---

[69] TNA:PRO HO 144/1540/A61535/80 (see Appendix VI).

# Introduction.

not be carried out in this case, as there exists a reasonable doubt in the matter.⁷⁰

The petition read as follows:

> To her Majesty the Queen of England and Empress of India.
>
> A French governess, Louise Masset, has been sentenced to death by an English tribunal and is to be executed on the 9th of January next. A number of French governesses implore your Majesty's grace for their abandoned colleague and miserable fellow-countrywoman. They petition the great Queen, who was herself a perfect mother, to have pity on this unworthy mother who killed her child.
>
> The moments of mourning for nations are those when royal clemency should be unbounded. Too much blood is being shed just now. Grant that the accursed stream may not be increased by that of a woman. Notwithstanding the monstrous nature of the crime, be forgiving, for pity would not be itself if it were extinguished by the unworthiness of the guilty.
>
> We have learned that it is no vain task to solicit one from whom Parliament withdrew the right of signing death sentences in apprehension of her pity.
>
> We therefore supplicate the pardon of Louise Masset with hearts full of hope. May your Majesty deign to accept the homage of our deepest respect.⁷¹

The petition was sent to the Queen by the Home Office, and returned without endorsement three days later. Following the rejection of this plea for *ex cathedra* intervention, Madame Téry actually travelled to Osborne House hoping to raise the question with the Queen in person. Instead, she was given an interview with Sir Arthur Bigge, who regretted that he had no authority to consult with the Queen, but promised to bring Mme Téry's concerns to the attention of the Home Secretary.

The *Daily Chronicle* also published a letter to the editor written, pseudonymously, by a former schoolfellow of Louise Masset's, who contended that, while the circumstantial evidence against her was strong, yet no evidence had been offered to prove that she had been at Dalston Junction that day:

> Sir – As an old schoolfellow of Louise Masset I join your other correspondents in invoking the aid of your powerful pen and great influence on behalf of this unfortunate woman. ... To one who knew the poor girl in happier days as an unusually gentle and kind-hearted creature a much more complete chain of evidence is required to carry conviction of guilt. I have just received from France a letter from another schoolfellow, who emphatically holds that Louise Masset

---

70   TNA:PRO HO 144/1540/A61535/39.
71   *Daily Chronicle*, 29 December 1899.

# Masset.

must be either innocent or mad – an opinion with which many people will agree.[72]

A week before Louise Masset was due to be executed, this letter was published in the *Daily Chronicle*, dated 2 January 1900, in which two new witnesses were identified. It was from Mr W. Gurney Winter of Ruddle and Gurney Winter, Solicitors, Southampton Buildings, Chancery Lane:

> Sir – It will be remembered that the prosecuting counsel in the case of Regina v. Masset stated that if the prisoner went down to Brighton on the four o'clock train she had been falsely accused of the crime and the learned judge in his summing up drew the jury's attention to the circumstance that there had been no evidence forthcoming to support the prisoner's story as to her movements in Brighton until after the arrival of the nineteen minutes past nine train.
>
> The prisoner stated in her evidence that on arriving in Brighton by the train which left London Bridge at four o'clock she proceeded down West Street, passed the Clock Tower, and afterwards went to 'Mutton's Restaurant' in the King's Road, where she had refreshment in the upstairs dining room, and where she remained for some time, as it was raining hard. She also said she had her waterproof with her.
>
> On Friday last I was at 'Mutton's Restaurant' (where I have been known as a visitor for some years), and in the course of a conversation with one of the waiters I happened to hear something which aroused an interest in the case, and on the following morning I called again, and made further inquiries of one Henry James Streeter, who is the waiter in the upstairs dining room. He informed me that he well remembered 27 October, as 'it was raining and a very wet and dirty day', and in consequence he had only two customers in the afternoon. One was a gentleman who upon further inquiry I have since been informed gave the name of 'De Levy'. The other was a lady dressed in black, who arrived about six o'clock. She took 'refreshment' and remained about three quarters of an hour.
>
> Mr. Mutton, jun., I am also informed, saw her in the room on two or three occasions, and both he and Henry James Streeter, I am told, believe that they could recognise her again if they could see her. After reading the press reports of the case, and seeing the importance of the matter with which I am now dealing, Henry James Streeter consulted Messrs. Bucknill and Co., solicitors at Brighton, and gave them a written statement of the evidence which he was able to give, and that firm, during the trial, I am informed, communicated by letter, sent by express delivery, with the prisoner's solicitors, from whom I am also informed they afterwards received a letter stating that they had satisfied themselves in the matter.
>
> Henry James Streeter informed me that no one called upon or saw him in the

---

[72] *Daily Chronicle*, 29 December 1899.

# Introduction.

matter, and even expressed surprise he had not been interviewed. As to the accuracy of this, I am quite unable to form any opinion. If that lady was the prisoner she must have journeyed down either before or by the four o'clock train, and it would become, therefore, an important piece of testimony in her favour, and entitle her to an acquittal. It being important to establish the question of identity, I telegraphed from my hotel at Brighton on Friday last to the prisoner's solicitors, requesting them to furnish me with a photograph of the prisoner, and expressing the hope that I might be of some assistance to them, and on Sunday I received a reply thanking me for my letter, and informing me that they had not got a photo of their client, but that if I were interested in the matter they would send me a copy of the petition, to which signatures could be obtained.

Meanwhile, I endeavoured to obtain through Messrs. Bucknill and Co. a written statement and declaration from Henry James Streeter, but this firm, on the ground of professional etiquette, hesitated to supply this to me without again communicating with the prisoner's solicitors, and up to the time of writing I have not been able to obtain the same, although I am pressing for it.

I have strong reasons to know, however, that both Mr Mutton, jun., and Henry James Streeter are ready and prepared to come up to London to see if they are able to identify the convicted woman. I also understand that, if the convicted woman can remember what refreshment she had, their system of business will enable Mr Mutton to test the accuracy of her story in a somewhat extraordinary manner. In these circumstances it seems to me that, whatever the result of the inquiry may be, justice demands a thorough and exhaustive search into the matter before the death sentence is carried out, and, if necessary, a short respite should be granted – I am, Sir, your obedient servant.[73]

This was at the very least an interesting twist on the matter, and, indeed, the earnestly hoped-for 'thorough and exhaustive search into the matter' then took place. Only the highlights can be represented here, however, and the best of these is the irritated remark of a Home Office mandarin on a docket dated 4 January 1900 – 'This letter shows what kind of person Mr Gurney Winter is'.[74] Gurney Winter had proceeded to trouble the Home Office not only on the question of the meal taken at Mutton's, but on other Masset-related matters besides; he had even been to the Home Office on New Year's Day, before his anxieties reached the press. The whole thing came down to the question of whether Louise Masset could recall what she had eaten when – in this rendition – she had been at Mutton's long before the 7.22 pm train reached Brighton Station. It seems that she could not decide, even when urged gently towards a definitive statement by

---

73   *Daily Chronicle*, 2 January 1900.
74   TNA:PRO HO 144/1540/A61535/45.

# Masset.

the enigmatic Taylorson. She eventually opted for two slices of hot meat with gravy and vegetables, bread and butter, cheese, and ale or beer, all for 2s 6d; Newton, apparently disliking the sudden precision of this doubtful recollection, reduced it to meat, vegetables, bread and cheese at 1s 9d; the records from the restaurant showed that the visitor, whoever she was, had had either a pot of tea with bread and butter at sixpence, or a pot of tea with bread and butter and a sole (total cost 2s 2d with table fee); the waiter thought the former, rather than the latter. The conclusion, ineluctably reached, was that, whoever had dined at Mutton's that evening, it was not Louise Masset.[75]

On 3 January, one John Hughes-Ellis of 128 Westminster Bridge Road came forward to the police at Bethnal Green Police Station. He had read a letter in the *Morning Leader*, and the experience had provoked memories which, suddenly, seemed to him to be of great significance. After visiting the newspaper offices and making a statement, he went the next day to the police station at Borough, and was sent from there to Bethnal Green. Inspector Forth takes up the story:

> He stated that between 3.00 pm and 4.00 pm on 27 October last, he was riding in an omnibus from Elephant and Castle to Cornhill. When the omnibus stopped at the foot of London Bridge, Surrey side, he noticed two women with a little boy standing on the rest in the centre of the road. The eldest one spoke to the conductor and both with the child entered the omnibus and rode towards Shoreditch. He alighted at Cornhill leaving the three inside.
>
> He describes the eldest as sixty-five years of age, medium height, and he believes she wore a cape; the second, thirty to thirty-five years of age, short. Both had the appearance of associates of low class prostitutes and from their conversation he is positive that they were not educated women. He cannot describe the child beyond his being about four years of age and he thought it looked of better class than the women. He does not think either of the women carried a parcel and he is satisfied that the child did not wear a red hat. ...
>
> I read to Mr Ellis the evidence prisoner gave at the C[entral] C[riminal] Court where she described the women as ladies of birth and education. I also told him how the deceased was dressed and he is satisfied that the child he saw was not the deceased.
>
> Mr Ellis was some time since the missionary at Lambeth Police Court and is now agent to the Borough of Lambeth Permanent Building Society.
>
> I am confident that the women and child Mr Ellis speaks of had nothing to do with the murder.[76]

---

75  TNA:PRO HO 144/1540/A61535/77.
76  TNA:PRO HO 144/1540/A61535/50.

# Introduction.

Under ordinary circumstances, that ought to have been that, but Hughes-Ellis began to have doubts about the veracity of his original convictions. He gave a new statement to Gurney Winter, whose collaboration with Newton was increasingly open, and between them the solicitors ensured that Hughes-Ellis's newly-revised opinion was transmitted to the Home Office. Newton had shown Hughes-Ellis a photograph of Manfred, taken after death: even Nellie Gentle, who had been more familiar with the child than anybody else, had described the deceased Manfred's face as 'dreadfully disfigured', and had declined to swear to his identity 'until,' as Inspector Forth noted, 'she had satisfied herself by other marks on its body'. When Hughes-Ellis had seen Forth on 4 January, he had 'said it would be doubtful if he could recognise the child by a photograph as he only saw him for a few minutes'. Despite these unhelpful auguries, however, Hughes-Ellis had disposed of any uncertainties under the heady influence of Newton and Gurney Winter: 'I conscientiously believe,' he stated, 'that the photo in question is that of the child whom I saw with the two women on the omnibus at London Bridge Station – or rather crossing London Bridge at the time and date above mentioned'.[77]

Other statements – not to mention scrawled postcards to the police – emanated from Hughes-Ellis over the following days. The infinite possibilities of his bespoke reality enabled him to reach conclusions without the bother of having to match these to any evidence. Perhaps the two women – the two on the omnibus, the two who were at least a class below Nellie Gentle, whose common linguistics had supposedly been a point of dissatisfaction for Louise Masset – had stripped Manfred practically at the moment of receipt, passed him along to 'their confederates', and then, hearing that 'their confederates' had murdered him, 'deposited such of the clothes as were found at the Brighton Station, there, in order to throw suspicion upon her'.[78] There was nothing to support any of these claims, and much to undermine them. At one time, according to one document emerging from the typewriter of Gurney Winter, Hughes-Ellis had 'been very uneasy in his mind' about his sighting of the two women and the child, and had wished that he had contacted the authorities earlier. He had even taken the trouble to go back to London Bridge, questioning several bus conductors and policemen, before realising that he would be unable to find anyone to substantiate his story.[79] No such qualms now affected him, and he complaisantly improvised to the rhythms established by his legal 'confederates', if we may use the word here.

---

77 TNA:PRO HO 144/1540/A61535/50.
78 TNA:PRO HO 144/1540/A61535/52.
79 TNA:PRO HO 144/1540/A61535/45.

Masset.

The matter became less evidential as it went along. Gurney Winter sent to the Home Office a statement from a gentleman called David Taylor, who lived at 36 Holywell Lane, Curtain Road, in which he said that he was on the same bus as John Hughes-Ellis (getting on after Hughes-Ellis had alighted) and that he saw the two women with the child as described. He had consulted with his friends about the matter after hearing about the murder, and composed a letter to Scotland Yard, but he decided against sending it.[80] Now, he had come forward to prop up the unsubstantiated claims of someone who had long since admitted to a policeman that the people he had seen on the omnibus were not like those described by Miss Masset, and whose subsequently-restored confidence in his original observations did nothing to advance the case for a commutation, and risked doing serious damage to its credibility. Nothing could be done to rescue these desperate last attempts to exonerate Louise Masset.[81] She was in her final days.

## X.

On Monday 8 January 1900, a syndicated newspaper report told the country that:

> Mr Arthur Newton, solicitor, has received a reply from the Home Secretary, stating that, having considered the whole case, he is unable to interfere with the sentence of death passed upon Louise Masset for the murder of her child at Dalston. Mr Newton, however, was at Brighton on Sunday further prosecuting his enquiries, and he hopes to be able to forward early today (Monday) such evidence as will cause the Home Secretary to alter his decision. The execution is fixed for tomorrow (Tuesday).[82]

This article appeared on the same day in the *Daily Chronicle*:

> Tomorrow Louise Masset is to be hanged. Today, therefore, while there is yet time we wish to ask the Home Secretary once and for all whether the case is so absolutely free from all element of doubt as to justify him in thus ruthlessly coming to an irrevocable decision. We hold no brief either for or against Louise Masset. She may be innocent or she may be guilty. Our only concern is that justice shall be done. Our only contention is that sufficient doubt exists and sufficient fresh evidence has come to light since the trial to justify at least an examination of these witnesses before the wretched woman is hurried out of this world.

80  TNA:PRO HO 144/1540/A61535/72.
81  TNA:PRO HO 144/1540/A61535/70.
82  *Derby Daily Telegraph*, 8 January 1900.

# Introduction.

Let us briefly review the reasons for and against revision. On the one side no sufficient motive was given for the murder, and the evidence was purely circumstantial. Louise Masset is a Frenchwoman, and would probably be more gently judged in France. She is a woman, and it is against the burden of precedent to execute a woman for the particular crime of child-murder. But we are not pleading for mitigation of the sentence, though it seems to us there is ample ground for a reprieve to allow time for the truth to emerge.

During the trial the prosecuting counsel pressed the case against the prisoner with unusual virulence; and since the trial various material points have come to light, which appear to have been kept back by the police. Mr Mutton testifies that a person resembling Louise Masset in every particular dined at his hotel at an hour which would have made it impossible for her to commit the murder. The police kept back this evidence at the trial.

Mr Hughes-Ellis identifies the photograph of the murdered boy as being that of a child which he saw in the company of two strange women on the day of the murder. The police interviewed Mr Ellis on the 4th inst., but did not show him the photograph of the child. Mr Ellis has been further corroborated by Mr David Taylor, who also saw the child in the same company. Miss Teahan, one of the ladies who found the body, states that she saw two women, answering to the same description, outside the lavatory, when she came out. She disclosed the fact to the police and it was kept back at the trial.

In three essential particulars, therefore, the police appear to have allowed their bias against the prisoner to influence their action in conducting the case. This alone supplies sufficient reason why the whole of the evidence should be carefully re-sifted, and the new witnesses allowed to identify the woman and the photograph of the child. On the other hand we fully recognise that bearing witness before the Home Secretary, under private conditions, is not the same thing as bearing the brunt of cross-examination in court. Moreover, it is not right that every case, after being tried by a judge and jury, should undergo a process of newspaper trial. In this particular case, however, we hold that important fresh facts have come to light. The danger of a miscarriage of justice taking place which cannot be rectified is infinitely greater than any that can occur on the opposite side.

If Sir Matthew White Ridley still refuses to allow this unfortunate woman even a chance of proving her innocence, he will lay himself open to the charge of that unworthy form of official cowardice, which shows itself in obstinately refusing to reopen a *chose jugée*.[83]

The *Daily News*, on 8 January, made this important statement in respect of a proposed change in the judiciary:

---

[83] *Daily Chronicle*, 8 January 1900.

## Masset.

The Home Secretary has refused to interfere with the sentence of death passed upon the French governess, Louise Masset, for the murder of her son, which will be carried out tomorrow. We are certainly not prepared to say that Sir Matthew Ridley is wrong. The evidence given against the prisoner at the trial was highly circumstantial, and the stories afterwards circulated had a very slender foundation. But we regret, and we think the public will regret, that an open inquiry could not by law be held.

Sir Matthew Ridley, like all his predecessors, gives, we do not doubt, the most sincere and anxious consideration to everything which can be said in favour of a prisoner under sentence of death, or, indeed, under any other sentence. He is assisted by the judges, and by the able members of the permanent staff at the Home Office. But the proceedings upon which the life of a man or woman condemned in court ultimately depend are secret and confidential. They are shrouded in a mystery which is not only unnecessary, but in some respects mischievous.

If there were a Court of Criminal Appeal, such as the present Lord James proposed when he was Mr. Gladstone's attorney-general, people could see for themselves the grounds on which an application for quashing a verdict or directing a new trial was granted or dismissed. Messrs Newton complain in their letter that the police have not followed up the clue furnished them on the prisoner's behalf since the trial, and that the Home Secretary will not allow important witnesses to be confronted with the prisoner.

Sir Matthew Ridley has no doubt taken a heavy responsibility upon his shoulders. But to take it is his duty if his mind is clear, and he has no conceivable motive for a decision which must be painful to him. The question is whether such a terrible burden should be laid upon any man, and we believe that this case, whatever else may be thought of it, will assist the movement for creating a Court of Criminal Appeal.[84]

Despite this comment and others couched in a similar vein, a reprieve was not granted, and the execution of Louise Masset went ahead on the morning of 9 January 1900.

The *Echo* reported the scene in the most graphic terms:

<blockquote>

WAITING ROOM TRAGEDY.

EXECUTION OF LOUISE MASSET TODAY.

A CONFESSION.

Louise Masset was executed at Newgate this morning for the murder of her illegitimate child at Dalston Junction Railway Station. Notwithstanding the heavy mist that enveloped the City, a crowd commenced to collect outside the

</blockquote>

---

84  *London Daily News*, 8 January 1900.

# Introduction.

prison walls before seven o'clock. By eight o'clock it had swollen to considerable dimensions, and when, at a quarter to nine, the prison bell began to toll, between 2000 and 3000 persons must have been present. The foreign element was conspicuous by its almost entire absence, though it was reported that a female relative of the condemned woman was present.

### THE BLACK FLAG.

Not more than a few seconds had elapsed after the hour of nine had struck when the black flag was run up from the quadrangle, announcing to the world that Louise Masset had met her doom. The appearance of the flag was greeted with loud cheers, but the crowd, which was a most orderly one, quickly dispersed. …

### THE ROPE TESTED.

The preparations for the execution were commenced yesterday morning. Billington, the hangman, with his son, as assistant, arrived at the jail in the course of the day, and in the presence of Colonel Milman, the Governor, Mr Under-Sheriff Metcalfe, who supervised all the arrangements, acting on behalf of the High Sheriff, tested the rope and the mechanism of the drop to safeguard against any possible mishap.[85]

### IN A DESPONDING MOOD.

The unhappy woman, who had been hopeful of a reprieve, was informed of the Home Secretary's decision on Sunday afternoon. Since Sunday Louise Masset has remained in a most despondent and dejected state of mind. In the course of yesterday she was transferred from the apartment she has occupied whilst under the death sentence to the cell set apart for condemned men, which is situate within a few paces of the scaffold. There was no visit from any relatives to the jail yesterday.

### RELATIVES' FAREWELL VISITS.

The condemned woman's two sisters and brothers-in-law paid 'farewells' on Friday and Saturday. Louise Masset retired to rest shortly after ten o'clock last night. She was very restless, and slept little. She rose at six o'clock this morning, attiring herself in the clothes which she wore on her trial. These were taken from her immediately after conviction, the prison officers supplying her with a special dress, which is usual in the case of condemned females.

### THE LAST MEAL.

Louise Masset presented a careworn and haggard expression, although she showed not the slightest symptoms of fear at her approaching fate. She scarcely touched her breakfast, which was brought to the condemned cell at seven o'clock,

---

85  As in the case of John Lee in 1885. James Berry tried to hang him three times, but the mechanism failed each time and Lee's sentence was commuted to imprisonment. See editor's book, *Deadly Service*.

# Masset.

and consisted of bread and butter and tea. The Rev. Mr Ramsey, the jail chaplain, who has been unremitting in his endeavours to bring the condemned woman to a proper frame of mind, was in attendance on her down to the last. The passing bell of the prison commenced to toll at a quarter to nine o'clock. Colonel Milman, the Governor of the prison, Dr Scott, the surgeon, and Mr Under-Sheriff Metcalfe and his brother arrived at the prison shortly before nine o'clock.

### A CONFESSION.

At three minutes to the hour Billington, with his assistant, entered the condemned cell and performed the process of pinioning. Louise Masset offered not the slightest resistance. Her last words were: 'What I am about to suffer is just. And now my conscience is clear.'

Louise Masset walked without any assistance to the scaffold. The final preparations were rapidly performed and the bolt drawn. A drop was allowed of 7ft. 8in. and death was stated to have been instantaneous. Louise Masset evinced wonderful firmness and self-control right up to the last.[86]

This account fails to mention that the person assisting Billington was, in fact, not his son but William Warbrick who later recalled the execution of Louise Masset in some detail:

A heavy mist hung around old Newgate on the Tuesday morning as we went about our mournful task of preparing to hang Louise Masset. A crowd of 2000 to 3000 gathered outside, and at a quarter to nine they knew that the fateful moment was near, for the bell of St Sepulchre's began to toll.

I had quite a shock when I entered the condemned cell with Billington. Her beautiful tresses had turned white since we saw her on the previous evening, and much of her facial loveliness had disappeared under the fearful strain occasioned by her night of soul-agony. She looked a nervous wreck.

Her face was haggard as she stood up to be pinioned, but despite this, she was perfectly calm and collected. I must confess that her firmness was a big surprise to me. She was a woman, and a young one at that, so naturally I expected her to display fear of the scaffold.

She hardly saw the execution chamber: Billington capped her too quickly for that. And she would hardly have realised that the rope was round her neck and that I had strapped her legs before the merciful release came.[87]

The *Daily News* added this comment on 10 January 1900:

---

86  *Echo*, 9 January 1900. 'Ramsey' should read, 'Ramsay', and he was the assistant chaplain.
87  *The Weekly News*, 12 February 1916.

# Introduction.

It will be a great satisfaction to many worthy people that the unhappy woman who was executed yesterday morning for the murder of her child confessed her guilt before she died. Even the mind of the Home Secretary, who deserves none of the abuse which has been showered upon him, will be relieved. A deeply-rooted instinct of human nature suggests doubt of unacknowledged crime. And in this case the motive seemed to be wholly inadequate for the commission of so cruel and unnatural an act. Whatever the motive may have been, it was probably not disclosed, and is not likely to be disclosed now.

The circumstantial evidence was clear and strong. People who say that there is 'only circumstantial evidence' do not seem to know what they are talking about. Murders are not as a rule committed in public. Privacy is always desired, and usually obtained. If nobody could be punished for an offence which nobody saw him commit, one gaol would hold all the prisoners in England. But that very desirable consummation must be reached by other and more legitimate means. The prisoner was the last person seen with the child. The railway station where the body was found is a station she knew and frequented. On the day of his death she took him from the family with whom he boarded, and gave them false reasons for doing so. The child's clothes were found at Brighton, where she went immediately after the murder. When she read in a newspaper that the body of a little boy had been discovered at Dalston Junction she went to her brother-in-law and told him she was being 'hunted for the murder of her son', which was untrue. Certain allegations made after the trial, and not worth discussing now, deserved inquiry, and we have no doubt that they received it. Some of them might have been, and were not, brought forward at the trial. The others were vague and inconclusive.

The prisoner gave evidence on her own behalf and told an ingenious story to explain away the evidence against her. It was wildly improbable, and unsupported by any testimony except her own. Her admissibility as a witness aided the cause of justice, because it showed that there was no valid defence.

All executions are horrible, and especially the execution of a woman. But if ever a woman deserved to be hanged, it was this one.[88]

The official announcement of Louise Masset's death, signed by the Under-Sheriff of the County of London, was sent to the Home Office that same day, along with a certificate signed by Dr James Scott, who had carried out the post mortem on her body.[89] As was customary, the body of Louise Masset was buried within the confines of Newgate Prison.

---

88  *London Daily News*, 10 January 1900.
89  TNA:PRO HO 144/1540/A61535/96.

# Masset.

## XI.

Louise Masset's story about the two Browning women doesn't bear close scrutiny. If they did exist and were, in fact, baby-farmers, they would never have bothered to take the parcel containing some of Manfred's clothes to Brighton Station – the clothes having been, in this scenario, altered to avoid identification – and leave it in the waiting room to incriminate her. They had given a false address and no undisputed witness had seen them; they could have simply slunk away and disappeared amongst the teeming tenements and alleys of North London, ready to repeat the scam with some other desperate mother. Louise would have been well aware of the nefarious activities of baby-farmers in London and elsewhere: she therefore concocted the story of the Browning women knowing it would seem perfectly feasible. It might well have been believed had not Mrs Ellen Reece challenged her statement that she had caught the 4.00 pm train to Brighton that day. It was extremely unlikely that, even in favourable traffic, Louise could have got from London Bridge – where she was seen by Mrs Reece at 3.05 pm or 3.10 pm – to Dalston Junction and back (committing the murder in the platform lavatory between the two journeys) in time to catch the 4.00 pm train to Brighton; and, even if she had, then the fact that the time of Manfred's death was, according to Dr Fennell, more likely to be closer to 6.00 pm than the earliest of Dr Bond's estimates, 2.55 pm, vitiated her story anyway. Louise's account of catching the 4.00 pm train, if true, gave her a strong alibi – or at least established reasonable doubt. The fact that Mrs Reece had seen her at London Bridge shortly before 7.00 pm demolished this alibi, and nobody can have required any further invitation to wonder about why Louise would lie about this matter. The exertions of Lord Coleridge were insufficient to shake Mrs Reece's compelling testimony.

The question must be addressed – why would an intelligent and hitherto affectionate mother hand over her child without receiving a receipt for the deposit paid, and without inspecting the 'school' to which he was to be taken? The story about the Browning women arriving to collect him an hour and a half late must have been intended to account for these two anomalies, but a couple of uncomfortable gaps remained. Louise should have realised that, even if her story had been true and the Browning women had arrived late, she could easily have gone to see the premises in Chelsea and caught a later train to Brighton. There was no urgent necessity for her to catch the 4.00 pm train from London Bridge that day, since Eudore Lucas would not reach Brighton until the following afternoon.

A more likely scenario is that the story of the two Browning women was

# Introduction.

a complete fabrication, and that Louise went to London Bridge intending to murder Manfred that afternoon in time to catch the 4.00 pm train to Brighton. After all, for what other reason would she have brought – if, indeed she did – the clinker brick from the garden of her sister's house in the Gladstone bag? She was seen waiting at London Bridge for at least one and a half hours. Was she not, as she claimed, waiting for the arrival of the fictional Brownings, but trying to pluck up the nerve to kill her son?

Or was it simply that the railway station at London Bridge was too crowded with potential witnesses? She must have been anxious to escape the scrutiny of both the attendants at London Bridge, Georgina Worley and Ellen Reece, who seemed bent on asking her questions, but these were not the only risks to her privacy. Mrs Reece said that as many as six hundred women and children might pass through the waiting room in any one day. Was that the reason she decided to go to Dalston Junction instead? Although she denied on oath that she had ever been in either the waiting room or the lavatory there, she was very familiar with the station: she travelled through it several times a week and often arranged to meet Lucas there. Though she denied it in court, surely she had sometimes found the need to use the lavatory after teaching until 7.00 pm – or at least to freshen up and make herself as attractive as possible before meeting young Lucas? She may well have known that the waiting room was unattended, and that the lavatory cubicles would provide a much more secluded venue for murder than the bustling concourses of London Bridge.

In other aspects, too, Louise's story falters very badly. She could not even make up her mind about what she had eaten at Brighton – the only thing which would conclusively prove her identity with the afternoon diner in black at Mutton's. Despite the passage of time, one would think that she would have remembered: it was not a normal, run-of-the-mill day, by any reckoning – not that anyone could have derived that conclusion from Louise's behaviour, as she, by all accounts, was coolness personified. The chambermaid, Alice Riall, didn't notice anything untoward about her demeanour when she checked her into the hotel at 9.45 pm that evening. Lucas also testified that she appeared perfectly calm and her usual self throughout their weekend together; her sister, Léonie Cadisch, said she seemed tired but calm and collected when she returned home on the Sunday evening. Most women, it might be supposed, would have been a little downhearted after saying goodbye to a child – let alone if she had brutally killed him. Under other circumstances, her chilling insouciance could have been construed as a sign that she was totally unaware that her son had been murdered and was lying in the mortuary at Hackney, but the evidence was piling up against her.

# Masset.

To accompany the icy control, there were errors, and even silly mistakes. Why did she take the parcel containing some of Manfred's clothing to Brighton and leave it at the station to be discovered and identified? She could so easily have tossed it from the window of the Brighton-bound train, over a cliff, or from the end of one of the piers on the seafront. She had already successfully disposed of some of the undergarments, so why not all of them? It is difficult to explain why the boy's clothes had been altered, seemingly to hamper identification, when they could just as easily have been destroyed or lost forever.

Why on earth did Louise take Manfred's favourite toy scales to the hotel with her and leave them in a drawer in room 11, knowing that they would be found and that Nellie Gentle would be able to identify them and thereby incriminate her? Had she, perhaps, taken the scales from the boy when he was being persistently fractious at the railway station and popped them into her pocket or the Gladstone bag, only to discover them later when she unpacked in the hotel room that evening? It would have been simple just to toss them into the sea. Or could it be that she kept the toy scales for sentimental reasons, as a memento of the little boy she had brutally murdered for some unfathomable reason earlier that day? If this was her reason for keeping the scales with her, it was a mistake that would ultimately help to hang her. A psychologist might suggest that these errors of judgement were engendered by guilt and that they were her subconscious way of being found out. And yet, if there is a *possibility* that Louise's story of the Browning women legitimately taking charge of Manfred was true, this might explain why she took the parcel of clothes and the toy scales to Brighton with her. Perhaps, as she said in court, she intended to give them to the child when she subsequently visited him at Chelsea. If she was innocent of the child's murder, she would have had no need to get rid of either the parcel or the toy scales. Their presence in Brighton was indicative either of innocence, or of error. The jury must have leaned towards error.

Why was little Manfred so unhappy that Friday? Knowing that he was frightened of trains, it seems odd for Louise to choose to take him to London Bridge, one of the busiest stations in the city, where his distress would no doubt escalate into a tantrum guaranteed to attract attention – unless, of course, she was telling the truth, and the two Browning women had stipulated the venue for the handing over of the child. Manfred would, no doubt, have picked up on his mother's anxiety and tension. Did he sense that he was in danger? Admittedly, he would have been very upset having to say goodbye to Nellie Gentle, but he was accustomed to spending time with his mother every Wednesday. Then again, Nellie was quoted as saying that the boy was always uneasy being with his mother and did not like her affectionate overtures, which might explain his

# Introduction.

distress.[90] The conductor of the omnibus from the Birdcage, Thomas Bonner, testified that Manfred was crying on the journey to London Bridge. For many boys of three and a half years of age, the twin prospects of a sea voyage and a family reunion would have been thrilling; but Manfred submitted to travel with his mother only with visible and almost portentous reluctance.

Where was Louise from 6.45 pm on the following Monday evening – when she left Mrs Haas's house – and 11.00 pm, when she knocked on the door of her sister's house in Croydon? Having read in the evening newspapers that the body of the dead child found at Dalston Junction had been identified, was she desperately constructing the story of the mysterious women on Tottenham Green to account for the death – or did she meet Lucas during those four hours to discuss the dilemma with him? This seems unlikely, as he professed to have no interest in the child – but her absence causes us to wonder.

Most chillingly of all, we read this trial with the disconcerting awareness that Louise could have changed her mind at any time. She didn't need to get rid of Manfred in order to spend the weekend with Eudore Lucas, as the child was living full-time with Nellie Gentle's family. Even after collecting him at the Birdcage, Louise could so easily have returned him to Nellie later that afternoon, saying that she had had second thoughts about taking him to France. In her 16 October letter to Mrs Norris, she had said that she would not stand in the way of Manfred's future prospects; but these are the sorts of awkward conundrums which affectionate mothers face all the time. She could simply say that she had had a change of heart. After she had off-loaded Manfred, restoring him to the safety of Nellie's humble care, she could have then caught the train to Brighton – any train, at any time – for her tryst with Lucas. And yet, horrifyingly, she went through with the murder.

Even Louise's 'confession' can be looked at in more than one way. On the evening of 8 January 1900, in conversation with Mr Alexander Keith Ramsay, the assistant chaplain at the prison, she said, 'What I suffer is just'.[91] Perhaps this was an acknowledgement of the correctness of the jury's verdict; or perhaps it was really a regretful admission that she had failed in her duty to protect Manfred from death at the hands of baby-farmers. According to one commentator, 'Louise Masset would never have been hanged had she confessed to the crime immediately it took place', and it is certainly true to say that there was a general distaste for imposing the sentence of death upon women, and

---

90   Mr Justice Bruce, writing to the Home Office, said that 'she had not gained the affection of the child'. (TNA:PRO HO 144/1540/A61535/30.)
91   TNA:PRO HO 144/1540/A61535/96.

then carrying it out.[92] Louise's case, however, shared few similarities with the majority of infanticide cases, which typically involved the murder of newborn children by mothers experiencing post-partum psychosis or the impact of social exclusion, shame or terror, rather than mothers deciding to dispose of children of three and a half years old. The careful premeditation which had been put into the murder of Manfred Masset placed it in a different class. To the last, Louise left the truth of her son's death to interpretation, surrounding it with improbabilities and near-impossibilities. It is difficult to know whether a last-minute mea culpa, expressed unambiguously, would have saved her life; it may not have done, and, either way, she may have preferred death to years of confinement in prison.

In an attempt to resolve some of the uncertainties which remained, attempts were made to invest Louise's crime with the characteristics of those of other, more typical, child-murders. It was suggested in a report in *Lloyd's Weekly Newspaper* on Sunday 24 December 1899, that 'it has transpired since the trial that the prisoner had not been helped of late by the mysterious father of the child and was in arrears for its keep'.[93] We have seen that similar suggestions emerged from Lord Coleridge and Arthur Newton. Mr Justice Bruce, writing to the Home Office on 2 January 1900, thought that 'the fact that her business engagements in October consisted only of six lessons a week seemed to me to render it probable that the payment of £1 17s a month might well be regarded by her as a drain on her resources,' although he also noted that '[t]here was really no evidence beyond the statement of the prisoner that she ever received any help from [Manfred's] father'.[94] The idea that Manfred's father might have discontinued his maintenance payments was worth little when there was no proof that he had ever made any such payments in the first place. Louise was not known to be in financial trouble. Léonie Cadisch, who had guaranteed the costs of Manfred's keep if Louise defaulted, testified that she had not been asked for any money; and Nellie Gentle did not describe any arrears. Maternal anxiety about the financial implications of child-rearing were common to many cases of child-murder, but arguments of this nature could not be applied to Louise's case.

But if not money, then why not shame? The puritanical views of the Victorian era were exemplified in the Masset family's attitude to Manfred's illegitimacy. George Simes tried unsuccessfully to keep the family names out of the court proceedings, and Léonie Cadisch made several telling remarks whilst giving evidence in the case. She admitted that she did not know the name of Manfred's father ('She never told me', she testified) but the family had rallied, providing

---

92  Felstead, S. T., *Sir Richard Muir: A Memoir of a Public Prosecutor* (The Bodley Head Ltd: London, 1927), 198.
93  *Lloyd's Weekly Newspaper*, 24 December 1899.
94  TNA:PRO HO 144/1540/A61535/30.

# Introduction.

her with free board and lodging and allowing her to keep all the money she earned from her teaching appointments. Léonie let slip, however, that Manfred's existence – on the periphery of the family unit but unavoidably in the centre of their consciousness – had been 'a sore point with the family for some time'.[95] It hardly made the situation better to say that they had 'forgiven her' and that they were 'making the best of it' – the inescapable conclusion is that little Manfred's illegitimacy had never really been accepted and accommodated.[96] Louise's stain had not been erased, but adjustments had been made to conceal it from sight as far as possible; Louise proceeded to examine the tolerance of these adjustments by speaking about Manfred 'very often ... as if she was very fond of him'.[97] 'As far as I know,' Léonie said, 'nobody made the fact of his existence unpleasant to her,' but the tension and embarrassment underlying the comment are palpable.[98] These remarks provide a sad reflection of the time, and attitudes which are largely, but not entirely, a thing of the past.

Despite their desperate efforts to persuade the Home Secretary to issue a reprieve, the family members did Louise and her son a great disservice by shutting their doors on Manfred instead of helping Louise to overcome her evident despair at her situation. Had the family been less judgemental – if they had welcomed Manfred, instead of rejecting him – this murder might never have happened. Yet, because of their small mindedness over Manfred's birth, their shame was to be compounded a hundredfold by Louise's infamous death at Newgate.

## XII.

A few more points. The fact that the murderer placed the shawl over the victim's body can surely be construed as indicative of Louise Masset's guilt. Baby-farmers wouldn't have bothered – it was their business to kill infants without remorse. The placing of the shawl was an act of private pity – the pity a mother, no matter how detached, might feel after subjecting her child to such a merciless attack and then leaving him on the cold floor of a public lavatory.

But, to the general public, and, no doubt, the jury, Louise Masset's actions were heartless. She had deliberately removed Manfred from the loving care of Nellie Gentle and had lied about her real motivation as part of a premeditated plan to kill him. S. Theodore Felstead believed that '[i]n all probability ... the

---

95 *Islington Gazette*, 3 November 1899.
96 *Lloyd's Weekly Newspaper*, 26 November 1899.
97 TNA:PRO CRIM 1/58/5.
98 Ibid.

ghastliness which attended her [Louise's] visit to Brighton ... finally determined the Home Secretary that the condemned woman must pay the extreme penalty', but her visible remorselessness must have contributed too.[99] It is interesting to compare Louise Masset's strength and determination with the painful distress of Sarah Drake – a notable mid-nineteenth century infanticide – who spent the duration of her trial cowering in the dock and covering her face in shame, agonised with grief at the death of her young son.[100] To the gentlemen sitting in judgement at Louise's trial – all, no doubt, bristling with sanctimonious outrage when her liaison with Eudore Lucas was exposed – her composure must have signified a character as cold as steel, and can hardly have failed to influence the verdict.

The difference, eventually, was a matter of life and death. Sarah Drake, Lucy Gould, Eliza Boucher, Eliza Adkins - and many other women who had resorted to murdering their children - were shown mercy in consideration of the catalogue of hardships and misfortunes they had faced in their lives; but Louise Masset had no such excuse and subsequently suffered the ultimate penalty of the law.[101] She was the first person to be hanged in England in the twentieth century.

The crux of the mystery remains – which train to Brighton did Louise catch? – the 4.00 pm or the 7.22 pm? We can only imagine the scene at London Bridge that day: amid the smoke, the bustle, and the jostling groups of bowler-hatted, city-suited gentlemen, do we see there the figure of an attractive woman in black, wearing a fashionably jaunty hat, boarding the 4.00 pm train to Brighton – or is that her, much later, at 7.22 pm, carrying a sturdy Gladstone bag and a brown paper parcel containing her dead child's clothes?

A year after Louise's execution, Queen Victoria was granted her dearest wish – to be buried in the mausoleum at Frogmore, laid to rest for eternity beside her beloved Prince Albert.

## XIII.

There is one last thing to mention. We saw a little earlier that the *Daily Chronicle*, which had been energetically pursuing the case for a commutation, at least, ever since Louise Masset's conviction, alleged that 'Miss Teahan, one of the ladies who found the body,' had stated 'that she saw two women, answering to the same description [as the Brownings], outside the lavatory, when she came

---

99  Felstead, 195.
100  See the editor's *Bad Companions* (The History Press; Stroud, 2013).
101  See the editor's *Deadly Dilemmas*.

# Introduction.

out. She disclosed the fact to the police and it was kept back at the trial.'[102]

This new evidence was provided by Newton to the Home Office on 5 January 1900. Miss Teahan's statement read as follows:

> I am single. I am a governess. I live at 46 Warple Road, Isleworth.[103] I gave evidence at the trial of Louise Masset, and am one of the ladies who found the body of the dead child at the Dalston Junction Railway Station about 6.20 on the afternoon of Friday 27 October last.
>
> I recollect that on the day in question, after I came out from the ladies' lavatory there, as detailed by me in my evidence, I saw two ladies dressed in black sitting on number 3 platform, facing number 4 platform, with their backs to number 2 platform, who correspond in appearance to those described by the prisoner in her evidence; and on the last day of the trial I was so struck by this fact that I mentioned it to Mr William Lewis of the Treasury, but nothing was said by anyone at the trial with regard to it, although I had mentioned this to Mr Lewis.
>
> I should mention that after hearing Miss Masset's evidence as to what the ladies had said with regard to the death of the husband of the elder one about six months ago, the fact of their being in black brought the matter back to my mind.
>
> I thought it only just and right that I should call and tell this to Mr Arthur Newton, which I did today, this 5 January 1900.[104]

As ever, this was only a copy of the statement – Newton had not forwarded the original, which would have allowed Miss Teahan's signature to be compared directly with those she had applied to other documents – but nonetheless there was obviously something here worth enquiring into. Slim hopes, perhaps ... but was it possible that Miss Teahan had really seen the Brownings? Charles Murdoch, at the Home Office, recommended that Mr Lewis, who had prosecuted the case in the magistrate's court on behalf of the Treasury, should be written to in order to obtain his side of the story, and indeed this was done the next day, 6 January 1900, as an annotation on the Home Office docket shows. Unfortunately, nothing – neither a letter in reply nor an annotation – shows us what the outcome was. We know that the surviving Home Office documentation is incomplete, but the routine 'weeding' (as it is called) of files in subsequent years normally did not take place at the level of individual documents. Whole dockets were retained, or whole dockets were scrapped – they were not opened and 'weeded' page by page. Elsewhere in the file, we read, in a briefing document compiled at the Home Office shortly after the execution – one perhaps intended

---

102   *Daily Chronicle*, 8 January 1900.
103   *Sic* in statement – should read: 'Worple Road'.
104   TNA:PRO HO 144/1540/A61535/46.

for distribution to the press, or for the Home Secretary to rely on in parliament – that 'Numerous ... representations were submitted to the Secretary of State besides those which appeared in the public press. They all received the most careful investigation. Many of them proved to be partly exaggerated and partly false, and none of them were of sufficient importance in any way to disturb the decision already arrived at in the case.'[105] And there can be no doubt that the official appetite was to learn the truth – it would hardly have been worth writing to Mr Lewis if it was not. We infer that Miss Teahan's late-arriving evidence was not found to stand up. And yet, without knowing Mr Lewis's response, an uncomfortable gap remains.

Of course, as always, there are contingencies which we cannot afford to overlook. Miss Teahan – if she really did make this statement, and let us suppose that she did – would not have been the first witness in a murder case to feel, quite reasonably, remorse about the destiny of the prisoner. The death sentence would do that to people, and there can be little doubt that other late-arrivers, such as Hughes-Ellis, were similarly motivated by their feelings about capital punishment. Every murder case attracted protests against execution, or otherwise manufactured, if well-meant, attempts to provide exonerating evidence, long after the verdict had been given. Newton can be faulted too, wasting his time on the hopeless evidence of Hughes-Ellis and Mutton's restaurant when Miss Teahan's statement would have been a better bet. But then we have the problem of the Brownings, who did not exist, apparently, except in Louise Masset's imagination. There was no proof of their existence, and the suggestion that there may have been two women in black at Dalston Junction an hour or more after Manfred had been murdered – well, if they had been the Brownings, and if they had killed Manfred, why would they still have been there? And could these women not have been anyone? The life expectancy of most men, especially those working in London's filthy and dangerous factories, docks and railways, was not much more than fifty. In this story, there were at least four named widows – Louise's mother, Elizabeth; Ellen Reece; Georgina Worley; Ann Skeet – and large hats, copious scarves and veils were common and often similar in style. On autumn evenings in Victorian London the presence of women in black at railway stations was commonplace and Louise's own mourning dress may well have made it difficult for witnesses to distinguish her from many other women similarly-dressed.

Eventually, we have to suppose that Miss Teahan's evidence was not enough to justify 'disturbing the decision', as the Home Office glossed it. But the procedural issue is unresolved by the documentation. She might have

---

105   TNA:PRO HO 144/1540/A61535/96.

# Introduction.

seen anybody, but if Miss Teahan did, indeed, on the last day of the trial, tell Mr Lewis about her sighting of the women in black, and if this was indeed ignored, then perhaps Miss Masset's commutation was not quite the distant prospect it might otherwise seem. We do not know what Mr Lewis said about the allegation; we do not know whether he said anything at all, although we ought, probably, to infer it from the Home Office's later statement. It is the absence of proof that troubles us. Perhaps the response was received, filed, for some reason not notated on the docket, and pilfered later on, as sometimes happens with publicly-available records – but it hardly seems likely, when much more interesting documents, which remain in the file, could have been pilfered instead. We are struggling to reach a position here. The Home Office's work in Louise Masset's case was thorough and transparent throughout; except, in this example, and only in this example, we know that we do not know what they knew. *Something* must have justified the Home Secretary in disposing of Miss Teahan's evidence. The question is: what?

*

## Note on the Text.

Only certain parts of the trial of Louise Masset are available in direct transcript, and as recorded, line by line, by the shorthand writer to the court. These include: the evidence of Mrs Ellen Reece; the evidence of the defendant; the summing-up of the judge; the verdict; and the judgement. The transcripts of these sections of the trial are available in TNA:PRO HO 144/1540/A61535.

Those parts of the trial which are not available in direct transcript have been interpolated from Central Criminal Court Session Paper, Vol. CX, Sessions I to VI (TNA:PRO CRIM 10/80; also www.oldbaileyonline.org, version 7.2, accessed 23 March 2017, December 1899, trial of Louisa [sic] Josephine Jemima Masset [t18991211-77]).

*

I would like to thank Mark Ripper (M.W.Oldridge) for his customary generosity in sharing invaluable research material : also the other members of the Notable British Trials editorial team - Adam Wood and David Green - for their constant support throughout the writing of this book. My thanks too to Andrew Firth for his excellent reproductions of the railway station maps used at the trial.

# Leading Dates in the Louise Masset Case.

| | | |
|---|---|---|
| 1896 | 24 April | Birth of Manfred Louis Masset at 17 Highgate Hill, Holloway, North London; the illegitimate son of Louise Josephine Jemima Masset, a thirty-six year old Anglo-French woman. |
| | May | Manfred becomes a nurse-child with Mrs Norris and her daughter, Eleanor Eliza (Nellie) Gentle, at 210 Clyde Road, Tottenham. |
| 1898 | August | Manfred's father, Maurice, returns to France; Louise Masset goes to live with one of her sisters, Léonie Cadisch, and her husband, Richard, at 29 Bethune Road, Stoke Newington. A young Frenchman, eighteen year old Eudore Lucas, takes lodgings with Louise Masset's mother, Elizabeth, at 31 Bethune Road. |
| 1899 | 20-22 May | Louise Masset, Eudore Lucas and a couple of friends spend a few days in Brighton, staying at Findlay's Temperance Hotel at 36 Queens Road. |
| | 4 October | Louise Masset meets two women called Browning in Tottenham Green and they suggest she places Manfred in their care. No decision is made. |
| | 11 October | Louise Masset meets the two Browning women again and she agrees to pay them £12 for a year's board and lodging for Manfred and 10s per month for his education. It is arranged that the child will be handed over at London Bridge Station on Friday 27 October. |
| | 16 October | Mrs Norris and Nellie Gentle receive a letter terminating their arrangement to care for the child as, according to Louise Masset, she intends to take him to France to live with his father's family. |
| | 18 October | Louise Masset instructs Miss Gentle to bring Manfred to London Bridge Station on Friday 27 October. |
| | 24 October | Louise Masset buys a large black woollen shawl from Maud Clifford at McIlroy's drapery store at 161 High Street, Stoke Newington. |
| | 25 October | Louise Masset visits Manfred at Clyde Road, as usual. Change of plan – that, on Mrs Norris's advice, Nellie Gentle is to hand over the child at the Birdcage public house, near Stamford Hill, at 12.45 pm, instead of London Bridge Station. |
| | | Louise Masset meets Eudore Lucas at Liverpool Street Station and suggests that they spend the following weekend in Brighton. That evening, she tells her sister, Léonie, that on Friday 27 October she is taking Manfred to France. |
| | 26 October | Nellie Gentle has a studio photograph of Manfred taken as a memento. |

# Masset.

| | | |
|---|---|---|
| 1899 | 27 October [12.45 pm] | Nellie Gentle hands over Manfred at the Birdcage public house, and Louise Masset takes him on the omnibus to London Bridge, saying she intends to catch the Newhaven ferry to France. |
| | [1.45 pm] | Mrs Georgina Worley, relief attendant in the ladies' first and second class waiting room at London Bridge Station, sees Louise Masset and Manfred and the child seems happy. When asked, Louise Masset says she is waiting for someone. |
| | [2.40 pm] | Mrs Ellen Reece, attendant in the ladies' waiting room at London Bridge Station, sees Louise Masset and Manfred, who seems agitated and is jumping on the seat. Mrs Reece asks why he is so unhappy. About 3.10 pm, Louise Masset takes him to the refreshment room to buy a cake. |
| | [2.45 pm] | In her version of events, Louise Masset meets the two Browning women, gives them £12, and hands over Manfred, saying she will visit him at 45 King's Road, Chelsea, the following week. They leave, taking the child with them and saying that they will return with a written receipt for the money. They do not return. |
| | [4.01 pm] | According to Louise Masset she catches the 4.00 pm train to Brighton (the departure of which was delayed by one minute), and arrives at Brighton at 5.19 pm. She goes for a walk along the seafront. At 6.20 pm, by the same story, she takes refreshment at Mutton's Restaurant, and then spends her time window shopping until shortly before 9.00 pm. She returns to the railway station to collect her Gladstone bag, checking into Findlay's Hotel at 9.45 pm. She has a brown paper parcel. |
| | [6.20 pm] | Mary Teahan and Margaret Biggs find the body of a dead child on the floor of the public lavatory at Dalston Junction Station. The two girls leave the station and go to their lecture as planned. Joseph Standing, porter, is called to attend the body. David Bunday, station-master, is called; also Dr James Patrick Fennell and the police. |
| | [6.54 pm] | According to Mrs Ellen Reece, Louise Masset enters the washroom at London Bridge Station. Mrs Reece turns on the water for her, gives her a towel and a clothes brush. She notices an untidy brown paper parcel near the washbasin stand. Louise Masset rushes off to catch the 7.22 pm train to Brighton, which actually leaves at 7.23 pm and reaches Brighton at 9.18 pm. There is no sign of Manfred. |
| | 28 October | Louise Masset goes to Brighton Station to meet Eudore Lucas's train from London, which arrives at about 3.20 pm. At 3.30 pm, a brown paper parcel is found by attendant Ann Skeet at Brighton Station and sent to the lost property office at London Bridge Station. |

# Leading Dates in the Louise Masset Case.

| | |
|---|---|
| 29 October | Louise Masset and Eudore Lucas return to London. Léonie Cadisch, believing that Louise has taken Manfred to France, notices nothing untoward. Louise Masset goes straight to bed. |
| 30 October | Nellie Gentle reads an account in the *Daily Mail* about the body of a child found at Dalston Junction and suspects that the murdered child is Manfred. She identifies Manfred's body at Hackney Mortuary and makes a statement to the police. |
| [1.30 pm] | Louise Masset leaves home to attend her usual lessons – first at the home of Mrs Haas, after which she escorts Mrs Sonnenthal's daughter to a school in Baker Street. She reads a newspaper account about the body of a child being found at Dalston Junction. |
| [About 7.00 pm] | On her way back to Bethune Road, Louise Masset sees a placard outside Dalston Junction which announces that the dead child has been identified. The *Evening News* confirms the identification of Manfred and states that the police are looking for the child's French mother. She panics and, instead of going back to Bethune Road as usual – where, unknown to her, the police are watching the house for her arrival – she makes her way to the home of her other sister, Mathilde, and her husband, George Simes, in Stretton Road, Croydon. |
| 31 October | In the early hours, after following George Simes and Richard Cadisch and questioning them about their sister-in-law's whereabouts, Detective Sergeant William Burch and Detective Constable Frederick Allen go to the house in Croydon and arrest Louise Masset. She declares her innocence but offers no resistance and is taken into custody at Dalston Police Station. She is later moved to Holloway Prison. |
| 1 November | The brown paper parcel found at Brighton Railway Station is inspected by Detective Sergeant Richard Nursey: he identifies items of the child's clothing – now damaged – as described by Nellie Gentle. |
| | A pair of toy scales belonging to Manfred is found in room 11 at Findlay's Hotel. |
| | Proceedings before magistrate (Mr Edward Fordham), at North London Police Court – first day. Louise Masset is charged with the wilful murder of her son, Manfred Louis Masset. She pleads not guilty. |
| 2 November | Inquest on the body of Manfred Louis Masset at Hackney Coroner's Court before Dr Wynn Westcott – first day. Louise Masset's solicitor, Mr Arthur Newton, attends proceedings on her behalf. |

# Masset.

| | | |
|---|---|---|
| 1899 | 4 November | Proceedings before magistrate – second day. |
| | 9 November | Inquest of the body of Manfred Louis Masset – second day. |
| | 11 November | Proceedings before magistrate – third day. |
| | 16 November | Inquest of the body of Manfred Louis Masset – third day. Louise Masset is committed to stand trial for the murder of her son on the coroner's warrant. |
| | 24 November | Proceedings before magistrate – fourth day. |
| | 1 December | Proceedings before magistrate – fifth day. Louise Masset is committed to stand trial at the Central Criminal Court, Old Bailey, on a charge of murder. |
| | 13 December | Trial of Louise Masset at the Central Criminal Court, before Mr Justice Bruce – first day. Mr Charles Mathews and Mr Richard Muir appear for the prosecution; Lord Coleridge appears for the defence, assisted by Mr Arthur Hutton and Mr Bovill Smith. |
| | 14 December | Trial of Louise Masset – second day. |
| | 15 December | Trial of Louise Masset – third day. |
| | 16 December | Trial of Louise Masset – fourth day. |
| | 18 December | Trial of Louise Masset – fifth day. The jury retires at 4.55 pm and, after half an hour's deliberation, returns a verdict of guilty. Mr Justice Bruce passes sentence of death. Louise Masset is returned to Newgate Prison to await execution. |
| | 29 December | Lord Coleridge writes to the Home Secretary to advise him that 'the prisoner had reason to think that she was abandoned by the father of the child'. |
| | 30 December | Arthur Newton submits a petition against the sentence to the Home Office. The petition is rejected by the Home Secretary. |
| 1900 | 3 January | Letter to Home Secretary enclosing statements from Vincent Mutton and Henry Streeter, who state that they saw Louise Masset in Mutton's Restaurant about 6.20 pm on 27 October. |
| | 5 January | Arthur Newton forwards to Home Secretary copy of statement from Mary Teahan. Ms Teahan claims that she saw two women in black at Dalston Junction Railway Station on the day she discovered Manfred's body, and that she mentioned this sighting to Mr William Lewis (a solicitor working for the Treasury) while Louise Masset was still being tried, but he took no action. No surviving Home Office documentation indicates how this matter was resolved (if at all). |

# Leading Dates in the Louise Masset Case.

6 January — Arthur Newton forwards to Home Secretary handwritten letter from John Hughes-Ellis – sighting of two women and a distressed child about 3.15 pm on 27 October, on an omnibus near London Bridge Station. Also a letter from David Taylor, who was on the same omnibus and saw the two women and the child. Also a letter from Thomas Evans casting doubt on Ellen Reece's identification of Louise Masset as the woman she saw in the washroom at London Bridge Station at 6.54 pm on 27 October.

8 January — Louise Masset's mother, sisters and brothers-in-law submit a petition against the sentence to the Home Office (via Newton). This petition includes transcribed copies of two letters supposedly written by Louise Masset to Maurice, the father of Manfred, on 30 September and 6 October 1899. The petition is rejected by the Home Secretary.

Plea for reprieve, addressed to Queen Victoria, submitted in person at Osborne House by Mme Andrée Téry, editor of La Fronde.

9 January — Execution of Louise Masset. After post mortem and inquest, her body is buried within the confines of Newgate Prison.

# CENTRAL CRIMINAL COURT

Before Mr Justice Bruce

Louise Josephine Jemima Masset
Indicted for the Wilful Murder of
Manfred Louis Masset

---

Mr Charles Mathews and Mr Muir
*appeared for the prosecution*

Lord Coleridge and Mr A. Hutton
*defended the prisoner.*

---

(Transcript from the shorthand notes of Messrs Barnett & Buckler of Chancery Lane [shorthand writers to the court].)[106]

---

106  Trial details from TNA:PRO HO 144/1540/A61535.

# First Day – Wednesday 13 December 1899.

## Arraignment and Plea.[107]

Louise Masset, 36, a governess, was indicted for and charged on the coroner's inquisition with the wilful murder of Manfred Louis Masset. The prisoner pleaded 'Not Guilty'.

## Opening Speech for the Prosecution.[108]

**Mr Mathews**

Mr MATHEWS, in opening the case, said the prisoner was charged with the murder of her illegitimate son, Manfred Louis Masset, a little boy of about three and a half years of age, and it was alleged that she committed the crime on 27 October at Dalston Junction Railway Station in a lavatory attached to the ladies' waiting room. The prisoner carried on the calling of a French governess giving French lessons to families in different parts of London, and in October she was residing with Mrs Cadisch, a married sister of hers, at 29 Bethune Road, Stoke Newington. In October, a young man named Lucas was living next door to 29 Bethune Road, and he had made the acquaintance of the prisoner prior to October. The little boy, of whose murder the prisoner was accused, was placed when he was three weeks old in the charge of Miss Helen[109] Gentle, who resided with her mother and stepfather in Clyde Road, Tottenham. Miss Gentle and her mother and stepfather became much attached to the little boy, and he also became much attached to them. The prisoner went regularly once a week to see the child, it being her custom to go on Wednesdays to see him, and she showed every sign of being an affectionate and loving mother to him. The prisoner paid Miss Gentle £1 17s a month for taking charge of him, which sum was always regularly

---

107 This account of the arraignment and plea is taken from *The Times*, 14 December 1899. The article was clipped by the governor of Holloway prison, Lieutenant-Colonel E. S. Milman, and retained by the Home Office in what is now TNA:PRO HO 144/1540/A61535/2.

108 This account of Mathews's opening statement is taken from *The Times*, 14 December 1899. The article was clipped by the governor of Holloway prison, Lieutenant-Colonel E. S. Milman, and retained by the Home Office in what is now TNA:PRO HO 144/1540/A61535/2.

109 *Sic* in article. Should read, 'Eleanor'.

## Masset.

**Mr Mathews** paid, it being sometimes paid in advance. The prisoner said that the father of the boy was a Frenchman, and she herself was half French, her father being French and her mother English. Letters bearing foreign postage stamps used to be addressed to the prisoner in the name of Mrs Mason at Miss Gentle's house. The young man Lucas's acquaintance with the prisoner seemed to have dated from September of last year, and it appeared to have ripened considerably by Whitsuntide in this year, because at Whitsuntide the prisoner and a female friend went with Lucas and a male friend of his to Brighton and stayed there from Saturday until Monday. After their return from Brighton, according to Lucas's statement, he and the prisoner began walking out together, and he commenced making love to her. The prisoner then mentioned the existence of the little boy, saying that she thought he ought to know before he continued to make love to her. Lucas said he was pleased that she had told him of the fact, that it was very fair of her to have told him, and he said he did not want to speak any more about the child. Lucas said that he never discussed with the prisoner the question of marriage, that that question was never mentioned between them, and that neither he nor the prisoner ever mentioned the existence of the child as an obstacle to marriage. Two of the families to whom the prisoner gave French lessons resided in the north of London, and she used to travel from Dalston Junction to the London Road Station[110] or the Finchley Road Station in order to give those lessons. On 16 October the prisoner wrote to Miss Gentle's mother stating that she had seen the father of the boy, and, as he considered that he was growing a big boy, he wished him to be brought up in his cousin's family. Although France was not mentioned in the letter, the letter indicated that the boy was to go to France. On the following Wednesday the prisoner saw Miss Gentle and made arrangements for the boy to be handed over to her on 27 October, as the prisoner intimated that she was going to take him to France on that day and would start from London Bridge Station. On 18 October, the prisoner told Mrs Cadisch that she had an opportunity of taking the boy to France to be brought up by his father, and that she was going to take him to France. On 24 October a woman who was alleged to be the prisoner bought a black shawl at a draper's in Stoke Newington. On 25 October the prisoner went to see the boy, and it was arranged that Miss Gentle should hand him over to the prisoner at 12.45 pm on the afternoon of 27 October outside a public house at Stamford Hill where the omnibuses for London Bridge started from. The prisoner told Mrs Cadisch on 25 October that she would have to go by the 2.30 train, that she would travel by way of Newhaven, and would cross by the night

---

110   *Sic* in article. Should read, 'Loudoun Road Station'.

# First Day – Wednesday 13 December 1899.

**Mr Mathews**

boat for France, and that she expected to be back at home on the following Saturday or Sunday. On 25 October the prisoner told Lucas that she was going to Brighton on Friday. Lucas said he would like to go down to Brighton to meet her, but he could not get away before Saturday afternoon. The prisoner said she would go to Brighton on Friday and would stay at the hotel where she had stayed at Whitsuntide and that she would go to the station on Saturday afternoon and meet Lucas on his arrival. Lucas told her that he would go down by the 2.00 train on Saturday afternoon, which was timed to arrive at Brighton at 3.20, and it was arranged between them that the prisoner should take the name of Miss Brooks while at Brighton and that Lucas should announce himself as her brother. At 12.30 in the day on Friday 27 October, the prisoner left 29 Bethune Road to go to Stamford Hill to receive the boy from Miss Gentle. The prisoner was carrying a brown Gladstone bag, but what it contained the prosecution were not able to say. Proof would be forthcoming that, in the back garden of 29 Bethune Road, there were some clinker bricks forming a grotto, and that there was an edging in the front garden formed of clinker bricks. Some clinker bricks were lying near the railings in the front garden. The prisoner went to Stamford Hill and Miss Gentle handed the boy to her. The boy was then wearing a blue serge frock trimmed with white braid and a blue cloth coat with gold buttons. Miss Gentle gave the prisoner a brown paper parcel containing some of the boy's extra clothing and also a pair of toy scales which he was in the habit of playing with. The boy cried at parting from Miss Gentle. The prisoner and the boy went in an omnibus to London Bridge Station, and arrived there at 1.35 pm. The prisoner went into a waiting room there and she told the attendant that she was waiting for someone. The prisoner afterwards went into another waiting room, near the refreshment room, where she remained until five or ten minutes past 3.00 pm. The boy was fretting. The attendant at the waiting room asked the prisoner what was the matter with him and she said that it was parting from his nurse. The prisoner added, 'Perhaps he is hungry. Have you a refreshment room at the station? If so, I will go and buy him a cake.' The attendant said there was a refreshment room on the left. The prisoner then left the waiting room with the boy and went in the direction of the refreshment room. That was the last time the boy was seen alive. At 6.30 that evening his dead body was found in a lavatory attached to the ladies' waiting room at Dalston Junction Station. There was no clothing on the body except a black shawl. A medical examination showed that the boy's death was caused by suffocation, and that just before or just after his death a serious injury had been inflicted upon his head with some hard substance. When his body was discovered a clinker brick was found

# Masset.

**Mr Mathews** lying immediately to the right of his head, that clinker brick being similar in its appearance to the clinker bricks in the garden at 29 Bethune Road. The body was still warm. The prisoner went to Brighton that evening, travelling by the 7.22 pm train from London Bridge, and she engaged two rooms at the hotel where she had stayed at Whitsuntide. On Saturday afternoon the prisoner went to the Brighton Railway Station to meet the train by which Lucas was travelling and which arrived at 3.30 pm, instead of 3.20 pm. There was found in the waiting room at the Brighton Station a brown paper parcel containing a blue serge frock and a cloth coat, a portion of the trimmings of which had been removed for the purpose, as it was alleged, of destroying the identity of the clothing. Miss Gentle, however, identified the clothing by means of a tear and a grease stain. The prisoner returned from Brighton on Monday 30 October, and according to her statement she bought an evening paper, which stated that the body of the child which had been found at the Dalston Junction Station had been identified. She went to the house of Mr Symes[111], her brother-in-law at Croydon, and said, 'I am hunted for murder, but I have not done it,' and she made a statement to the effect that she last saw the boy alive at London Bridge Station, that two women, who gave an address in Chelsea, had told her that they were setting up a home, and asked her to let them have the boy to take care of, and that she gave him to those two women, together with £12 to pay for his keep for twelve months. The prisoner was afterwards arrested, and she denied the charge and repeated the statement which she made to Mr Symes.[112] A pair of toy scales was found at the hotel at Brighton.

## Evidence for the Prosecution.

**Frederick Humphreys**  FREDERICK HUMPHREYS (Policeman 49J) produced and proved the plans of London Bridge Station, and of the waiting rooms there.[113]

**Eleanor Gentle**  ELEANOR ELIZA GENTLE, sworn and examined.

I am single, and live with my mother and stepfather at 210 Clyde Road, Tottenham. My mother's name is Norris. We have been living at Clyde Road about seven years, as near as I can say. We were living there

---

111  *Sic* in article. Should read, 'Simes'.
112  *Sic* in article. Should read, 'Simes'.
113  First day's evidence from Central Criminal Court Session Paper, Vol. CX, Sessions I to VI (TNA:PRO CRIM 10/80, subsequently CCCSP; also www.oldbaileyonline.org, version 7.2, accessed 23 March 2017, December 1899, trial of Louisa [sic] Josephine Jemima Masset [t18991211-77]).

The clinker brick found at the murder scene
*from The Police Encyclopedia, Vol II (1914)*

Mr Charles Mathews QC
*Author's collection*

# First Day – Wednesday 13 December 1899.

**Eleanor Gentle**

when I first made the acquaintance of the prisoner, which was about three or four years ago.

The deceased was born on 24 April 1896, and I took charge of him when he was three weeks old. I had advertised that I was willing to take a nurse-child, and in answer the prisoner came to Clyde Road and saw my mother and I.[114] She asked what my proficiency and experience was, and I told her I had been a nurse for a clergyman's family, and that I was willing to take the child. I was to be paid £1 17s per month, and I was paid the first month in advance.

It was arranged, a few days after the first interview, that I was to go and fetch the child from Mrs Ballard's, of 17 Highgate Hill, Islington. I took the child back to Clyde Road, and the prisoner came with me. From that time up to 27 October, with a few exceptions (when the child was in the hospital for an operation for circumcision), it remained with me. The child had three operations: two at home, and one at the hospital.

While the deceased was in our care, the prisoner came and saw him once a fortnight at first, but about eighteen months ago she began to come once a week. It was about then that she went to live with her sister, Mrs Cadisch, in the Bethune Road. She seemed very fond of the boy, and the boy of her. I became very fond of him, and he of me. We were all very fond of him, and he of us. He never seemed quite so well since he has been circumcised, and I told his mother so. He seemed weaker.

The £1 17s per month was always paid, and if the prisoner came on a Wednesday and the money was due on the Saturday, she would not wait till then, but would pay me on the Wednesday. The boy was about the same in October; he did not get weaker. The prisoner generally came on Wednesdays. I remember [her] coming on Wednesday 4 October, and taking the deceased out. I remember her coming on the eleventh and taking him out, and my meeting them in the Seven Sisters Road, and we went on to Tottenham Green. We got there about 3.30 pm, and stayed there till about 5.00 pm. The prisoner and I sat about, and the child was playing. We were talking about the boy. We always had something fresh to ask about him. At 5.00 pm, we thought it was time to go home to tea. We were very upset that day because the boy was so sick. We were sitting on a seat, and the prisoner said, 'I think Manfred looks rather heavy about the eyes'. I said, 'Yes, he does,' and she said, 'Don't you think we had better be getting home?' and so we went, and the little boy came over very pale. I thought he was tired, and his mother carried him home, and when we got home he was very sick. His mother was there then; she stayed till between 6.00 pm and 7.00 pm. A doctor was not sent for while she was there.

---

114   *Sic* in CCCSP.

# Masset.

**Eleanor Gentle**

When she left, the boy still seemed to be very sick, and I sent for a little brandy. After she had gone, I went for a doctor, and I met the prisoner. She had said she was coming back to see the boy; she was to sleep at the house. I said to her that I was going for a doctor, and she saw him when he came. He prescribed for the boy, and he got better. I was with the prisoner the whole of the time after she and the boy left the Seven Sisters Road. She did not speak to anyone else. From the time that she took the boy out till I met her in the Seven Sisters Road was between a quarter and half an hour. The arrangement to meet was made at home.

The next day, the boy seemed worse: he came out in a rash, and I sent for the doctor again. The prisoner had promised to come on the Friday, the thirteenth, but she did not come. Her next ordinary visiting day would be the eighteenth, but on the eighteenth[115] my mother got a letter. This is it, and it is in the prisoner's writing [produced]. Before we received it, we had had no intimation that the prisoner intended to remove the child from our care. It came as a great surprise to me. This stated that the prisoner had seen the child's father, and that the child would be sent for to be removed from the care of Mrs Norris, as his father wished him to be brought up in his cousin's family, and to start learning French; that she was very sorry to have to remove him, but did not like to raise objections, as she thought she would be in the way of his future prospects. On Wednesday, the eighteenth, the prisoner came. Both I and my mother saw her, and 27 October was fixed for the child's departure. She did not say where she was going to take the child to. She did not name any country. It was first arranged that I should take the child to London Bridge, and she said that they would put up for an hour or two at an hotel until the boat started. I did not know where the boat started from: I was to leave them at London Bridge. The prisoner never made any statement as to the nationality of the child, or say[116] anything about the father. She told me to take a change of clothing for the child, and told me what to take. She told me to put into a parcel a flannel shirt, a chemise, a petticoat, a white serge dress, and two overalls, and bring them with the child.

I next saw the prisoner on Wednesday, the twenty-fifth, my mother being again present, and an alteration was made in the plans. My mother suggested that I had better leave Manfred at the Birdcage public house on Stamford Hill, where the buses start from, because the farther I went with him the more he would be opposed to parting with me. The Birdcage is not very far from Clyde Road or from Bethune Road. I was to be at the Birdcage at 12.45 pm.

---

115   *Sic* in CCCSP, but should read: 'sixteenth'.
116   *Sic* in CCCSP.

# First Day – Wednesday 13 December 1899.

**Eleanor Gentle**

On the Friday, I dressed the child. He had on a little red sailor hat – it had black ribbon round it, with H.M.S. Raven on it in gold letters – [and] a blue serge frock trimmed with white braid, and a little band of white braid to form a cuff, a turndown collar trimmed with white braid, [and] a little waistband of same material, with white braid on it. He had a blue cloth coat on, with brass buttons, with an anchor on each – it had fawn-coloured cuffs, with two capes of fawn colour. He also had on two petticoats – one of white flannelette and one of a grey striped flannel – a pair of white flannelette drawers with lace at the bottom, a white cotton shirt with lace round the neck and sleeves, a pair of black socks which had been a good deal darned, brown shoes with little brown straps, fawn gaiters, and a white silk tie round his neck. This blue cloth coat [produced] he had last winter, and this blue serge frock [produced] he had in the summer. The coat had a greasemark on one of the sleeves. This [produced] is the dress he had on: I see now that the white braid is taken off, and the collar and the band, [and] also the braid which made the cuffs. I can see where the braid has been: there is a piece of it here now, and there is the cotton where I should think the collar has been taken off. I am sure that this is the little child's dress. This [produced] is the little boy's coat: the cuffs have been taken off, and the capes, the buttons, and the turndown collar. I have got one of the capes in my bag, which matches: it was taken off some time ago by the prisoner. The grease-spot is here now. I have no doubt that this is the coat which was worn by the child when I took him out on 27 October.

When I took him out, I took the change of clothing which the prisoner had spoken to me about in a brown paper parcel. I also took a little pair of toy scales [produced] in a separate brown paper parcel. The boy was accustomed to weighing things. He had had some sugar and currants on the morning of the day he went away. This [produced] is a photograph of the boy; that is how he looked on the twenty-sixth, when that was taken.

We left on the twenty-seventh, and went by tram to the Birdcage, where we got out and met the prisoner. We got there first, and waited for her a few minutes. There was a bus standing by the Birdcage. I think the prisoner got in, and I got in with the boy, but I would not be sure who got in first. I put the two parcels in the bus. I got out and waited till it drove off. Both the boy and I were a good deal upset at parting – he screamed when I left him. That was the last time I saw him alive.

I had asked the prisoner if she would give me a letter of reference – I said I had one from a doctor and from a clergyman, and she said she would give me one, and, on Monday 30 October, this letter arrived, addressed to my mother, from her. [This stated that she was very sorry to have had to take the boy from Mrs Gentle's, that he had been thoroughly

# Masset.

**Eleanor Gentle**

taken care of, and that she would be very pleased to answer any inquiry.] Letters had come from time to time to Clyde Road, addressed to Mrs Mason; they had three stamps on them with a kind of a three on them; I should say they were foreign ones. The prisoner had asked me that, if a letter came for Mrs Mason, would we kindly forward it to 29 Bethune Road, addressed to Miss Masset. There was a second letter in the envelope which we received from her on 30 October. [This stated that the prisoner had just returned from her journey, that the boy cried until she got to London Bridge, that she was very ill on the boat, that she enclosed the letter promised, and that the boy sent his love.] I do not know what time those letters arrived – I was not at home – but I should say between 9.00 and 10.00 on the Monday morning.

By then, I had heard of something in the newspapers, and on the Monday morning I went to the Hackney mortuary, between 9.00 am and 10.00 am. I read something in the *Daily Mail*, and I thought it seemed to tally, and, before I did anything further, I went to our family doctor for advice, after which I went to the mortuary. That was before I went to the police. I was shown the body of a child which I identified as Manfred's. I did not identify him by the face. There were signs of injury to the face and head. It was dreadfully disfigured. It was like this photograph [produced].

I think Sergeant Burch came to the mortuary while I was there. I made a statement to him, and then I made out a list of the clothes contained in the brown paper parcel. The sergeant took them down in writing. At that time I spoke from memory. I had not been shown any of the clothes. I was afterwards shown the serge dress, the blue coat – which I identified – and the little toy scales. There was some sugar in them which the child had been playing with in the morning. I was also shown a piece of brown paper which I had received from a Mr Shaw, who is a draper at Tottenham; it had 'E. Shaw, draper, Tottenham' on it [produced]. The piece which I received from Mr Shaw was too large for what I wanted it, and I cut a piece off, and in doing so I cut part of the name off. In the piece which I cut off I wrapped up the extra clothes for Manfred: the piece which I kept and the piece in which I had wrapped up the clothes were afterwards fitted together in my presence. These [produced] are the scales and the little pans in which Manfred weighed the sugar on the twenty-seventh. I have no doubt that the body which I saw in the mortuary on the thirtieth was the body of Manfred Masset.

*Cross-examined.*

I saw the account in the paper of my having identified the child, but it said a middle-aged person. I will not be sure whether it said that the

# First Day – Wednesday 13 December 1899.

**Eleanor Gentle**

child was the child of a Frenchwoman. I read it in the *Evening News*. [This stated that the poor little victim of the Dalston murder had been identified by the child's nurse, that it was the child of a Frenchwoman who took it away from her, that the police had an important clue, and that the nurse had frequently seen the mother, and that it was believed to be an illegitimate child.] During the last eighteen months, the visits of the mother had been weekly, sometimes oftener; the visits were generally on Wednesdays. Tottenham Green is about ten minutes from our house. We generally went to the Downhills. The prisoner might go with the child to Tottenham Green, but not often. By the little boy's conversation with his mother, I think they had been there on 4 October. I did not go with them. I did on the eleventh. The prisoner went first, and I went afterwards. We arranged to meet at the Seven Sisters Road. We stayed from about 3.00 pm to 4.30 pm or 5.00 pm. There were no other people there. It was very quiet. The child did not play with any other children. We were sitting down talking, and the child was playing just in front of us. I can swear that he did not play with any other children on that day. That was the day the boy was not well. The doctor came in the evening. I do not remember him saying it was indigestion or a bilious attack.

The prisoner came on the eighteenth. She did not take the child out; the eleventh was the last day she took him out. He cried very much on the eighteenth; his mother noticed it. I think she stayed till about 6.00 pm.

After I put the child in the omnibus at the Birdcage, I got out at once. I could not stay, I was so upset.

I never had any difficulty in getting my money for the child. I was paid in full up to the time of the child being taken from my care. The prisoner was always very fond of the child. She was very worried when he underwent the operations. I did not pay for the operations. I do not know if anybody paid for them at the London Hospital.

The child was hasty, but only the same as other children. He was always a good boy to manage; I could always manage him. I know I spoilt him a bit. I cannot remember the prisoner saying that she thought I spoilt him; she might have said, 'You give way to him too much,' or something like that. She said once or twice that the child exhibited a little temper when out with her.

**Léonie Cadisch**

LÉONIE CADISCH, sworn and examined.

The prisoner is my sister. I live with my husband, Richard Cadisch, at 29 Bethune Road, Stoke Newington. My father was a Frenchman, and my mother was English. My sister was thirty-six last June; she is unmarried. For some years she has followed the occupation of a daily

# Masset.

**Léonie Cadisch**

governess. She was living at home with our mother just before the birth of Manfred, on 24 April 1896. This is the certificate [produced] of his birth. I knew that after its birth it was placed with Mrs Norris and her daughter, and I guaranteed to them the payment monthly of £1 17s; I was never called upon to pay any part of that. After the birth of her child, the prisoner did not live at home with her mother any longer. We had a stepfather living then; he died on 27 September, since when I and my sister and the other members of our family have been in mourning for him. Since August 1898, up to the date of her arrest, the prisoner was living with my husband and myself at 29 Bethune Road. She went to her teaching, among other places, to a Mrs Haas and to a Mrs Sonnenthal, from my house. She went by tram to Dalston, and then by train, but I cannot say what station she went to on the North London Railway.

She first mentioned to me that she was going to change the custody of the child from Mrs Norris at the beginning of this year. She simply said it would be better for the child's education; that is the only reason she gave. Nothing was done then. She next mentioned it on 18 October, when she said that she was going to take the child to a cousin of its father in France, to be brought up. I did not know who the father was: she never told me. On the twenty-fourth or twenty-fifth, she told me she was going to Newhaven with the child on the Friday, and would be back on the Sunday or Monday. She said she was going by the 2.30 pm train, because she had to be in Newhaven at 5.00 pm to meet the boat, I suppose. I do not remember her saying anything about the boat. I last saw her on Friday, the twenty-seventh, at 12.30 pm – she was not dressed to go out. Her hat and jacket, which I saw at the police court, are the clothes she was in the habit of wearing. She did not say anything about her journey to me on the Friday. After 12.30 pm on the Friday, I next saw her at 9.00 on Sunday night; she was wearing the same hat and jacket as she was wearing at the police court. I did not speak to her that night: she was tired and went to bed. Next morning, I asked if the child had been troublesome, because I knew it was fond of its nurse; she replied, 'Only at London Bridge'. I asked her if she had had a good crossing, and she said the sea was better going than coming, or coming than going – I cannot remember which.

I have never seen this shawl [produced] in her possession. I have never seen her with a black shawl of any kind.

We have got in our back garden a rockery made of clinker bricks, and in the front garden there is an edging of the same kind of bricks. These bricks [produced] are similar to those in the front garden. This one also [produced] is like ours.

My sister never mentioned to me that she ever intended giving the

# First Day – Wednesday 13 December 1899.

child into the charge of two women at Chelsea. Mondays were the days she taught at West Hampstead. She left on Monday, 30 October, at 1.30 pm. She usually returned about 8.00 pm. We used to dine about 7.45 pm. She did not come home that night. She had not said she would not be home. We expected her.

My sister was in no monetary difficulties, as far as I know.

*Cross-examined.*

Bricks like these are in most of the back gardens in our neighbourhood. There is no regularity in the placing of the bricks round the edging. I said that you could not see where any brick had been taken from, except those taken by the police.

The whole of our family knew of the existence of this child. My sister always seemed to have enough money for her wants. I and my husband housed her free of charge.

She was very fond of her child. She spoke in terms of affection of him to me. When she came back on the Sunday night, she was in her usual state of mind, and quite calm. Next morning, she had breakfast and went to her work as usual. Nobody was unpleasant to her because of the boy's existence; we had all forgiven her. She went several times to her brother-in-law's, at Croydon. It was not unusual for her to go and stay there.

*Re-examined.*

She went there last in August, I think. She had not said anything about going to Mr Simes.

MAUD CLIFFORD, sworn and examined.

I am an assistant to Mr McIlroy, a draper, of 161 High Street, Stoke Newington. I sold this shawl [produced] on 24 October. This is the bill for it [produced]. I remember selling it. On 4 November, I picked out the prisoner as the person to whom I had sold the shawl. I am nearly certain that she is the person. When I sold it, she asked for a black shawl, and I showed her one at 1s 6¾d, a size smaller than this one, but otherwise the same. She said she wanted a little larger one, so I showed her this one for 1s 11½d, and she had it. I was marking the shawls off. We had only had them for a week. There were only three like this in the parcel. This one [produced] is one of the other two—I think this one is the one I sold on the twenty-fourth.

*Cross-examined.*

I am prepared to swear that I sold that shawl to the prisoner on 24 October. I said before the coroner, 'I won't swear positively she is the

**Léonie Cadisch**

**Maud Clifford**

# Masset.

**Maud Clifford**

woman,' and, when before the magistrate, I said, 'At the inquest I said I won't swear positively she is the woman; I won't swear that now'. I do not wish to differ from those two statements. I should not like to swear, but I think she is the woman. Ours is a busy shop; there are about twenty assistants. I cannot remember what I sold before I sold the shawl, or what I sold immediately after; I cannot remember anything I sold on that day. I sold a good many things that week. I know this is the shawl I sold, by the pattern. This shawl is the same pattern, and wool, and size – I do not see any difference in them. I have been six years in the trade.[117]

*Re-examined.*

These are all new shawls. A detective brought the shawl in and asked me if we sold shawls like that, and I brought out a box and showed him some, and we saw they were the same. That was on a Friday. I knew nothing about the Dalston murder then. I gave my evidence before the magistrate on 11 November. The detective brought the shawl in on the Friday week before that, the third. I told the detective I remembered selling the shawl. Next day, I was taken to the Dalston Police Court, where I picked out the prisoner as the person to whom I had sold the shawl.

**Ernest Mooney**

ERNEST HOPKINS MOONEY, sworn and examined.

I am manager to Mr McIlroy, draper, of 161 High Street, Stoke Newington. On 16 or 17 October, I purchased a quarter of a dozen woollen shawls, trade number 310, from Rylands & Sons, Wood Street, City.[118] Anyone going to Rylands could get the same shawls. I have compared this one, which was sold on 24 October, with the two remaining in our possession. The three are all the same. I have had twelve or thirteen years' experience in the trade.

*Cross-examined.*

I should call this shawl rather a striking pattern, not an ordinary pattern. I think I said, when before the magistrate, 'I suppose it would be an ordinary shawl,' not, 'an ordinary pattern'. I said that they could be bought by anyone.

---

117 At the magistrate's court, it was similarly recorded that Miss Clifford had six years of experience in the drapery trade. This was amended to 'two' before she signed her statement. (TNA: PRO CRIM 1/58/5.)

118 In fact, Mooney had purchased fifteen shawls from Rylands, but only three of them were black, and only one of these three had been sold (TNA: PRO CRIM 1/58/5). The judge's notes give the trade number as 110 (TNA:PRO HO 144/1540/A61535/7).

# First Day – Wednesday 13 December 1899.

*Re-examined.*

These were not made specially for us. I have never seen this pattern before.

**Ernest Mooney**

THOMAS BONNER, sworn and examined.

I am an omnibus conductor employed by the London General Omnibus Company. My bus starts from the Birdcage, Stamford Hill, for London Bridge. We started at 12.48 pm on 27 October; we got to London Bridge at 1.35 pm. I remember a woman and a child travelling with me from the Birdcage to London Bridge. This is a photograph of the child. It had a red hat on. I do not recognise the prisoner at all. The child was crying inside the omnibus. They had a brown paper parcel. That is all I remember.

**Thomas Bonner**

GEORGINA WORLEY, sworn and examined.

I am a widow, and relieving waiting room attendant at the London Bridge Station on the London, Brighton and South Coast Railway. My waiting room is on the south side, near the parcels office. It is number 2, first class waiting room.[119] I was on duty there from 7.30 am, till 2.30 pm, on Friday 27 October. I saw a little boy in the waiting room. I cannot positively say that this is a photograph of him. He had a little blue serge dress and a little blue serge coat. I do not remember what kind of a cap he had on. The coat had one or two bright brass buttons, and a little collar round the neck, of either red or brown. This is the frock [produced]. This is the coat, only there was something round the neck.

A lady was with the boy; she was dressed in black – a black round hat. I afterwards went to Dalston Police Station and saw a number of women, but I did not identify anybody; I had not seen the woman's features sufficiently; she came into the waiting room and hurried to the far side and put the boy on the settee and sat down on it herself; she never looked up whilst she sat there. This is like the hat she was wearing [produced].

It was about 1.45 pm when they came in, and I left at 2.30 pm to book my money in. I was relieved at 2.30 pm by Mrs Swaker. While I was on duty I wore a white cap. I went and paid in the money which I had taken. When I left, the lady and the boy were in the waiting room. I had spoken to the lady. I said, 'You look very tired'. She said, 'No, I am waiting for someone to come'. I could not see her face because she had

**Georgina Worley**

---

119 There were four waiting rooms at London Bridge Station. On the main line there was a first class ladies' waiting room (attended by Mrs Reece), and on the London, Brighton & South Coast line there was a combined first and second class ladies' waiting room (attended by Mrs Worley and Mrs Swaker). Both of these waiting rooms had adjoining general waiting rooms that were unattended.

# Masset.

**Georgina Worley**

her head down. She put the parcel down on the floor. It was concealed by her dress. I never saw her look up while she was in the room. I returned about 2.40 pm. They were not there then.

*Cross-examined.*

I cannot say if the boy had a red hat on. I did not speak to the lady till just before I was ready to go out. The child kept running up and down the settee. It appeared quite happy. I asked the lady if she was going by train, and she said she was waiting for someone.

**Kate Swaker**

KATE SWAKER, sworn and examined.

I am married, and waiting room attendant at the same waiting room as Mrs Worley. I was there to oblige her, and relieved her at 2.30 pm on 27 October. I did not notice a lady and a little boy there.

The court adjourned.

*******

# Second Day – Thursday 14 December 1899.[120]

ELLEN REECE, sworn and examined by Mr MATHEWS.

**Ellen Reece**

Your name is Ellen Reece? — Yes, sir.

You are a widow living at 18 Raul Street, Tottenham? — Yes.[121]

Are you an attendant in the first class waiting room main line section of the London Bridge Station? — Yes.

And is that a waiting room which is not far distant from the refreshment rooms? — Yes, sir.

And were you in attendance in that waiting room on 27 October of this year? — Yes, sir.

At what hour did you go on duty? — At 2.30 pm.

And how long did you remain on duty on that day? — Till 12.10.

Mr Justice BRUCE: At midnight? — Yes, sir.

Mr MATHEWS: In that waiting room, after you had gone on duty, did you see anybody whom you see here today in court? — Yes, sir, I saw the prisoner.

At what time did you see her? — I first observed the little boy about 2.40 pm, as near as I can say.

It was the little boy that you first observed, was it? — Yes, sir.

And how soon after you had observed the little boy did you observe the prisoner? — After I had looked at the little boy – his back was to me – I looked at the prisoner to see what she was doing to the little boy.

Where was she at that time? — Sitting at the end of the couch.

Is that a photograph of the little boy that you have spoken of [handing photograph to the witness]? — That is the little boy, but he had a coat and a hat on.

He was not dressed like that but that is a photograph of him? — Yes.

You say he had a hat on – did you notice the colour of the hat? — A little red hat.

Now, what was there in the little boy as he sat with his back to you which caused you to look up to the prisoner with the object of seeing what she was doing to him? — While I am in the waiting room – there

---

120  Testimony of Ellen Reece from TNA:PRO HO 144/1540/A61535; remainder of second day's evidence from CCCSP (TNA:PRO CRIM 10/80; also www.oldbaileyonline.org, version 7.2, accessed 23 March 2017, December 1899, trial of Louisa [sic] Josephine Jemima Masset [t18991211-77]).

121  *Sic* in transcript. In fact, Ellen Reece of 8 Raul Road, Peckham.

# Masset.

**Ellen Reece**

are two doors and, if anyone is talking to me in the lavatory, I have a habit of always looking at this door to see if there is anybody there that ought not to be – and there I saw the little boy going backwards, and I looked then at the prisoner.

The child was going backwards, away from the prisoner? — Yes, sir: backwards.

Did you see any sign in the child of his being upset or distressed in any way? — I observed that he did not want to go to the lady that was with him.

Did you speak to the little boy? — Not then.

After a time did you speak to him? — I saw him again but still he was side-face to me then. He was going that way [describing], sideways.

And about how long after that – when you first saw him – was it that you spoke to him? — Quite a quarter of an hour.

And are you able to say that during that whole quarter of an hour the prisoner and the little boy remained in the waiting room? — Yes.

Did she remain sitting upon the couch? — As far as I saw.

Now, at the end of the quarter of an hour or thereabouts, you tell us that you spoke to the child. What did you say to him? — I was putting away my mantle and bonnet in a cupboard where we hang them and I saw the little fellow near the prisoner's knee, and he looked up, and I said, 'What are you grizzling about?' He came towards me and I said, 'There is nothing in here for little boys'.

He came towards the cupboard in which you were in the act of placing your mantle and bonnet? — Yes.

You said, 'There is nothing here for little boys'? — Yes.

And what next? — He looked up again at me as I locked the door, and I looked towards the prisoner and said, 'What is he fretting about?' and she said, 'His nurse'.

Then just continue. — I looked intently at the prisoner because I am very fond of children, and especially little boys, and if I see a little boy unhappy I generally go to them. I looked intently at her and she said, 'Perhaps he is hungry. I will get him a cake.'

Was there anything said about the age of the child? — She said, 'Yes, perhaps he is hungry'. I said, 'He is a fine little fellow'. I looked at the prisoner: 'He is a fine little fellow – how old is he?' – and she said, 'Four next April'.

Mr Justice BRUCE: 'Perhaps he is hungry'? — 'I will get him a cake – have you a refreshment bar here?' I said, 'Yes, on the left as you go out of the door.' She got up and turned round and picked something up with her right hand – but I do not know what it was – and took the little boy by the right hand by her left, and went out of the door. She picked

# Second Day – Thursday 14 December 1899.

**Ellen Reece**

up something from by a chair and took the little boy by her hand and walked down towards the door.

Mr MATHEWS: And went towards and out of the door? — The door has a spring – you have to hold the door a little. As she was going out she turned round and looked at me and I thought she was looking to see which way for the bar, and I put up my hand like that [indicating] in the direction of the bar.

And then she went out? — Yes.

Now, about what time, as near as you can fix it, was it that she left the waiting room? — I should think the time took about ten minutes – it might be twelve minutes. The 2.58 pm bell rang as I came out of the lavatory.

What time was it, as near as you can fix it, that she went out of the swing door with the little boy? — I cannot fix it nearer than that. I know the 2.58 pm bell had rung before I spoke to the little boy. That is a Thornton Heath train.

Mr Justice BRUCE: And you say it was about 3.00 pm? — No, it was more than that – it was about 3.05 pm or 3.10 pm, as near as I can fix it.

Mr MATHEWS: I suppose you cannot say in what direction she went? — No, sir, the door was shut.

You remained on duty until something past midnight on that day? Did you see the prisoner again in the course of the evening? — Yes.

Where was she when you next saw her? — She was coming up the room, but I did not notice that it was the prisoner then until I went to draw the water she asked for to wash. She had her hat on.

What time did you recognise her as the woman who had been there in the afternoon? — About 6.55 pm of the same day.[122]

Where was she then? — In the lavatory.

There is a lavatory attached, is there not? There is the first class waiting room and the door, as we see, leading to a number of water closets and a cupboard and some basins, I suppose. — Three basins. She washed in the one opposite the looking glass.

And what was she doing when you saw her opposite the middle basin? — She was drawing up her sleeve, and I turned the water on. I looked at her in the glass and I said to myself, 'Where have I seen you?' I thought, 'Oh, you are the lady I saw this afternoon with the little boy'. I was alongside of her and the glass was in the front.

Mr Justice BRUCE: You saw her reflection in the glass and you

---

122  *Sic* in transcript, but apparently a mishearing of the evidence. The judge's notes (TNA:PRO HO 144/1540/A61535) indicate that Mrs Reece said that the sighting occurred at 'about 6 minutes to 7'. Mr Justice Bruce adhered to this timeframe during his summing-up.

# Masset.

**Ellen Reece**

recognised her as the lady with the little boy? — Yes, in the afternoon.

Mr MATHEWS: You turned on the tap for her? – Yes, I do it for everyone.

You did it for her? That is what we are concerned with. — Yes, I did.

And did she wash her hands? — Oh, yes. I then went to the cupboard to get the towels – we lock them away.

She washed her hands? — Yes.

You gave her a towel, I daresay. — Yes.

Did she do anything to her hair at all? — That I do not know – I was making my tea.

Did you go out of the lavatory to make your tea? — Yes, sir.

Do you remember her making any request of you about a clothes brush? — After I had made my tea, I remembered I had not got any sugar and I went into the cupboard for some sugar, and she was brushing her jacket down, and she said, 'Have you got a clothes brush?' I said, 'Yes'. I said, 'Shall I brush you down?' She said, 'No'. I said, 'You will have to hurry up because it is 7.15 pm now'.

Had she said anything to you? — When I was drawing the water, she said, 'What is the next train for Brighton?' and I said, '7.20 pm'.

Mr Justice BRUCE: You returned to the lavatory to get some sugar from the cupboard and she said, 'Have you a clothes brush?' — Yes, and I said, 'Shall I brush you down?' She said, 'No'. I said, 'You must hurry up, because it is 7.15 pm now, if you mean to catch that train'.

Mr MATHEWS: Did you give her a clothes brush? — Yes.

You handed that to her? — I handed it to her.

Did you see whether she used it? — No.

You cannot say that? — No.

Did you go back to the waiting room? — To my tea.

That would be, to the waiting room having got your sugar? — Yes.

And you made your tea? — I had it made there.

And then what became of her, can you tell us? Did you see her leave? — I saw her go out of the waiting room.

Out of the waiting room door? — Yes.

And that would be at what time? — It must have been quite close on 7.15 pm – it might have been 7.20 pm, but I do not know. The last time I looked at the clock it was a quarter past, and the train is twenty-two past, but we call it twenty past. It had gone for so many years at twenty past that we always call it at twenty minutes past.

So far as you could see, did she take anything away with her in the shape of luggage? — She had a brown paper parcel and her gloves on it – not a tidy looking parcel. I did not pay much attention to that.

That was at the end of the washing slab? — Yes.

# Second Day – Thursday 14 December 1899.

Did you notice if she had something else with her? — I did not notice.

Mr Justice BRUCE: The end of the washing stand? — Yes, towards the left.

There she put her clothes on it? — Yes.

Mr MATHEWS: At that time the little boy was not with her? — No, sir.

You are quite sure of that? — [The witness made no answer.]

Now come to a later date. I think you saw no more of her until you went to the Dalston Police Station, was it? Did you go there to a courtyard which is attached to the Dalston Police Station? — Yes, sir.

Are you able to fix the date of your visit to the Dalston Police Station, to the courtyard which is attached to the police station? — No, I cannot – still, I ought to.

Was it on the morning of the same day that you gave your evidence before the magistrate? — Yes, the same day.

We can fix the date, my Lord, as 24 November. [To the witness] When you went into the courtyard, into the Dalston Police Station, was there a number of woman there? — Yes.

Mr Justice BRUCE: About how many? Do you know? — Well, I cannot say – there seemed to be a cluster.

But were there a dozen or more? — It looked more than a dozen?

You cannot tell us exactly? — [The witness did not answer.]

Mr MATHEWS: And amongst them did you see, Mrs Reece, the woman who had been in your waiting room on 27 October? — I did.

Did you pick her out? — Yes.

Who was the woman that you picked out on that occasion? — The prisoner.

Have you any doubt about her identity? — I have not.

*Cross-examined* by Lord COLERIDGE.

You were not called before the coroner? — No.

And this incident at the Dalston Police Station was about a month after you say you saw the prisoner in the waiting room? — I should say it was about the fourth week.

In the meantime had you read about this case in the newspapers? — Oh, yes.

In many newspapers? — Any newspaper which is left about I generally read.

And it interested you perhaps? — On account of London Bridge being mentioned in it.

And because of London Bridge being mentioned in it, you took a special interest in it? — Yes.

**Ellen Reece**

# Masset.

**Ellen Reece**

And I daresay followed it in the papers from time to time, whenever it was mentioned? — No, I would not say that. I am not fond of reading the papers too much lately.

Did you read a description in the newspapers of the supposed murderess? — I do not think I have.

Just reflect. — I have read nothing that has been going on about it.

Did you read a description of the child in the newspapers? – I saw one likeness of a child, but I cannot tell you the paper – but it was not like the child.

Then it was not a likeness? — It was a supposed likeness.

Did you read a description of the child? — No, I have not.

Had a description of the child been furnished to you? — No.

Did you say this when you were before the magistrate? 'I wondered if this was the child from the description I saw.' — No, I did not. I said, 'I wonder if that is the boy?'

I am reading from your own deposition, which was read over to you and signed by you, was it not? — Yes.

Well, be careful, do not answer in haste – did you say that?

Mr Justice BRUCE: Just read the passage again, please, Lord Coleridge.

Lord COLERIDGE: 'I wondered if this was the child from the description I saw.' — I said I wondered if it was the little boy.

Mr MATHEWS: I think Lord Coleridge ought to read the two earlier passages.

Lord COLERIDGE: I will.

Mr Justice BRUCE: 'I saw the back of the boy three Sundays ago.' [Reading the deposition.]

Lord COLERIDGE: Were not you drawing an opinion between a description and a drawn description? Did you say this? 'I cannot say whether I read an account in the *People*.' — I have the *People* every Sunday.

Is that what you said? — Yes.

'I do not remember the exact description of the prisoner and the child – how they were dressed, et cetera. I saw a picture of the prisoner without her hat.' — Yes.

'I think it was three Sundays ago. I do not remember seeing a description of the child. When I read about the Dalston murder, I wondered if this was the child from the description I saw.' — I wondered if it was the child with the red hat. I would know the lady with him. That was in my own mind before I came before the magistrate or anyone.

You wondered if that was the child – was that not because of something you had read? — Oh, no.

Lord Coleridge QC

*Author's collection*

# Second Day – Thursday 14 December 1899.

What did you mean by saying, 'I wondered if this was the child from the description I saw,' if you had never seen a description of the child? — I did not think I ever said such a word – I do not think I ever uttered 'description'.

It was read over to you and signed by you. — Yes, but I did not read it: you must bear that in mind. The clerk read it. If it had been given to me, I should have scratched it out.

Do you mean to say that the clerk did not read it properly? — I do not suggest anything.

Mr Justice BRUCE: You mean that you did not hear it? It was a long document, and you did not hear it? — Yes.

Lord COLERIDGE: Now, you saw a picture of the prisoner? — I saw a picture, but that was after I had said that it was –

Never mind – you are so anxious in this case. — I am not anxious at all.

Did you see the prisoner without her hat? — I did.

Mr Justice BRUCE: I should just like to know what time that was. Was it before or after you went to the police station? — Oh, long before; it was after the first hearing at the court.

Lord COLERIDGE: Now you have spoken, you know; I am going to test your memory. You remember all these little details. Do you think you have told us all? — I remember everything that I say and I can say again.

I will take you to the first interview, the interview at 3.00 pm. After you had been examined and cross-examined, did the magistrate put some questions to you? — He did.

Did you say this to him, in answer to the magistrate? 'I was putting the kettle on when the prisoner came back.' That is the later interview? — The magistrate – the first question asked me was –

Did you say that? — Not the first question.

'I was putting –' — Not the first question.

Kindly answer my question. I was not asking you if it was the first question. — Oh, yes, I did say it.

I was asking you whether, in answer to the magistrate, you said this? 'I was putting the kettle on when the prisoner came back.' Did you say that? — Yes.

Did you go on to say, 'I said nothing to her earlier in the day'?–

Mr Justice BRUCE: '–about having seen her earlier in the day.'

Lord COLERIDGE: Very well. Did you say to the magistrate, 'I said nothing to her about having seen her earlier in the day'? — Yes, quite right.

Did you ask her where her boy was? — I did not.

**Ellen Reece**

# Masset.

**Ellen Reece**

I put it to you, Mrs Reece, that even at that time you were not convinced that she was the woman that you had seen earlier. — I have not a doubt now when I see her without a hat. Now that I see the prisoner without a hat, she is the same woman who had the child in my waiting room at 3.00 pm.

That I understand you to say, but what I am putting to you is this: that after you saw this woman later in the day, about 7.00 pm – the second interview, we will call it – you were not then convinced that she was the same woman that you had seen earlier in the day, and that you have since become convinced that she was the same woman, but you were not convinced then. — I was convinced then; so far as that I saw the prisoner I should be convinced, but when I saw her amongst the other women, I did not see her without a hat.

Mr Justice BRUCE: When you saw her in the lavatory washing at that time --? — I recognised her as the same woman with the little boy.

Lord COLERIDGE: I put it to you that, at that time, you were not then convinced that she was the same woman that you had seen earlier in the day. — I do not think I had altered my mind.

Were you of opinion then --? — My opinion was the same.

As it is now? — Yes.

Mr Justice BRUCE: The question is this: whether, at that time, when you saw her at 7.00 pm, were you then able to make up your mind, or did you then make up your mind whether she was the same woman you had seen earlier in the day? — I did make up my mind.

Lord COLERIDGE: Why did you not ask her where her child was? — I had no business to ask questions.

You seem to have talked a great deal, but did not take notice if the child was about? — [The witness did not answer.]

Was the gas alight then? — We generally have it alight at that end.

Was it alight? — Yes. I thought you meant in the afternoon.

It was gas? — Yes.

Then the incident about the towels and the brush is a usual incident. Do a great number of ladies go to the lavatory? — Many come to the lavatory.

You have not got it right. Do you mean yes or no? — No, but a great many ladies do come.

How many towels do you use in a day? — Sometimes we use twelve.

And does every person have a clean towel? — Not everyone.

For everyone? — I cannot say. It all depends on who the customer is.

Mr Justice BRUCE: Do they pay extra for a clean towel? — Extra for the washing.

And that includes the towel? — Yes.

# Second Day – Thursday 14 December 1899.

Sometimes a clean towel and sometimes a partially clean towel? — Yes, it all depends on what the lady is.

Lord COLERIDGE: Then we may take it that more than a dozen people go through this ceremony? — Oh dear, no! Sometimes we do not have wash at all in the day – not in the quiet season.

Is this the quiet season? — The Brighton season is coming on now and we have a good many good ladies who have a clean towel.

And the beginning of November would be the beginning of the Brighton season, would it not? — Yes.[123]

Now, how many people in the day use the lavatory, on an average? — Sometimes two hundred to three hundred.

Mr Justice BRUCE: That, I take it, means using the water closets? — Yes, not using the room.

Lord COLERIDGE: I am asking about the three closets, my Lord.

Mr Justice BRUCE: When she speaks of two hundred, she means the lavatory and the water closets, I think?

Lord COLERIDGE: How many people use the lavatory and the closets in the day? — I am not there all day.

I am sure you can tell me. — In the tenure of my office, two hundred. There may be more.

Did you say before the magistrates sometimes four hundred, sometimes five hundred, sometimes six hundred use your waiting room during one period of duty? — Yes, I did.

Now, how came you to tell me just then that it was two hundred? — You are taking the average.

Mr Justice BRUCE: When you say the waiting room, do you mean the lavatory? — The lavatories. I cannot say how many in the waiting room.

When you say five hundred, do you mean the waiting room or the lavatory? — The lavatory.

Lord COLERIDGE: Sometimes six hundred? — Yes, I have taken £4 or £5 odd in the day.

In pennies and two pences? — Pennies.

That is four hundred and eighty.

Mr Justice BRUCE: Is that in one period of duty? — That was the Sunday before the Jubilee.

That is a special occasion? — That was on the Sunday before the Jubilee day.

More than usual? — Yes, a great deal more, and in the excursion season a great deal more.

---

123 The 'Brighton season' referred to the autumn months when the middle classes came to Brighton on holiday after the lower classes, who generally arrived during the summer, had gone home.

# Masset.

**Ellen Reece**

Do you say you took £5 in pennies? — I did.

That would mean 1200, would not it? — I cannot say. It was £5 odd. Sometimes it is £2 10s, sometimes £1 15s.

That Sunday before the Jubilee was a very special day? — Yes, it was.

Lord COLERIDGE: But there are fewer trains on Sundays than on weekdays? — There may be more people. I do not know the trains – how many trains go.

How many years have you been in the waiting room? — Since the twenty-fourth day of July, 1877.

And you stand there and tell me – and tell the jury – that you do not know whether there are fewer trains on Sundays? — Of course there are fewer trains.

May I take that answer as a specimen of your evidence? — You can if you like.

As a specimen of your accuracy? — I am not going to tell any stories for anyone.

During this month, you tell us, you interested yourself in the case … During the month which elapsed between 27 October and 24 November, you interested yourself in the case? — I have not at all.

You have read the papers. You say you have followed the case. — Well, anyone reads the papers.

Do you still say that you did not interest yourself in the case? – I did not.

You had no interest in it? — No.

Yet you followed it? – I read it.

You followed it. You wondered whether the little boy was the little boy, and yet took no interest in it? — I took interest in it. I did not want to have anything to do with it.

Did you or did you not take an interest in it, wondering whether the little boy was the little boy? — Of course I did take an interest in it, so far as that.

Did you first communicate to the police, or did they communicate with you? — No.

One or the other must have.

Mr Justice BRUCE: Did you go to the police first, or did the police come to you? — Neither.

Lord COLERIDGE: One or the other must have. — He went to the superintendent of the station. There are two Mrs Reeces at London Bridge, and he did not know that the superintendent sent for me. That is the station-master.

Mr Justice BRUCE: The superintendent at the station sent for you? — Yes.

# Second Day – Thursday 14 December 1899.

**Ellen Reece**

Lord COLERIDGE: What did the superintendent say to you? — He said, 'All right, Mrs Reece, walk in'.

That is very important. — That is all he said, and I walked in. He had nothing to say because there was a gentleman with him that I did not know anything about.

The gentleman was the gentleman from the police? — Yes.

What did the gentleman from the police say? — He asked me if I had seen anyone on such a day, seeing the lady and the little boy.

Did he mention a day? — I think he did.

You are not sure? — I am not sure of that because, of course, I did not want to have anything to do with it.

But you have had something to do with it. — Yes, at last. I am sorry.

Did you deny it? — No.

You did not say that you had not seen the little boy? — No, I could not say that. It would have been a story.

Was the day mentioned? — I cannot say. I cannot say what was mentioned at the first.

Just try to remember. We are dependent upon your recollection in this case. Will you try to recollect what the superintendent said to you – the police officer? — He said, 'I am a police officer. I have come to –'

Did he ask you if you had seen the little boy? — Yes.

Did he mention the date? — I cannot say whether he mentioned the date or not. I suppose he did, but I do not know.

Did he describe the little boy? — No, he did not.

All he said was, 'Have you seen a little boy?' — No, he said, 'I am a police officer'.

And after that he said, 'Have you seen a little boy?' — I cannot say what he said.

Try. — I cannot, because I was taken off my guard.

I do not want to take you off your guard. — I am not taken off my guard now.

Are you easily taken off your guard? — No.

Why were you taken off your guard? — Because I had such a horror of having anything to do with such a thing.

Now, just tell me – try and recollect whether you were off your guard or not. Did the police officer mention the date to you? — I suppose he did, but he did not say anything about that.

Mr Justice BRUCE: Can you recollect whether he did or not? — I cannot say.

Lord COLERIDGE: Is it because you do not want to say? — No, it is not because I do not want to say. It is because I cannot. He said he was a police officer and I said, 'Oh!' I did not want to have anything to do

# Masset.

**Ellen Reece**

with it.

Did he describe the little boy to you? — No, he did not.

Or the woman to you? — No, he did not.

If he did not mention the date or give a description of the boy or the woman, how came you to the police station? — Because I was summoned to the police court.

May I take it that you are not at all sure of a single detail which took place? — Yes, I can tell you all.

On 21 November, you know that you were sent for? — Yes.

Do I understand that it has passed from your mind? — No.

Tell us what took place. — When I got into the office, I was asked to sit down.

He said he was a police officer, we know that. — If you know all that, you had better not ask me.

Well? — He said he was a police officer and he wanted to know if I knew anything – if I had seen a lady and a little boy in the room.

What little boy? — Oh, in the case.

The Dalston case? — Yes.

And he mentioned that then? — Yes. Then I told him what I knew.

What was that? — That I had seen her.

Seen whom? — The prisoner. The lady with the little boy.

What lady? — The prisoner, and he said, 'Would you know her again?' I said, 'Yes'. I said if I saw the woman I should know her.

I thought you were taking no interest in the case? — You cannot help knowing what is true.

You jumped at once to the conclusion, then, that the little boy and the woman that you had seen at the Dalston station – the woman and the boy whom the policeman asked about --? — I did not. I said, 'I must see the woman first'.

I thought you told the policeman that you had seen the woman. — I saw the woman with the little boy in the room, but I did not identify her then. I said I could identify her if I saw her.

Now, when you got to the police station, had you any hesitation in identifying her? — Not at all.

When you went to the police station, did you go with your mind fixed upon identifying the woman that you had seen with the little boy? — I did.

You tell us you identified the woman at once? No hesitation? — No hesitation. I saw her as she stood on the steps at the station.

Before you got up to her? — Yes. I said in my own mind, 'There you are'.

Is it true to say that you stopped two or three times before reaching the

# Second Day – Thursday 14 December 1899.

prisoner and looked up all the persons? — I cannot say that I stopped. I never passed the prisoner.

Is it true – or is it not true – that you stopped two or three times before reaching the prisoner and looked up and down all the persons? — No, that is not true.

Mr Justice BRUCE: Just tell me what did take place. Do you say that is not true – that you stopped two or three times and looked up and down all the persons? Tell me what happened. — Some door shut, and I stood on some steps, and I understood that I had to identify the woman that I saw in the waiting room. I put my glasses on and I looked at the cluster of women. I saw the woman I wanted and I said, 'There you are,' to myself. I walked down and a voice said to me, 'Look steadfastly at them and touch the one you want.' When I came to the prisoner, I stood a minute and looked at her. The voice said again, 'That will not do. You must touch her,' and I touched her. I did not like doing it, but I put my hand to her shoulder and the voice said again, 'Walk this way,' and I walked on.

Were you standing, or stopping, or how? — Walking on.

Lord COLERIDGE: Did the inspector stand just behind you? — I do not know.

Was it in a yard? — It was in a yard.

Paved with gravel? — There was gravel, and asphalt.

So that footsteps could be heard? — I do not know anything about that.

I am asking you, was it that you could hear persons walking? It was not like a carpet. When you walk on a carpet, you do not hear footsteps. — I did not hear anything but a man's voice.

Will you swear – do you say that the inspector was not there? — I will swear that I do not know if he was.

You will not swear he was not? — I will only swear to the voice of the man who called to me, but no footsteps.

Whose was the voice? — He told me what to do.

Was that Inspector Forth? — I do not know the name of anyone.

Will your Lordship allow Inspector Forth to come in?

Mr Justice BRUCE: Let him come in. [Inspector Forth was brought into court.]

Lord COLERIDGE: Do you know Inspector Forth – is that the man? — That is the one.

Was he the man who called out, 'What do you say?' — Yes.

Was not he just behind you? — No. I think he was near. There were some words.

Are you sure? — No, I am not sure, but the voice seemed not behind

*Ellen Reece*

# Masset.

**Ellen Reece**

my ear.

Is it true that Inspector Forth stood quite still behind you when you stopped? — I do not know that. The voice that told me to 'walk this way' seemed a few yards from me. I did not know anyone was behind me. I thought I was all alone.

You will not swear that anyone was behind you? — I do not know. I cannot say behind me. When I left those steps, I had only one thing to do: that was to walk straight to the person and point her out.

When you identified the woman, as you say, had you your glasses on? — Yes.

How close did you stand to her? — About two feet from her.

You had your glasses on? — I had. I was a step or two away from her and put my hand on her.

Are you short-sighted? — No, not at all.

Long-sighted? — I do not know.

Poor sighted? — If I want to see, I put my glasses on.

Do you wear the glasses in the waiting room? — Only when I am reading, but not to look at anyone ... except when I want to look minutely at anyone.

You do not ordinarily use them in the waiting room? — No.

Had you them on when the woman and the child were there? — No.

In the waiting room? — No.

On neither occasion? — No.

And may I take it that between the time [of] 27 October and 24 November, you had seen in that waiting room thousands of people, at any rate? — Yes.

Was there any peculiarity about the prisoner in dress or appearance? — No – unless she was all in black, nothing peculiar.

That is not peculiar, is it, to be all in black? — No.

Black is a very prevailing colour? — Yes.

Especially for travelling, is it not? — Yes.

And I suppose a great many people are continually travelling? — Oh, yes. Numbers of children.

And coming into the waiting room? — Yes.

Can you give me a personal description of anybody who was in the waiting room on 27 October, besides this woman and the little child? — No. I had no reason to look at anyone.

You cannot? — I cannot.

Or the day before? — No.

Or the day after? — No.

Or any day between then and now? — I can recognise hundreds of ladies who go in and out of the room.

# Second Day – Thursday 14 December 1899.

If you know them, of course. There are a number of people who are constantly at the station. Can you give me a description of a single woman, not personally known to you, who has been only in one day? Can you give me a description of any person from that day to this? — I can tell the profiles of a lot. I can say I could recognise one or another.

I ask you to give me a description of any person not otherwise known to you. Can you give me a personal description of any person who has come into that waiting room from that day to this? — I do not know what you mean.

Tell me whether they were tall, or fair, or short, or dark? — Lots of people, but simply the –

Who they had with them? — No.

*Re-examined* by Mr MATHEWS.

Tell me, after 27 October – the Friday, when the woman and the child were there – did you see anything of this matter in the public press? — I saw it on the Sunday.

In one of the newspapers? — Yes.

And you read the account in the newspaper? — Yes.

You did not communicate with the police, nor did the police communicate with you? — No.

But, Mrs Reece, did you make any statement to anyone that you know in relation to the case, after you had seen the account in the newspaper on the Sunday? — Oh, no, because I did not think it concerned us in any way, because there was nothing about London Bridge in it. That was on the first Sunday.

Did you go back to your ordinary work on the Monday 30 October? — I did.

Did you upon that day, or upon any day about that time, make any statement to anyone not at all connected with the police? — Of course I had a conversation about it when we saw it was connected with London Bridge.

With whom did you have a conversation? — Marion Fitzgerald.

She is the book-keeper at Bertram and Roberts', the refreshment room at London Bridge Station? — Yes.

At that refreshment room which is so close to your waiting room? — Yes.

And you had a conversation with her upon that day, the Monday? — I do not know the Monday, but in that week when it came out about London Bridge.

My friend has put it to you that you were anxious in this case. Have you any anxiety in the case? — I was in very great fear that anyone

**Ellen Reece**

## Masset.

**Ellen Reece**

should find out that I knew anything about it.

That is your only fear? — That is my only fear.

You did not want to give evidence in this case? — I did not.

And you remained in that condition of mind until you were sent for, as you have told us, by the station-master? — Yes.

Whom you found in the company of the police officer, Police Sergeant Nursey?[124] — Yes.

How long was that – how many days was that before you went to the Dalston Police Station? — It was on the Tuesday evening.

Mr Justice BRUCE: Tuesday before? — Tuesday before.

Mr MATHEWS: Tuesday 21 November. Did the interview which occurred take place at the station, the Superintendent's office? — Yes.

Mr Justice BRUCE: The station-master.

Mr MATHEWS: Yes, my Lord. [To the witness.] And, Mrs Reece, did you then make a statement which was taken down by the officer? — Yes.

Who took it down in writing? — Yes.

After he had taken it down, did he read it over to you and did you sign it? — Yes.

Is that your signature, Mrs Reece [handing document to the witness]? — Yes, that is my signature.

And is that the signature which you attached to the document which he took down in writing at that time? — Yes.

My Lord, I take your Lordship's opinion upon that.

Mr Justice BRUCE: I do not think you can put it in, Mr Mathews.

Mr MATHEWS: After you had made that statement and signed it, you were told, were you, to attend at the police station at Dalston? — Yes.

And in consequence of being told that, you went there on Friday morning? — Yes.

And there pointed out the prisoner? — Yes.

Is there any ground for the suggestion that, at the Dalston Police Station, you were assisted in any way by the police or any other people in the identification of the prisoner? — No, none whatever.

Had you any doubt about her identity then? — No, I had not.

Have you any doubt about her identity now? – No.

Something has been put to you with regard to the likeness which you saw in the public press. I think you answered that you did see a picture in the public press of the prisoner without her hat? — Yes.

And a picture of the child – did you see that? — Yes.

---

124 Nursey would more conventionally be described as 'Detective Sergeant Nursey'. Many detective officers – that is, those in the Criminal Investigation Department – were accustomed to describing themselves and being described as 'Police Sergeant, C.I.D.', or 'Police Constable, C.I.D.'.

# Second Day – Thursday 14 December 1899.

Ellen Reece

Do you take the People? — Yes, every Sunday.

Just look at that and tell me, was it in that copy of the People on Sunday 5 November that you saw the likenesses of which you have been speaking? — Yes. I said the little boy's hair was not so curly –

And those were the likenesses.

CLARA HAAS, sworn and examined.

Clara Haas

I am the wife of Maximilian Haas, and live at 72 Greencroft Gardens, West Hampstead, which is about seven minutes' walk from the Loudoun Road Railway Station on the North London line. The prisoner has acted as daily governess in my family since 1895, with the exception of about five months in 1896, when she did not attend. At first, she came four times a week; the last two years, twice a week. She always used the Loudoun Road Station. She always came on Mondays and Thursdays, in the afternoon. She came on Monday 30 October, at 5.15, and left at the usual time, twelve or thirteen minutes to seven.

*Cross-examined.*

On 30 October, she was in her usual spirits, and quite cheerful. She gave every satisfaction in her capacity as governess. I had not thought of parting with her then.

MARY TEAHAN, sworn and examined.

Mary Teahan

I am single, living at 46 Worple Road, Isleworth, and am a daily governess. On 27 October, I travelled with a friend, Miss Biggs, from Richmond, in Surrey, to Dalston Junction. Our train was timed to leave at 5.19 pm, and reach Dalston Junction at 6.05 pm. We arrived rather late. We got out at Dalston at number 3 platform, and we went at once to the ladies' waiting room on that platform. I left my friend in the waiting room, and went to the floor leading to the passage which leads to the water closets. I went into the one which is nearer to the passage door, and, as I was in the act of closing the door, I saw a dark object on the floor, lying at right angles to the door when it was closed. I saw a child's face, and I immediately opened the door, and went out. I had not quite closed the door. I went into the waiting room, and rejoined Miss Biggs. I spoke to her, and we left the waiting room together, and she, in my hearing, spoke to a porter who was on the station. She and I left the station, and went to a lecture to which we were going in Tottenham Road. The schoolroom, where we were going to, is about five minutes' walk from Dalston Station. We went on foot, and were seated there comfortably, when we noticed it was 6.30 pm by the school clock. On Sunday 29 October, I saw something in Reynolds's Sunday paper, and

# Masset.

**Mary Teahan** in the evening we communicated with the police.

**Margaret Biggs** MARGARET ELLEN BIGGS, sworn and examined.

I am single, and live at Twickenham. I am a friend of the last witness, and, on the evening of 27 October, travelled with her from Richmond to Dalston Junction, to attend a lecture in the schoolroom, which is close to the station. The 5.19 pm train was rather late in arriving, but on arriving we went into the waiting room, and Miss Teahan left me and went into the passage which leads out of the waiting room. She was away a short time, and then returned and spoke to me, and we both went out onto the platform. I spoke to a porter named Standing, and Miss Teahan and I left the station and went to the school. When we were comfortably seated, we noticed by the clock it was 6.30 pm. The lecture was to begin at 7.00 pm. The room is about five minutes from the station.

**Thomas Hall** THOMAS HALL, sworn and examined.

I am a guard on the North London Railway, and live at 10 Chadbourn Street, Bromley-by-Bow. I was in charge of the 5.19 pm train from Richmond to Dalston Junction on 27 October. It was due at Dalston at 6.05 pm; it did not arrive till 6.19 pm. I booked it at that time in the course of duty.

**Joseph Standing** JOSEPH JOHN STANDING, sworn and examined.

I am a porter in the employ of the North London Railway at Dalston Junction. On the evening of 27 October, I was on duty at number 3 platform when Miss Biggs and Miss Teahan spoke to me. I was wheeling a barrow, and I went straight over to the inspector, Mr Bunday. I spoke to the foreman porter, Cotterell, first. I spoke to the inspector at 6.38 pm. He told me to go and see what it was. I went into the ladies' waiting-room and to the back w.c. first, and then to the one nearest the entrance; I pushed the door, and found there was something behind it. I saw a shawl behind the door; then I saw the body of a child. I came out directly, and went over to the inspector and informed him. He came out, and I lit a lamp and went across the metals. I did not touch the body till after Mr Bunday got over, when I left it in his hands. I stayed till the police came. The body was not disturbed in any way till then, that I know of. If anybody had touched it I should have seen them.

There was a very dull light before I brought in the lamp; there was only the gaslight on the partition between the two closets; we could not see without the lamp. I saw a clinker brick on the floor. There are no bricks like that about the station, that I know of. I have been there about six months. I left the brick on the floor, and it was taken possession of

# Second Day – Thursday 14 December 1899.

by the police.

**Joseph Standing**

*Cross-examined.*

I looked at my watch when I fetched the inspector and it was then 6.40 pm. My watch was exactly right by the station time.

DAVID BUNDAY, sworn and examined.

**David Bunday**

I am a station inspector at Dalston Junction. I have been there eleven and a half years. I was called to the ladies' waiting-room on number 3 platform on 27 October by Standing. He came to me first at 6.40 pm, and shortly afterwards I went to the waiting room. Behind the door of the first lavatory, I found the body of a child clothed simply in a black shawl, which was round the body – the head, throat, and feet being exposed. I put my hand under the shawl on the chest and I found the body was slightly warm, although the child was dead. I sent for the police and for a doctor.

The face of the child was smeared with blood, and there were two or three wounds on the face, one above each eye. This photo shows the state of the face as I saw it [produced]. I also saw on the floor a clinker brick. I did not see any blood on the floor. I did not examine the floor. I touched nothing after finding that the child was dead. I did not touch the feet or hands of the child.

The ladies' waiting room on number 3 platform has never had an attendant while I have been at the station – only two charwomen, first thing in the morning and last thing at night, to clear it up. They are not there between 4.00 pm and 7.00 pm. There is a bolt on the middle of the door of the lobby where the closets are, and anybody coming into the lobby can prevent anybody from coming into either closet from the general portion of the waiting room. There is no entrance except from the waiting room. The closets themselves are also provided with a small catch in the locks. The quick trains from Loudoun Road arrive at number 3 platform, and the slow trains to Loudoun Road leave the same one. All trains from Finchley Road arrive at number 3 platform, except the 8.05 am and the 11.45 pm, except on Sundays. The train due to leave Loudoun Road at 6.55 pm and arrive at Dalston Junction at 7.14 pm runs in at number 2 platform. That is a slow train.

*Cross-examined.*

If the trains were running late, I should say that probably a little more than a hundred people would use the lavatory on number 3 platform. I should say that there would be over two hundred trains arrive at number 3 platform in a day. There are four platforms at Dalston Junction; you

# Masset.

**David Bunday**

can go from one to the other without giving up your ticket. The partition between the two closets is made of stained match-boarding. There is an opening common to each closet over the door of about a foot, and one gas light which lights them both. I should say that any noise in one compartment could be easily heard in the next. It would be easy for anyone who wanted to make a noise and not be heard to bolt the door in the passage; it would not require two. If an accomplice went into one closet while the murder was done in the other, the public would be excluded. It would be easier to be done like that than by a single person.

*Re-examined.*

If one person bolted the door from the waiting-rooms, he or she would be free from any interruption. Dalston Junction is the third station from Broad Street. Fast trains do it in five minutes, stopping trains in seven minutes. There are about eight trains in the hour from Broad Street to Dalston between 3.00 pm and 5.00 pm stopping at number 3 platform, and about eight or nine going back. Between 5.00 pm and 6.00 pm, there might be ten or eleven trains going to Broad Street from number 3 platform. They would rather increase as the evening draws on. I do not know of any clinker bricks about the station.

**James Patmore**

JAMES PATMORE (Policeman 108J), sworn and examined.

I was called to Dalston Junction on 27 October at 6.48 pm. I arrived in the ladies' waiting-room, where I found the station-master, who pointed out to me, in a water closet, the dead body of a child. Lying near its head, there was a clinker brick. I did not disturb the body or anything till Dr Fennell came. Just after he came, a police sergeant named Burch[125] came, and, after the doctor had seen the position of the child the police sergeant took charge of the brick. A black shawl partly covered the body.

**Eudore Lucas**

EUDORE LUCAS, sworn and examined.

I am a clerk, and live with my father at Le Havre, in France. I am a Frenchman and nineteen years old. I came to England in August 1898, and went to live at 31 Bethune Road, which is next door to number 29. I lived at 31 till early in last November.

I first made the prisoner's acquaintance at the end of last year, when she was living with Mrs Cadisch at number 29. I knew Mrs Cadisch first; I was a visitor at her house, where I met the prisoner. I continued my visits up to last Whitsuntide, when I paid a visit to Brighton with the

---

[125] Detective Sergeant William Burch. All subsequent references to 'Police Sergeant Burch' are to this officer.

# Second Day – Thursday 14 December 1899.

prisoner and a lady and gentleman. We all four stayed at an hotel kept by a Mr Findlay at 36 Queens Road, Brighton; we occupied rooms number 10 and 11, two adjoining bedrooms on the first floor. We stayed there from a Saturday till the Monday, and then returned to London.

**Eudore Lucas**

After our return, my relations with the prisoner became more friendly, and I began to walk out with her about a month after. That was not known to her sister and brother-in-law. I wrote to her sometimes, and she wrote to me. She addressed her letters to me at my office. I have not preserved any of her letters. Sometimes I met her at the Loudoun Road Station about 6.45 pm, when we would go to Dalston Junction by train. I went from Broad Street to meet her at Loudoun Road. We would return from Dalston Junction to Bethune Road by tram. We would leave the tram at Manor Road and go together on foot to the Bethune Road, and I would part with her at the door of 29. I went in on other occasions, but not on these, because I did not want Mrs Cadisch to know that I had been out with the prisoner. I met the prisoner at other places, but most often at Loudoun Road.

She told me that she had had an illegitimate child. She first mentioned it about the beginning of September – I cannot remember where we were walking when she told me. I had been walking out with her for some time before she told me. I do not think I had been making love to her before she told me. I do not call that love. When she told me she had a child, I said, 'I am glad to know that'. I did not want to know any more about the child, and that I was very pleased to know that she had told me, and that it was fair of her to tell me. I was not making love to her then, specially.

I met her sometimes once and sometimes twice a week. I wrote sometimes one or two letters to her in a fortnight. They were letters of appointment or friendship. I threw them away because I did not want anybody to see them; I do not know why. I did not want them lying about in my pocket. I said before the magistrate, 'They were love letters; they were about meeting; there were loving terms in them'. We do not understand that in France as one does in England. Love is not the same thing in France as it is in England. I do not think they would be called love letters in England. I think you cannot call them loving terms in English.

On 24 or 25 October, I met the prisoner at Liverpool Street Station by appointment. I think I made the appointment, but I cannot remember whether by letter or word of mouth. I had met her there before a few times. I did not know anything about Tottenham. She had not told me where the child was; I did not know that it was at Tottenham. On this occasion, she told me she was going to Brighton on the Friday from

# Masset.

**Eudore Lucas**

London Bridge by the 4.00 pm train. I said I should like to go too, to meet her on the Saturday at Brighton. She said she intended staying at Mr Findlay's Hotel, in the Queens Road, where we had stopped at Whitsuntide. I said I would go down by the 2.00 pm train on Saturday from London Bridge, which arrives at Brighton at 3.20 pm. She said she would meet me at the station there. I said I would not go in my own name, and should like to take another, and I gave her the name of Brooks as that which I should go in. She also was to take the name of Brooks, and we were to go as brother and sister. She was to take two rooms. I was to write to her and tell her what train I was to take at London Bridge. I had already told her, but I was not quite sure. When I met her at Liverpool Street, we went to Clapton by train, and then we went home to Bethune Road, where I parted from her. She did not mention the child during that interview: she only mentioned it a very few times after the first time. She said she had seen it – that was all. She never told me that she intended taking it to France, or that she intended to hand it over to anybody in London.

On Friday, the twenty-seventh, I wrote to her in the name of Brooks at Findlay's Hotel, when I knew that I could get away by the 2.00 pm train from London Bridge on the Saturday. I went by it; we arrived punctually, and the prisoner met me on the platform. We walked to the hotel, I carrying my luggage. I did not give any name at the hotel then. I found the rooms, numbers 10 and 11, which we had had at Whitsuntide, engaged. The prisoner seemed calm and quiet – nothing extraordinary about her. We stayed there together that night, and slept in the same bed. That was the first time that I had had connection with her. She did not mention the child. We remained there all day Sunday. She seemed very quiet, the same as usual. She did not make any statement with regard to the child on Sunday, and we travelled up together on Sunday evening to London Bridge. The prisoner had a brown bag [produced]. We went home to Bethune Road by cab to Stoke Newington Station, and walked from there – it is about five minutes' walk. I parted from her at the corner of St Kilda's Road, about sixty yards from her door. I left her at 9.00 pm, and I did not see her again till after she was arrested. The question of marriage had never been discussed between us.

*Cross-examined.*

I do not remember the suggestion of going to Brighton again – after Whitsuntide – being discussed from time to time. That she had had a child was not at all material to me. My income was not sufficient to offer marriage to anyone; I was earning £3 a month. I continued on exactly the same terms with the prisoner after she had told me she had had a child

# Second Day – Thursday 14 December 1899.

**Eudore Lucas**

as before. I did not know that she would have to make excuses to enable her to go to Brighton. I said before the coroner, 'I knew she would have to make an excuse to get to Brighton'. Her age is thirty-four, and mine eighteen.[126] I never wrote her letters promising her marriage, nor love letters in that sense. When I got to Brighton her demeanour was as usual. I asked her what train she came by: she said the 4.00 pm from London Bridge. I went freely in and out of her room; her door was not locked against me.

*Re-examined.*

I arrived at the hotel about 3.20 pm or 3.30 pm. I fetched my luggage from the station. It was about ten minutes' walk. The rooms did not communicate. I went outside of mine to reach hers in the night. I was in her room once or twice on the Sunday. We were staying at the hotel as brother and sister. I knew that. She did not tell me what her excuse was to get to Brighton. I was earning £3 a month as correspondence clerk. My object was to learn English. My father is well-to-do. On the return journey, the prisoner brought a grey light waterproof, in addition to the Gladstone bag. She carried it over her arm. I only saw it on that occasion.

ALICE RIALL, sworn and examined.

**Alice Riall**

I am chambermaid in the hotel kept by Mr Findlay, in the Queens Road, Brighton. On Friday 27 October, the prisoner arrived, about 9.45 pm. She stayed till Sunday evening, 29 October. She occupied number 11 bedroom, on the first floor. On Saturday afternoon, she was joined by a gentleman I now know to be Lucas. She ordered number 10 bedroom on the Saturday night. I took the arrival. She said most likely she would want number 10 for her brother, who would arrive between 4.00 pm and 5.00 pm. Lucas came about 4.10 pm. They slept in those adjoining rooms, as far as I know. The prisoner gave the name of Brooks. A letter came on the Saturday morning in the name of Brooks. I took it to her bedroom about 9.30 am. There was nothing unusual in her condition or demeanour. She was very particular about having number 11 room.

*Cross-examined.*

I said before the magistrate that she had a small Gladstone brown bag and a wrapper or rolled up parcel; that on the Sunday afternoon I still saw the two articles. I call it a wrapper: it was a little plaid, bound round

---

126  *Sic* in CCCSP. He had previously testified to being nineteen. This is almost certainly an error in the transcription, rather than an accurate account of a witness at a murder trial testifying to being two different ages at once. He was almost certainly no more than nineteen.

# Masset.

**Alice Riall**

with leather. It was plaid pattern. I saw the luggage opposite the coffee-room door. I remember it because I asked the boots to take it up. I saw it in the bedroom about 1.45 on Sunday. I was off duty after that. It was by the side of the fireplace and the table. It appeared to be in the same position as it was on the Saturday. I saw some French fancy cakes in a drawer – not cakes bought in the hotel. They fitted in the little papers—I did not see any name on the paper.

**John Findlay**

JOHN FINDLAY, sworn and examined.

I keep an hotel in the Queens Road, Brighton. On Friday 27 October, I saw the prisoner in the lobby about 9.45 pm. She had two packages. The succeeding Wednesday, I found in a drawer of number 11 room the small scales produced. One scale had grains of what appeared to be sugar. I handed them to Police Sergeant Burch.

**Ann Skeet**

ANN SKEET, sworn and examined.

I am a widow of 19 Buckingham Road, Brighton. I am assistant in charge of the first and second class ladies' waiting-room at Brighton Railway Station. I was on duty on Saturday 28 October from 9.00 am till 9.00 pm. There is a small inner room which adjoins the lavatory, in which I have a little box to keep my caps. On that Saturday afternoon, about 3.30 pm, I found in my cap-box a brown paper parcel. I am sure it was not there before. I kept it till about 5.40 pm, when, in accordance with my duty, I took it to the cloakroom, and handed it to Henry Court.

**Henry Court**

HENRY COURT, sworn and examined.

I live at 23 Over Street, Brighton. I am cloakroom porter at the Brighton Railway Station. About 5.40 pm on Saturday 28 October, Mrs Skeet handed me a parcel. I kept it in the cloakroom till Monday 30 October, when I opened it. I attached this label, and sent it to the lost property office, at London Bridge, on 31 October. I forwarded the same paper. That was in the usual course of my duty.

**William Brown**

WILLIAM JAMES BROWN, sworn and examined.

I am chief clerk at the lost property office at London Bridge Station of the L.B. and S.C. Railway. On 1 November, I received a parcel with this label on it. In my presence, it was handed to Sergeant Nursey that afternoon. It was opened the same Wednesday afternoon.

**Richard Nursey**

RICHARD NURSEY (Detective Sergeant, J Division), sworn and examined.

On 1 November, I saw this parcel opened. It contained this serge

# Second Day – Thursday 14 December 1899.

**Richard Nursey**

frock and this little blue coat. The next day, I received this brown paper from Brown. I kept them till they were produced in court. On Friday 3 November, I received from Eleanor Gentle, at her residence – 210 Clyde Road, Tottenham – another piece of brown paper. I fitted them together, and found they corresponded [produced]. On one piece are the letters 'E. S' Part of the other piece is torn off.

I was in charge of this case from 1 November. Before that, I made inquiries as to the identity of the child. With Burch and Forth, I kept observation on 29 Bethune Road from 3.30 pm on Monday 3 November.[127]

Information came to me from Mrs Reece, the attendant at the ladies' waiting room at London Bridge. On 21 November, I attended at the station superintendent's office. Mrs Reece was sent for. She made a statement, which I took down in writing. She signed it. She was ordered to attend on 24 November at the North London Police Court. I was present in the yard and saw her identify the prisoner.

I have tested the time of the trains between Dalston Junction and Broad Street. The express trains take five and the stopping trains seven minutes. I went from Dalston Junction to the foot of London Bridge by bus and walked into the station in twenty-three minutes. Walking to the bus at the foot of the bridge, and going to the corner of Liverpool Street, and walking to Broad Street Station, took twenty-five minutes. I selected number 3 platform on the first occasion and then took my chance, but happened to come in at number 3. There may be variations in time caused by stoppages.

*Cross-examined.*

About seven or eight persons were present. There is no practice for the inspector to stand or follow at the back of the person identifying who is asked to touch the person she or he knows. Mrs Reece stopped and put on her glasses, stopped and looked, and then pointed with her umbrella at the prisoner. I said, 'Touch the one you mean,' and she touched the prisoner. The inspector was not behind her, that I remember. Such a thing did not strike me. Part of the yard is gravelled and part paved.

*Re-examined.*

Persons are placed on the asphalted pavement in a semicircle for identification. They are allowed to choose their position. Persons are collected like the accused, and great care is exercised according to instructions, which were carried out in this case.

---

127 *Sic* in CCCSP, but an obvious error: should read, 'I kept observation on 29 Bethune Road from 3.30 pm on Monday 30 October.'

# Masset.

**Richard Nursey**

*By the court.*

We at first, in watching 29 Bethune Road, did not go near the house till dark, before 7.00 pm; we tried to avoid observation.

**Richard Cadisch**

RICHARD CADISCH, sworn and examined.

I live at 29 Bethune Road. I am the prisoner's brother-in-law. I remember her return home on Sunday 23 October. She brought this brown bag. It is mine. I did not notice any waterproof. I let her in. I did not see her again till Monday.

About 2.00 am on 31 October, my brother-in-law, Mr George Richard Simes, came to the house. Mr Simes made a statement and remained some time with me. He and I went the following morning to London Bridge Station, with the object of going to his house at Croydon. It was about 8.00 am. We noticed, in Stoke Newington, that we were followed to the station. We found they were police officers. We spoke to them at the station. In consequence of what we stated, they came with us to Mr Simes's house at Croydon.

*Cross-examined.*

When the prisoner returned on Sunday evening, she seemed exactly in her usual spirits. I have four children. She has lived in our house about eighteen months. She was kind and affectionate, and very much liked by the children. She earned from teaching enough for her wants. She was not distressed for money, so far as I know. She retained some pupils for several years. She went for two or three years to the same houses.

**Alice Sonnenthal**

ALICE SONNENTHAL, sworn and examined.

I am the wife of George Sonnenthal, of 30 Belsize Park, Hampstead. The nearest stations are Hampstead Heath and Finchley Road, or East London, about a quarter of an hour off, and Loudoun Road, which is the nearest. The prisoner Masset has given lessons to my daughter since October 1895, with several interruptions, including the summer vacations, when we were away, and when she was away in the spring of 1896 down to Monday 30 October, last. I recommended her to Mrs Haas. Sometimes she came to me first, and sometimes to her. I did not see her on the Monday; I heard her voice. Thursday would be one of her days for coming. She came three or four times a week.

*Cross-examined.*

She gave every satisfaction. I had the fullest confidence in her.

The court adjourned.

*******

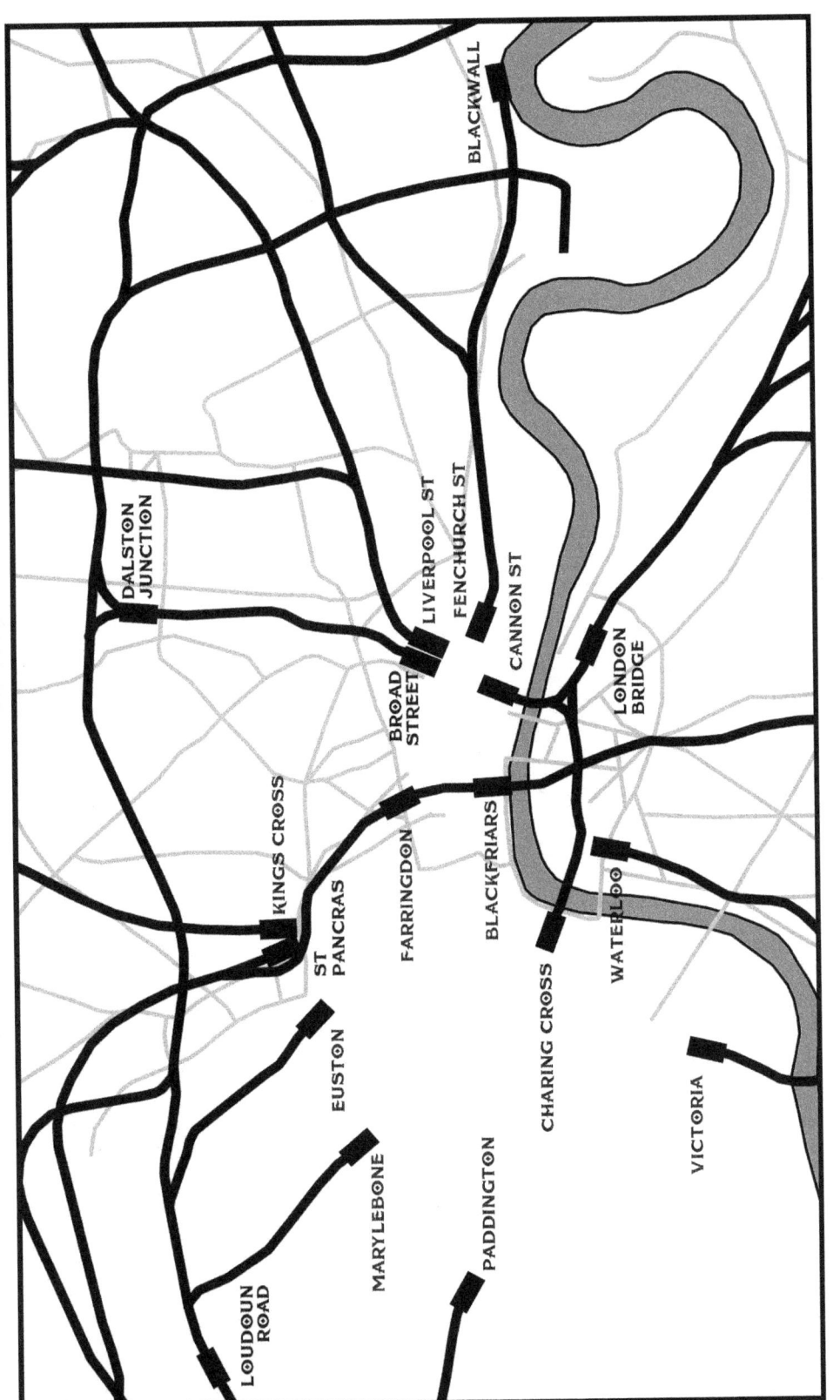

London Railway Schematic

*Courtesy Andrew Firth*

# Third Day – Friday 15 December 1899.[128]

**GEORGE RICHARD SIMES**, sworn and examined.

George Simes

I am an auctioneer at Stretton Road, Croydon. I am married to the prisoner's sister. She visited us, from time to time, at Croydon, before 30 October. I think the last time she came was at the beginning of August. I did not expect any visit from her on 30 October, but about 11.00 pm I answered the door and found her there. She said, 'Can I speak to you?' I said, 'Yes, what is it?' She said, 'I am being hunted for murder, but I have not done it'. I said, 'The child found at Dalston was not yours, was it?' I think she said, 'Yes, I am sure that it is,' or something like that.

I asked her what she knew, and she said that she had seen at Dalston that evening a placard of an evening paper stating that the body had been identified, that she had bought a paper, and from the description she was sure that it was her child. She was very much agitated, and I tried to calm her before I said much more to her. I was fairly successful in calming her, and then I asked her to account for her movements on the Friday. She said she had handed the child over to two women at London Bridge Railway Station (South Coast), and had afterwards gone by the 4.00 pm train to Brighton; that she arrived a little before 6.00 pm, I think it was; that she went to Mutton's restaurant and had something to eat, and afterwards went to Mr Findlay's Hotel and engaged a room there; that Mr Lucas was at Brighton on the Saturday. That was the first I heard of the visit to Brighton. By that time it was nearly 12.00 am. I then left home and went to my brother-in-law, Mr Cadisch, at Bethune Road, leaving the prisoner with my wife, her sister.

I got to Bethune Road about 2.30 am, where I saw Mr and Mrs Cadisch, and had a conversation with them. I stayed the night there, and next morning left with Mr Cadisch to go back to Croydon. We went to London Bridge Station on foot, when I noticed that we were being followed; and, on our arrival at London Bridge, finding that it was the police who were following us, I spoke to them and made a statement, in consequence of which they accompanied us to Croydon, where we arrived about 10.00 am, when the prisoner was arrested.

---

128   Third day's evidence from CCCSP (TNA:PRO CRIM 10/80; also www.oldbaileyonline.org, version 7.2, 23 March 2017, December 1899, trial of Louisa [sic] Josephine Jemima Masset [t18991211-77]), except testimony of Louise Masset (from TNA:PRO HO 144/1540/A61535).

# Masset.

**George Simes**

*Cross-examined.*

The prisoner was in a very hysterical state when she came to me. I told her that if she would tell me all about it, whatever it was, I would do my best for her, and I think she said, 'How could you think I could kill my own child?' Then she told me about Lucas going to Brighton, and that the story about the child going to France was untrue. I think I had heard of it from my wife. It was then that the prisoner told me of the meeting with the two women at Tottenham – I think she said at Tottenham Green – at any rate, one day when she had the child out. She said that they had found out that it was a nurse-child, and that they were forming a home at King's Road, Chelsea, and that they said they would take the child for £12 a year; that she had agreed to hand over the child to them at London Bridge Station on the Friday, I understood in the general waiting room; that she was to pay the £12 down in advance. I am not sure that she told me that she had gone to another waiting room first. She said that she had met the two women, that she had given them the £12, and that they had left to go to the refreshment room, taking the boy with them, for the purpose of getting something to eat. She said that she knew Lucas was coming on the following day, and asked me not to mention the fact to her people. She did not say she would go to the police station if she was wanted. I told her she must go, and she said, 'Very well'. She made a statement to Sergeant Burch at my house, in my presence, which he took down in writing.

I know Dalston Junction and number 3 platform fairly well, and that there is large traffic there. I went with the prisoner to the station, where she twice asked to see the dead body of the child. Her request was not granted then. I had an interview with her in the cells after she was remanded, and she urged me to arrange for her to see the child; which she did, in spite of my telling her it was not in a condition to be seen. I was aware of the existence of the child, and we all considered her to be very fond of it.

*Re-examined.*

I never saw the child myself. I knew it was at Tottenham. I believe I heard of its intended removal to France on the Friday when the murder was committed. I heard that the pair had gone to France with the child to hand it over to some relations of the father, who would take care of it in the future. I did not hear that the father had been in England in the week which ended on 14 October. The prisoner told me of more than one meeting with the two women prior to 27 October. I believe she said that the place of meeting on each occasion was at Tottenham Green, at about 2.00 pm. She told me that she waited in the waiting-room on the

# Third Day – Friday 15 December 1899.

twenty-seventh for the purpose of getting a receipt for her money, which she had paid the two women. It was from her that I first learned of the visit to Brighton, as well as the fact that Lucas had been down there from the Saturday to the Sunday night.

*George Simes*

WILLIAM BURCH (Detective Sergeant, J Division), sworn and examined.

*William Burch*

I and other officers kept watch on 29 Bethune Road on the afternoon of 30 October. We got there about 3.30 pm. Sergeant Nursey was with me. The prisoner did not come to that house at all that evening.

Next morning, I followed Mr Cadisch and Mr Simes to London Bridge Railway Station, and then went with them to Mrs Simes, at Croydon. I saw the prisoner. I was with Detective Allen. I said to her, 'We are police officers; you had a child which you took from its nurse last Friday. Can you account for it to me?' She said, 'I last saw my child, Manfred Louis Masset, aged three and a half, on Friday, at London Bridge Railway Station, in the waiting-room. I gave it to two women, who gave the address at 45 King's Road, Chelsea, with £12, mostly gold, to take care of it for a whole twelve months. I had seen them at Tottenham Green four Wednesdays ago; that would be 4 October; they first spoke to me and by their conversation with me they found out it was a nurse-child. They said they were setting up a home, and would I mind letting them have mine for £12 a year.' I took this statement down in writing at the time. She said that at first she did not agree, but that she would see them again next Wednesday; that she had the child with her, and decided to leave it with them for that sum, and arranged to meet them at London Bridge on the twenty-seventh; that she met them, but before doing so she went into the waiting room near the parcels office, where there was a woman attendant who had a cap on, and another attendant came to relieve her while the prisoner was there; that the woman took the bag, and went out as they asked the child if he would like a cake; that she waited there two or three minutes for a receipt for her money, but they never came back; and that she had never seen her child since.

When that statement was made, I did not know that Miss Teahan and Miss Biggs had communicated with the police. I said to her, 'You will have to go to Dalston Police Station'. She said, 'I will go willingly'. She was taken to the station and charged by Inspector Forth.

On 1 November, I was at Brighton, and Mr Findlay handed me some toy scales [produced]. I also produce the clinker brick found in the lavatory at Dalston Junction. I saw the body of the child in the lavatory on the night of the twenty-seventh, and one part of the brick was on one side of the head, and the other part on the other side. There was a portion

# Masset.

**William Burch**

broken off. This black shawl was round the body of the child. On 28 November, I took a journey from number 1 platform at Dalston Junction to Broad Street by train, and then by bus to London Bridge. I left Dalston at 5.42 pm, and arrived at London Bridge at 6.17 pm. I waited about five minutes for a bus.

*Cross-examined.*

The statement I took down is in the identical language in which she spoke. This [produced] is the original note, and part of it is the result of my questions and her answers.

*Re-examined.*

The language used is the language of the prisoner. I repeated everything she said, while I was writing it down, so that I should have it correct.

**Henry Willis**

HENRY WILLIS, sworn and examined.

I live at 45 King's Road, Chelsea, where I carry on the business of a dairy; I have had the place for ten years. There is no home for nurse-children kept there. I employ four female assistants in the business, and also a female domestic servant. My wife lives there, and those are the only females in the establishment. I got a visit from a police officer soon after 27 October. I am quite sure that none of the females at my address were away on 27 October; they were all there between 8.00 am and 8.00 pm. I have no lodgers.

**William Bowers**

WILLIAM BOWERS, sworn and examined.

I am a guard employed on the London, Brighton and South Coast Railway, and was in charge of the train due to leave London Bridge at 4.00 pm on 27 October for Brighton. We left at 4.01 pm, and arrived at 5.19 pm, four minutes late.

**John Whittle**

JOHN WHITTLE, sworn and examined.

I am a guard employed by the London, Brighton and South Coast Railway, and was in charge of the train due to leave London Bridge for Brighton at 7.22 pm; we left at 7.23 pm, and arrived at 9.18 pm, eight minutes late.

**Frederick Forth**

FREDERICK FORTH (Inspector, J Division), sworn and examined.

I am the inspector in charge of this case. There are two lines of omnibuses between London Bridge and Stoke Newington. I was present at the Dalston Police Station when Mrs Reece identified the prisoner on 24 November. She picked her out without any aid from me, or anyone.

# Third Day – Friday 15 December 1899.

**Frederick Forth**

On 31 October, the prisoner was first brought to the station, and Sergeant Burch showed me a statement made by the prisoner, which he had taken down. I read it, and then said to the prisoner, 'You will be charged with the murder of your child'. She said, 'Impossible'. The charge was read over to her. She said, 'Cannot I say something to clear myself?' I said, 'Yes, if you like'. Mr Simes, who stood near, said, 'You had better not say anything now,' and she said nothing.

On 2 November, I was at the coroner's inquiry, and also the prisoner, and she asked to see the child. The permission was given, and I accompanied her into the mortuary, where the dead body lay. When she saw it, she said, 'Oh! My child, my poor boy!' She was affected. This [produced] is a photograph of the child after death, which I had taken about noon on 28 October. It correctly represents the condition of the child's face at the time. There had been a great change between 28 October and 2 November.

I went to 29 Bethune Road, and in the back garden there is a grotto or rockery formed of clinker bricks. I took these two bricks [produced]. When I took them away there were no traces left of their having been taken. There are also some clinker bricks in the front garden, forming a border, and there were some loose on the ground. I took away three and compared them with the clinker brick found by the child's body. They are apparently of the same kind.

On 28 November, I took a journey from number 2 platform at Dalston Junction to Broad Street. I left Dalston at 6.05 pm, and, after waiting a few minutes at Broad Street, I went by bus to London Bridge, arriving there at 6.35 pm. The distance from Bethune Road to Dalston Junction is one and seven-eighth miles, and from Dalston Junction to the Birdcage public-house one and three-quarter miles. From the Birdcage to Tottenham Green is about one and a quarter miles; from Tottenham Green to King's Road, Chelsea, is about eight and a half miles.

*Cross-examined.*

I could not see any place from where the bricks were missing. The loose ones had been lying loose on the ground some time, apparently.

HORACE BAKER (Policeman 41N), sworn and examined.

**Horace Baker**

I was present at the identification of the prisoner by Mrs Reece on 24 November. No indication was given to Mrs Reece to help her in her identification.

*Cross-examined.*

Mrs Reece halted two or three times before getting to the prisoner.

## Masset.

**Horace Baker**

*Re-examined.*

She then went up to her and identified her, about six or seven yards in front of Inspector Forth.

**Marion Fitzgerald**

MARION FITZGERALD, sworn and examined.

I am a book-keeper at Bertram and Roberts' refreshment room at London Bridge Station. I know Mrs Reece, who is the attendant at the ladies' waiting room nearest the refreshment room. I remember her making a statement to me, as near as I can possibly say, on Wednesday or Thursday, 2 or 3 November.

**James Fennell**

JAMES PATRICK FENNELL, sworn and examined.

I am a registered medical practitioner, and live at 20 Dalston Lane. On Friday 27 October, I was called to Dalston Junction at 6.55 pm. I went at once to the water closet, which is attached to the ladies' waiting room, arriving there about three minutes after being called.

On the floor, I saw the dead body of a child. It was behind the door, a few inches from the partition, with its head towards the corridor, and its body towards the seat of the closet. The left leg was bent at the knee, the outer surface of the leg resting on the ground, and the foot under the right thigh. The body, with the exception of the head and legs, was loosely covered with a black shawl; it was simply laid over it, not tied round it. I felt the body on my arrival, and found the trunk was warm; stiffening had not set in, the extremities were cold. I saw some bruises and abrasions on its head. I should say it had been dead about one hour, but I cannot fix the time. In my opinion, the longest period that it could have been dead was two or three hours; four hours would be the outside time. I think the shortest time within which it could have died would be within an hour.

The photograph which has been produced shows the condition when I saw it on 27 October. I did not then come to any conclusion as to the cause of death. I noticed that the tongue protruded slightly between the teeth, which is one of the signs of death by suffocation. There were bloodstains on the head and forehead, and a small clot on the floor to the left of the child's head. I saw a clinker brick there, and I afterwards made an examination of it. There appeared to be bloodstains upon one corner of it, but I cannot say that it was bloodstains. There were also two hairs corresponding to the hairs on the eyebrows of the child. The brick was an instrument with which the injuries to the child's head might have been inflicted, and I believe it was the implement with which they were caused.

I do not attach any importance to the position of the left leg. I believe

# Third Day – Friday 15 December 1899.

the child died in the closet, and was not removed there after death. The child's bowels had been evacuated, which, I should say, took place at the time of death. The clot of blood on the floor could have been covered with a florin. The blood being there would indicate, I think, that death had taken place in the closet. The lips were blue, which would be another indication of death by suffocation. The upper lip was slightly swollen. The tip of the nose was bruised, which might indicate pressure over the nose.

Under my instructions, the body was conveyed to the mortuary, where I made the post mortem examination, when I found a bruise on the forehead extending from above the centre of the left eyebrow to the outer side of the right eyebrow. It was of recent infliction, but I cannot say positively whether before or after death – but it was immediately before or after death. It would require much violence to inflict. It was a bruise only, not a wound. It might have been inflicted by a clinker brick.

There was a lacerated, punctured wound one inch above the inner side of the left eyebrow, a quarter of an inch long. There was a small wound of the same character immediately beneath it, and at the outer end of the right eyebrow there was a lacerated, penetrating wound, and a very small wound beside it. At the inner end of the right eyebrow, there was a small lacerated wound. Outside the left eyebrow, there was a small abrasion and a bruise. There was a curved bruise extending from the right side of the nose across the cheek to the outside of the right under-eyelid, about half an inch wide at its widest part. A bruise of a similar character extended from the left side of the nose across the cheek to a little beyond the centre of the left lower eyelid, ending in a small lacerated wound. There must have been a good deal of violence used to cause those wounds and bruises. In my opinion, they were all caused by some hard substance; a clinker brick would have caused them.

The post mortem was made at 10.00 pm on Saturday night. I and Dr Jackman, the divisional surgeon of police, made it together.

When at the closet, I saw a depression in the centre of the forehead about the size of half-a-crown, with some gritty dust on it; it was gritty to the feel of the fingers. At the post mortem, I found the surface of the body pale, with the exception of the face; the body was clean and well-nourished. The child had been circumcised. There was no disease of the organs. The brain was congested, and the large venous channels in the interior of the skull were full of blood, which was indicative of death from want of air. It is a sign I should expect to find in death from suffocation. I believe the child died from suffocation. I speak of suffocation as quite distinct from strangulation. The injuries on the child's head were not sufficient by themselves to cause death. It is not possible to say whether

*James Fennell*

# Masset.

**James Fennell**

the external injuries were caused immediately before or after death; the appearance would be the same. Probably the child would be stunned, and probably the stunning and suffocation would be quite close to each other; they might almost be simultaneous.

*Cross-examined.*

I said before the coroner, 'I think he must have been dead at least half an hour; I think the child had certainly been killed within an hour of my seeing him.' I cannot say if rigor mortis takes place sooner after suffocation than in ordinary circumstances. I do not think rigor mortis would intervene more rapidly if there had been struggling immediately before death, unless it had been prolonged. I do not think the ordinary struggling in suffocation would be sufficient to induce rigor mortis to set in earlier than normally.

*Re-examined.*

It is most difficult to fix the precise time when this child died. I think it had been dead about an hour.

**Charles Jackman**

CHARLES HOWARD JACKMAN, sworn and examined.

I am divisional surgeon of police and live at 69 Kyverdale Road. I assisted at the post mortem examination on the body of the child on 28 October. I agree with Dr Fennell that the injuries on the face and forehead must have been caused by violence and with some hard substance, as the clinker brick which has been produced. I say that it is impossible to say whether the injuries were inflicted either immediately before or after death. I agree that the general condition of the organs were healthy, and also that the death was caused by suffocation, which may have been caused by pressure of the hand over the nose and mouth. The tongue protruding through the teeth is another indication of death from suffocation. It is difficult to say precisely how long the child had been dead.

*Cross-examined.*

I did not have an opportunity of judging how long it had been dead by its temperature; I think it is impossible for Dr Fennell or for me to say how long the child had been dead. He did not tell me what the temperature was; he did not say that the w.c. was draughty. I wish to differ from Dr Fennell when he says that the child had been dead an hour when he saw it.

# Third Day – Friday 15 December 1899.

*Re-examined.*   **Charles Jackman**

Heat may remain in the body for eight or sixteen hours after the death, if you wrap it up; under the conditions in which this body was found, it might be from eight to four hours.

THOMAS BOND, sworn and examined.   **Thomas Bond**

I am a Fellow of the Royal College of Surgeons, and consulting surgeon at the Westminster Hospital. I have had much experience in giving evidence in courts of justice. I have studied the depositions in this case, and I have heard the evidence given in court today. I cannot form any certain opinion as to how long the child had been dead when seen by Dr Fennell, but I should say between one hour and four. I quite think an hour would elapse.

*Cross-examined.*

I think I am much more qualified to give an opinion than Dr Fennell. I have seen so many hundreds of dead bodies with regard to giving evidence; but a man who is present has a better opportunity of judging than one who comes afterwards.

*By the court.*

The study, observation, and examination of questions like this does not form part of the practice of an ordinary practitioner. I have given special attention to questions of this kind.

INSPECTOR FORTH, re-examined.   **Frederick Forth**

I have been in the water-closet on other days since the one on which the body was found, and I have made experiments with matches and so on, and I find that it is not cold or draughty.

*Cross-examined.*

I heard Dr Fennell examined at the police court; I cannot remember him saying that the closet was cold and draughty.

DR FENNELL, re-examined by Lord COLERIDGE.   **James Fennell**

I said before the magistrate that the closet was a cold and draughty place; that is true.

*Cross-examined* by Mr MATHEWS.

I was speaking generally; I had made no tests.

# Masset.

## Evidence for the Defence.

**Louise Masset**

LOUISE MASSET, sworn and examined by Lord COLERIDGE.

You are the daughter of French and English parents? — Yes, sir.

Your father is dead and your mother is alive? — Yes, sir.

And we know that three and a half years ago you became the mother of the little boy whose death is being enquired into. — Of Manfred Louis Masset.

Was his father a Frenchman? — He was. I am quite willing to give his name, but I would rather do it in private.

But he is not at present resident in this country? — No, he has not been since August twelve months.

And have you for some years past maintained yourself by the giving of lessons to pupils? — Yes, sir; for the last sixteen, seventeen, eighteen years I have.

Mr Justice BRUCE: By giving French lessons?

Lord COLERIDGE: Not only French lessons? — No: English and music.

And about three weeks after the birth of Manfred did you respond to an advertisement which was inserted in the newspaper by Miss Gentle? — Yes.

And she tells us that you met and arranged that she should take charge of your son? — That was so.

Did she give references? — Well, she wished me to have two or three, but I only wrote to one woman, a friend of hers, simply to know whether the child would be comfortable.

You did not think it necessary to verify all her references? — No, I had seen her and liked her as a person.

As an individual? — [The witness did not answer.]

Did she take charge of your child for the sum of £1 17s a month? — Yes, sir. She had him from 22 May 1896.

Your sister, Mrs Cadisch, I believe, guaranteed the payment of the sum? — Miss Gentle, I suppose, was frightened that she would not get the money, so Miss Gentle came to her and she guaranteed it.

And she tells us that she was never called upon for her guarantee? — That is so.

Did the father of the child regularly subscribe to the maintenance of the child? — Yes, sir. He has continued to do so, and would now.

We hear that Miss Gentle took great care of the little boy. — She was exceedingly fond of him.

And did you used to go once a fortnight and, during the last eighteen months, at least once a week to see your boy? — Since I have been with

# Third Day – Friday 15 December 1899.

my sister, I have been once a week.

That has been for about eighteen months? — Since August twelve months.

And, now you have mentioned your sister, it is true, is it not, that you went to live with her free of charge? — Quite so. I have had the offer between two sisters and I chose that one because my lessons were in London. That is why I did not go to Croydon.

It was nearer to your work than Croydon. We hear that the little boy as a rule enjoyed good health. — Till his operation.

And we hear of an operation which was twice unsuccessful and successful the third time, I think in the spring of this year – January or February, I think it was. — January, I should say. I cannot quite localise it.

Were you anxious and distressed about the boy at that time? — Very much so.

Now, you have told us that Miss Gentle was uniformly kind to the little boy. Did you ever have any conversation with her with reference to her being too kind and spoiling the little boy? — Yes, I did not think she was quite judicious enough.

Not quite judicious. She has said to us that you may have said to her that she spoiled him, and that she said that the little boy was difficult to manage. — I beg your pardon: was –

She has said that you said to her that she spoiled him and that she, Miss Gentle, found a difficulty in managing him? — Yes, I think she did. He was of a very hasty temper and given to crying.

Mr Justice BRUCE: I thought Miss Gentle said she had no difficulty in managing him.

Lord COLERIDGE: But the little boy was hasty and given to fits of crying? — Yes. I thought the reason was, if I may speak, that they said things in front of him which he ought not to hear. For instance, they would speak about the operations which he had had, and he was so sensitive that if he heard it he would go into a fit of screaming.

And you had conversations with her from time to time with reference to this? — Yes.

Now I take you to 27 September, which I think was a Wednesday; but before I go to that more particularly, may I ask, were you in the habit of taking out the boy when you went to him? — Nearly every time I went, if the weather was sufficiently fine, I took him out. The rooms were very small there and I thought he ought to get as much air as possible.

Did you go to Tottenham Green? — In the daytime, I used to go to the Downhills.

Mr Justice BRUCE: What weather? — When the weather was dry. But

**Louise Masset**

# Masset.

**Louise Masset**

when it was damp I went to Tottenham Green. It was paved with gravel or asphalt.

Lord COLERIDGE: Now I take you to 27 September, which, I think, is a Wednesday. Did you take the little boy on that day to Tottenham Green? — No, sir, I did not. It was the day my stepfather died. We expected him to die any moment. That is why I went in the evening, instead of the morning. I had no time to take him out.

Did you go on the twenty-seventh? — No, sir.

Mr Justice BRUCE: You went to see the boy but you had no time to stay? — No, because I was so anxious to get back, for my stepfather was so ill. In fact, he had died when I got home.

Lord COLERIDGE: When was the next time you went to Tottenham Green? — On the fourth, the next Wednesday.

Mr Justice BRUCE: 4 October, do you mean? — 4 October – yes.

Lord COLERIDGE: Did you take the little boy with you? — Yes.

Mr Justice BRUCE: You took the boy to Tottenham Green? — Yes.

Lord COLERIDGE: I understand you constantly did it: when it was at all wet weather, you went to Tottenham Green. I mean, that was not the first time you had been to Tottenham Green? — Oh, no, several times.

Well, after you got there with your little boy did you see anybody? — When I got there, the first person I saw was a little girl whom I had met several times and who used to play with Manfred. He said, 'Hello, Millie!' and she said, 'Hello, Manfred,' like children do when children meet.

Did you see anybody else? — There were two ladies. They looked perfect ladies, sitting on the seat where this child was playing.

Did you accost them or did they accost you? — The first thing that I remember was when one of them said, 'Oh, is this the little boy whom my daughter has spoken so many times about?' I said he had played with her, and at the same time they made a movement, and made room for me on the seat.

And you sat down? — Yes.

Mr Justice BRUCE: They made a movement and did what? — I sat down by them.

They made a movement to invite you to sit down? — Yes.

Lord COLERIDGE: Yes? — We began talking first of all and the children – we played with them, in fact. And I suppose they saw that I had no ring because I had my gloves off.

No wedding ring. — Yes. They began talking of the child and they said, 'Are you married?' Of course, I said, 'No'. One other thing they said before I sat down: 'How was it that they had not seen me before, and the little girl had?' I explained that I only came on that green once

# Third Day – Friday 15 December 1899.

a week, and it was only on Wednesdays that I could be there. They said, 'How was it they had not seen me before?'

They said it to you, not you to them? — Yes.

And you said you only came on Wednesdays.

Mr Justice BRUCE: 'How was it that they had not seen you before, as I have seen your little girl'? — Yes. They would say, 'How is it that we have not seen you before, as you have seen our little girl?'

'I explained I was only there on Wednesdays.' — Yes, and they said that generally they brought their little girl from Philip Lane – no, it was a road leading into the Philip Lane. I cannot remember the name; it was where they lived, it was near Philip Lane … That they used to leave her to play, and would go and do their shopping while she played there. It is rather a safe place for children.

Lord COLERIDGE: Is Philip Lane in the neighbourhood? Where is Philip Lane, do you know? — I cannot say exactly where it is.

But that is what they said to you? — Yes, I cannot describe the place. I cannot say exactly where Philip Lane is.

Go on, Miss Masset. What further took place? — Then it was that they spoke to me and asked me if I had been married; or they said, 'You are not married'.

They saw that from your not having a ring? — I suppose so; I had my gloves off. I answered, 'No,' and they inquired where the child was, whether he lived with me or not. I said, 'No,' that he was a nurse-child, but I had placed him in the care of people in Tottenham, but I did not give the address, and that he had been there – but I did not give the Gentles' address.

Mr Justice BRUCE: You did not give the address? — I did not give the address of the Norrises.

Yes. Did you tell them that he had been there three and a half years, or not? — Yes.

Lord COLERIDGE: Go on with the conversation. — Of course, it was in conversation they spoke of this. I cannot say the very next thing, but they asked me if I was pleased with his being there, if he had got on nicely. I said I was satisfied, with the exception of his education. In fact, the way he spoke was enough to prove it to them.

You say the manner in which the little boy spoke – what do you mean? — Well, he used the word 'ain't' a good deal more than was necessary. He would say, 'Look at them things'.

He did not speak like educated people? — Far from it.

Had you mentioned that fact to your sister, Mrs Cadisch? — Yes, I have said it more than once.

Before that? — Oh, yes.

*Louise Masset*

# Masset.

**Louise Masset**

And these ladies whom you met, how did they speak? — Very nicely. They were what I should call perfect ladies, both in appearance and education.

As far as you could judge? — Yes.

What next took place? — They began talking about themselves. Then the elder lady – she must have been forty-five – she had been a widow about six months, she told me. She was not dressed in weeds. This other lady was her husband's sister. She gave me the name of Browning. She was Mrs, and the other Miss, Browning.

Mr Justice BRUCE: Her husband's sister? — Yes. She might have been about twenty-seven or twenty-eight.

She gave you the name of Brown? — Browning.

That was the younger lady? — One was Mrs, and the other Miss.

Was it the younger woman who gave you the name of Browning? — I cannot say which mentioned it, but they told me their name was Browning.

Lord COLERIDGE: Yes? — They said that since her husband had died, her means were rather reduced, and she had thought of taking two children – no more. There was no baby-farming.

Mr Justice BRUCE: They had thought of what? — Of taking a house – they were only in apartments.

Yes? — They would like to have two children to bring up with their little girl. The sister was to have a kind of kindergarten.

The younger lady? — Yes. She was to have several children she hoped to get to come to her daily.

Lord COLERIDGE: Did she say where she contemplated setting up this establishment? — No, she did not. She had not decided where she would go.

Yes? — Then she asked me whether I would let her have my little boy, because, she said, they were rather difficult to get – people who were sure. I suppose she meant people who were sure to pay properly.

Which of them said this – the elder one or the younger one? — The elder lady.

Was anything said about terms? — Yes, that was the first thing afterwards that I asked. She said that it would be £12 per year for the child's board and lodging.

How paid? How was the £12 to be paid? — That did not happen at the time. I will tell you now if you like. It was to be paid in advance because she wanted money to set up the house.

Mr Justice BRUCE: Was it said at this time, or afterwards? — It was said at this time.

Because she wanted ready money? — Yes, for moving and starting

# Third Day – Friday 15 December 1899.

her house.

Lord COLERIDGE: Yes? — She would require – it was the younger lady who was then to undertake the child's teaching for ten shillings monthly.

Mr Justice BRUCE: In addition to the £12? — Yes, and the other was simply for the board and lodging. The younger lady was to undertake the teaching.

Lord COLERIDGE: What did you say to that? — I said I could not be sure if I would let her have him or not. I could not make up my mind in a hurry.

Did you say anything about further meeting, or anything of that kind? — Yes, we were to meet the next week. She was to see what house she was to get. She was to look about and see what house she could get, and to tell me the next time.

Have you now told us all that you can remember that is of importance that took place at this interview? — I think so. Several other things, of course, were said at the time, but nothing of importance.

Did you mention this to Miss Gentle? — No. It would have been a very sore point with her.

It would have been a very sore point? — I could not tell her that she did not speak properly, or anything like that.

When did you next go to Tottenham Green? — It was the following Wednesday. I got to Miss Gentle's rather earlier that day. For one reason I remember the day: I had had one extra lesson that morning, and when I had extra lessons in the morning, I always came straight through by the tram to the bottom of Seven Sisters Road, and I got there earlier. I did not go home to my sister's house on those days.

You did not go to your sister's house? — Not on those days.

When you had an extra lesson in the morning, did you have a lesson in the afternoon? — No.

The afternoon was quite free? — Yes.

Mr Justice BRUCE: 'When I had an extra lesson in the morning, the afternoon was free, and I would go to my sister's house in the afternoon.' Do you generally go to your sister's house in the middle of the day? — On any other day, when I had a lesson in the morning, I should return for my lunch.

Did you take the tram? I think you said -- — From Dalston I might have an omnibus. For all I know, I might have taken an omnibus to the Birdcage.

You took a tram or omnibus from where? — From Dalston Junction.

To? — Seven Sisters Corner.

Lord COLERIDGE: How far is that? From Miss Gentle's to Seven

**Louise Masset**

# Masset.

**Louise Masset**

Sisters Corner? — Ten minutes' walk.

And how far from Tottenham Green? — Three minutes from Tottenham Green.

What time do you say you got to Miss Gentle's? — It must have been about 2.30 pm. I was earlier then, because I generally get there about 2.45 pm.

You got there on this occasion at what time? — About 2.30 pm. I would not swear to the time.

No, no: but about. — About that.

Did you take your boy out at once, or did you wait? — I waited while it was being dressed. I asked Miss Gentle – because I always ask her – at what time she was going to take her father's shirts and collars to the cleaners. She said she could not come out at once, but she would meet me later on.

Mr Justice BRUCE: I thought you said you waited until she was dressed. — Until the boy was dressed. She dressed him for me, so that I could take him out at once. She would have to dress herself and go to the cleaners and all before she could meet me, and I arranged to meet her at Seven Sisters Station.

Seven Sisters Station? — Yes, Seven Sisters Station.

Now then, Miss Masset, what were your movements after that? — I went straight down the Clyde Road to the Green, as I said I would.

Did you meet Miss Gentle at Seven Sisters Station? — Afterwards – not then. We arranged before I left. She would not be able to meet me before the half hour.

Lord COLERIDGE: Miss Gentle tells us that she met you at 3.30 pm. — That would be about it.

Mr Justice BRUCE: You went down to the Green with the boy? — With the boy.

Lord COLERIDGE: To the Green? — Yes.

And there? — I met the same two ladies and their little girl; they were all three there.

Mr Justice BRUCE: Yes? — The lady told me that she had been looking out for a house.

Which lady? — Mrs Browning – she was the spokesman.

The elder lady? — Yes. She was spokesman generally, and she thought of taking 45 King's Road, Chelsea.

Yes. — I thought it was rather far, and I said so. I did not know Chelsea in any way, but I thought it might be rather far.

Yes. — But she overruled my objection by saying it was a very nice house.

Lord COLERIDGE: Yes. — And she then asked me whether I had

# Third Day – Friday 15 December 1899.

decided whether I would let her have the boy.

And what did you say? — I said I would.

Did you then go --? Was that all that took place at that interview? — No. We made arrangements for meeting. She was to let me know whether there was any change in her plans, and she was to let me know at 29 Bethune Road.

You gave her your address? — Yes.

That was Mrs Cadisch's, where you were living? — Yes.

Mr Justice BRUCE: You gave her your address there, then? — Yes.

Lord COLERIDGE: If there was any change in the plan? — Yes. I mean by that, if she had any bother in getting the house – she had not taken it then – she only thought of getting one. She wanted time to move in. I wanted time to give notice to Miss Gentle, so we arranged that we should meet at London Bridge on the twenty-seventh.

Do you mean London Bridge, or the station? — The station. The child never would go in a train; he always screamed. They have had many a time to walk home with him late at night, because he never would go in a train. That was why it was arranged that they should go as far as London Bridge. It was so the child should have no train. I thought it would be easier for him to go by tram, straight on from the bottom of Clyde Road to London Bridge.

You can get from Clyde Road to London Bridge without going by train? — Yes, straight there.

Was that all that took place? — That was all for the time.

Then where did you go after that? — Well, they walked up – whilst they were talking, they walked up to Clyde Road together, and I took some of the little turnings that there are which lead into the West Green Road.

Was that where you had appointed to meet Miss Gentle? — That is where I had appointed to meet her.

Mr Justice BRUCE: Just one moment. This, I understand, is 11 October, is it not?

Lord COLERIDGE: It is, my Lord. Miss Gentle has told us that she went out and met you in Seven Sisters Road. — Yes, that is so. When I came out of this road just above the station, she was there.

Mr Justice BRUCE: You say you turned down somewhere? — I was in the Clyde Road. I took one – there were several of them from Clyde Road to the West Green Road, and I turned into the West Green Road. Seven Sisters Station is in the West Green Road.

When you got into the West Green Road, what happened then? — I met Miss Gentle.

Lord COLERIDGE: Is that near Miss Gentle's house? — Yes. She was

**Louise Masset**

# Masset.

**Louise Masset**

returning to see if she could find us.

Then did you go to the Green? — Yes, we went again to the Green.

Miss Gentle tells us that she got to the Green about 3.30 pm. Would that be about the time? — Yes, about that. I got to her house, as I said, about 2.30 pm.

Were the women gone then? — I did not see them go, but they had come part of the way up the Clyde Road with me, you see.

Mr Justice BRUCE: You say the women had gone then? — Yes.

Lord COLERIDGE: They had accompanied you part of the way to Seven Sisters Station? — Yes.

Mr Justice BRUCE: What became of them? — I cannot say. I know they came as far as this street, which I took to get into the West Green Road.

Lord COLERIDGE: Did they go into the West Green Road? — No, they did not. There is Clyde Road, and there is West Green Road.

Mr Justice BRUCE: 'They had come so far before I met Miss Gentle.' — Yes.

Lord COLERIDGE: Very well. That concludes the incident of 11 October. — Yes, the child was ill that day.

Yes, we remember about the child being ill. — I returned there that same evening and stopped there till 10.00 pm.

The doctor was sent for?

Mr Justice BRUCE: You stayed some time on the Green? — Yes.

Lord COLERIDGE: Miss Gentle has told us that the child was swollen in the eyes. — Yes, I carried him home.

Did you go home in the meantime, and come back again? — Go home where?

That evening, you know. — Ah, yes, I did. I returned to Bethune Road. I knew they would expect me. I returned about 7.00 pm and I told them that he was not well, and then I went back to the boy about 8.00 pm, and stayed till 10.00 pm.

Mr Justice BRUCE: You reached home about 7.00 pm? — Yes, I reached home about that time.

And returned to Miss Gentle when? — About 8.00 pm to 8.30 pm. I only took time to have my dinner, my evening meal.

And stayed till 10.00 pm? — Yes, 10.00 pm or 10.30 pm. I waited till the doctor came, anyhow.

Just let me see if I follow this. You say the women left you and you went on to the Green? — Yes. Miss Gentle knew about the little girl because the child had often spoken about her. She had met her several times.

Lord COLERIDGE: Now I wish to hark back a little bit. We know that

# Third Day – Friday 15 December 1899.

living next door to you was the young man, Lucas, and we know that you had gone down with another lady and another gentleman, all four of you? — At Whitsuntide.

At Whitsunside, to Brighton. At that time, were your relations those simply of friends? — Yes.

We have heard of two bedrooms being occupied. Did you and the lady sleep in one. And the two gentlemen in the other? — Yes.

Gradually, did a greater amount of intimacy grow up between you and Mr Lucas? — Yes.

And, he has told us, you used to walk out together and meet each other by appointment? — Yes.

Now I wish to draw your attention to the letter of 16 October, which you wrote to Mrs Norris. 'I thought I should be able to see Manfred last Friday.' You remember the letter – I need not read it – about taking him away. When did you first form the intention of going with Mr Lucas to Brighton? — I think it was on the eighth.

On 8 October? — I formed it by myself, not with him. I did not speak of it to him until the twenty-fifth.

We know that, but when did you form in your own mind the intention of going with him to Brighton? — The ninth or tenth. I had a piece of poetry sent me on the eighth, passed over the garden wall.

By him?

Mr Justice BRUCE: Was it the eighth, or ninth, or tenth? — The verse was sent me on the eighth.

Lord COLERIDGE: May I ask you --

Mr Justice BRUCE: Just tell me. 'I think it was on the eighth that I first formed my intention of going to Brighton.' You said something about a bit of poetry over the garden wall? — It was given to me over the garden wall.

By Lucas? — Yes.

Lord COLERIDGE: Did you know he had his Saturdays and Sundays free? — Yes. I knew he was occupied on Saturdays till three and sometimes four, and then he was free till Monday morning.

You knew that Saturday evenings and Sundays were free? — Quite free.

Had you formed any opinion when you wrote the letter of 16 October? — I had.

Now, your relations with Miss Gentle were always those of the most friendly character? — I treated her like a sister for the sake of the boy.

Did you find it a matter of some difficulty how to break to Miss Gentle --? — That I was going to take the boy away?

The news that you were going to take the boy away? — Yes.

**Louise Masset**

# Masset.

**Louise Masset**

Miss Gentle knew, did she not, that the father of the boy was abroad? — She must have known it.

How? — Letters used to come that she sent on to me. Besides, she had toys sent to him which came from the father, and registered letters. I have had, too.

Was it with a view of sparing Miss Gentle's feelings that you wrote the letter of 16 October? — Yes.

Making excuses about the father? — I did not want her to know that I was giving the child into the care of anybody else in England. She would have been heartbroken.

The excuse was not a true one about the father? — Nothing was true in that letter, except about the education.

Did you see Miss Gentle, after writing the letter of the sixteenth, before the twenty-seventh, or not? — Miss Gentle?

Yes. — I saw her on the eighteenth, a day I well remember.

What do you say? — I say I remember the day well.

Did anything of importance take place on the eighteenth? — When I went in, the child was sobbing bitterly, and we could not quiet him.

That was the day that you meant to take him out. — Yes, they had been talking to him about leaving; at least, they had said it in front of him, and of course the child was feeling it very much.

Mr Justice BRUCE: He felt it very much, you said? — Yes, it had upset him very much.

And you were not able to take him out that day? — No, I was not.

Lord COLERIDGE: Was it then the final arrangement was made with reference to the twenty-seventh? Handing the child over to you on the twenty-seventh? — Not the final. The final was on the twenty-fifth.

Mr Justice BRUCE: An arrangement was made about the twenty-seventh, was it not? — I think it would be the twenty-seventh. I said at the time I was not sure, because I might have had a letter, you see, at any time.

When did you finally --? — On the twenty-fifth, I settled it. It was on the twenty-fifth that the change was made, because it had been decided that she should come to London Bridge Station with the boy; that I should meet them at the station.

Lord COLERIDGE: You know it was suggested that Miss Gentle should not accompany the child because of the parting?[129] — That was not my suggestion.

It was her suggestion? — It was her mother's suggestion.

---

129   This appears to be an error, and the questions have been attributed to Lord Coleridge by the editor.

# Third Day – Friday 15 December 1899.

Mr Justice BRUCE: It was her mother's suggestion that she should go no further? — No further than the Birdcage.

Lord COLERIDGE: By this time, had your relationship with Mr Lucas become closer? — Yes.

And when was it that you and he determined to spend the Saturday and Sunday at Brighton? — On the twenty-fifth, I made the arrangement with him. I met him at Liverpool Street, after I left Miss Gentle. I went to Liverpool Street from Miss Gentle's by the 5.38 pm or the 5.48 pm.

Mr Justice BRUCE: Which day was this? — The twenty-fifth.

Lord COLERIDGE: That is the Wednesday? — The Wednesday. The same Wednesday that I made final arrangements with Miss Gentle.

Mr Justice BRUCE: On the twenty-fifth, did you see Mr Lucas? — I went to meet him on the twenty-fifth at Liverpool Street Station.

Lord COLERIDGE: Then you arranged with him to spend the Saturday and Sunday at Brighton? — Yes.

Was your relationship – the intimacy between yourself and Mr Lucas – known to your sister and her husband? — It was known to no-one.

Mr Justice BRUCE: Which sister do you mean, Lord Coleridge?

Lord COLERIDGE: Mrs Cadisch, my Lord.

Mr MATHEWS: Known to no-one?

Lord COLERIDGE: And you were desirous that it should not be known? — No, he was going back to France. He was not going to be here later than December. He only came for a year when he first came.

Now, Mr Lucas has been asked as to whether there was any talk between you of marriage, and he has said, 'No'. Is that a fact? — Certainly, not the slightest talk of it in any way.

You never suggested it to him, or he to you? — No, it would have been absurd.

He is a young man, earning £3 a month. You, perhaps, did not know what he was earning. — I know it was from £2 to £3.

And you, being a Frenchwoman, do you know what control parents have over their children? — Yes. He has to serve his time in the army.

Had he served his time? — No, he is only nineteen, and they begin when they are twenty-one.

And they serve how many years? — Three. Of course, there are occasions when they serve only one – that is, when there is a dispensation.

But you did not say anything about marriage? — I never had any idea upon the subject.

Now we will go to the twenty-seventh. A great deal of it is common ground. You did meet at the Birdcage? — I did.

You did have the child handed over? What luggage had you with you? — I had a Gladstone bag, a brown one, with my mackintosh, which is a

*Louise Masset*

# Masset.

**Louise Masset**

brown one, in case it rained. There are two straps to the Gladstone bag, and my mackintosh was put in between, in case I should want it.

Did you take from Miss Gentle a brown paper parcel containing the underlinen of the little boy? — She gave me a parcel of things which I had asked her to put up, and also a smaller parcel with some clothes which I had asked her to put up for the journey. I had taken them to the boy the preceding Wednesday. I never went to see the boy without taking something.

What was in the Gladstone bag? — Oh, necessary things.

Your nightclothes, et cetera? — Yes. Not very much, because I carried it myself.

Is there any truth in the suggestion that it contained a brick? — None whatever.

Mr Justice BRUCE: You carried it yourself to the omnibus, did you? — Yes.

Lord COLERIDGE: Now you came finally to the London Bridge Station. What time did you get there? — I should not have been sure of the time, but I have heard the conductor say it was 1.33 pm; but I should not have known it myself.

Did you proceed with the little boy to the waiting room? — I had made arrangements for where the trains go for Littlehampton.

It is close to the parcels office? — Yes. When I made my statement, the detective or officer did not understand when I said to Littlehampton Station. I have used that station for nine years, backwards and forwards to Littlehampton.

And there, we know from the evidence, that you waited – or is it a fact that you waited for about three quarters of an hour? — Yes, I had given the meeting for 2.00 pm, and one woman had a cap.

And one woman had a cap on? — Yes. I gave that in my statement.

Then were you there when Mrs Worley, who had the cap on, was relieved? — Yes, the person who relieved her.

Did you have a conversation with her? — Yes. She asked me something about a train.

She tells us that she asked you if you were going by the train, and that you said, 'No'. Is that so? — Yes.

And then she said that you looked very tired, and that you said that you were waiting for someone to come. — Yes, I gave that to Mr Newton, and I think he asked, 'Did you not?'

I am asking you – who was the person for whom you were waiting to come? Who was the person indicated by that statement? — These two ladies, Mrs and Miss Browning.

And, shortly after Mrs Worley was relieved, did you go away from

# Third Day – Friday 15 December 1899.

that waiting room? — Yes, I came out of it, because I thought it seemed a very long time. It was past two, and I came out to see what the time was. The boy ran out, and we went into another waiting room.

That is the waiting room near the parcels office? — That is so, the ladies' waiting room. We simply went in to see if the ladies had made a mistake and gone in there.

Mr Justice BRUCE: That is where Mrs Worley was? — Yes, on the Littlehampton side.

And you left that, and went into another waiting room? — Yes.

Lord COLERIDGE: This is a plan which has been produced. [The plan was handed to the witness.] Never mind the pink and green piece; take the upper part. There you find the platform? — Yes.

And you see at the bottom the ladies' first and second class waiting room with the parcel office nearest to it? — The one I went into was the ladies' waiting room, main line, as marked here.

That is marked pink? — Yes.

There is a general waiting room adjoining? — Yes. That is the one I gave in my statement. I simply went into the other to see if they were there, to see if they had made a mistake.

Now, when you found that the ladies had not turned up at the waiting room close to the parcels office, you then went to the general waiting room? — No, I went to the ladies' first class waiting room.

Mr Justice BRUCE: To see if they had made a mistake? — To see if they had gone in there instead of going to the other one.

Did you find them there? — No, I did not.

Lord COLERIDGE: That is where Mrs Reece is? — I did not see Mrs Reece.

Were you there until about 3.10 pm? — I could not possibly have been.

Mr Justice BRUCE: 'She went to look into this ladies' waiting room and did not find them there.' Did you stay there? — About five minutes, not more.

Lord COLERIDGE: You stayed there an appreciable time? — I did not give them any special one. I said the Littlehampton: that is where we were to meet.

As I understand, she went from the ladies' waiting room to the Littlehampton waiting room. Now, what did you do after that, after you had waited in the first class waiting room, main line? — I do not know if you have the same plan as mine. Have you the same plan as mine?

Yes. — I think it is a different paper. This is marked 'Ladies' first class waiting room'. That is the position of it, I know.

Mr Justice BRUCE: You went there for about five minutes? Where did

# Masset.

**Louise Masset**

you go after that? — I went outside, and we met the ladies outside on the platform, and we turned into the general waiting room.

Lord COLERIDGE: Which is next to the waiting room? — It has two doors.

Were they the two ladies whom you had seen and made this arrangement with? — Yes.

Mr Justice BRUCE: We have now, Lord Coleridge, come to a point. I should like to finish, but I have an important engagement which makes it necessary for us to stop.

The court adjourned.

*******

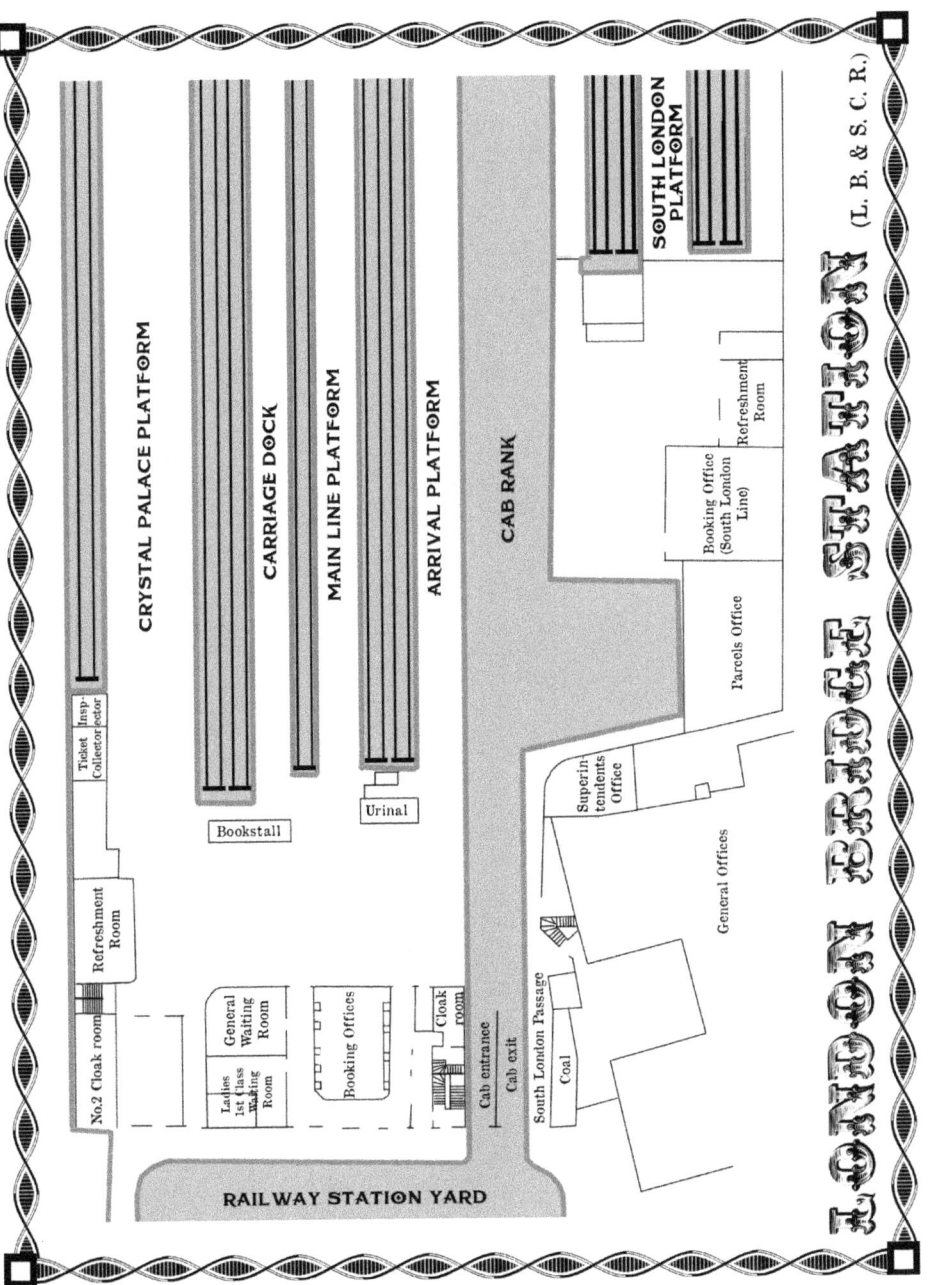

Diagram of London Bridge Railway Station

*Courtesy Andrew Firth*

# Fourth Day – Saturday 16 December 1899.[130]

LOUISE MASSET, recalled and further examined by Lord COLERIDGE.

**Louise Masset**

Mr Justice BRUCE: The last thing you told us yesterday was that you went outside and you met the ladies on the platform. — Yes.

And returned into the general waiting room. That is the last I have got. 'Soon after I came out of the waiting room to see what the time was, I went into the ladies' waiting room, pink on the plan. I went in there to see if they had made a mistake. I did not find them there. I stayed there five minutes. I went outside and we met the ladies outside on the platform, and we went into the general waiting room.'

Lord COLERIDGE: Now, Miss Masset, you had had handed over to you by Miss Gentle a brown paper package containing the child's underlinen, as you believed. — Yes.

When you got into the general waiting room, just tell us what further occurred. — The first conversation was on the platform. I came out of the waiting room.

Mr Justice BRUCE: You mean the first conversation with the ladies? — Yes. I came out onto the platform by a little passage there is there, and they came from one of the booking places – so we met on the platform.

Did you see anyone in that waiting room? — There was one man there.

No attendant? — No, no attendant at all.

In the ladies' waiting room? — Yes, there was an attendant. I did not see her at first.

You mean the waiting room you went in to see whether they had made a mistake? — Yes, sir.

Is that the Waiting Room, Lord COLERIDGE?

Lord COLERIDGE: Yes, my Lord.

Mr Justice BRUCE: You saw no attendant in the general waiting room? — No. I did not see one in the ladies' waiting room at first.

Lord COLERIDGE: When you went in there, was Mrs Reece in there? — I did not know her name. She came forward because the little boy was jumping about on the seats. She came afterwards.

Mr Justice BRUCE: 'When I was in the ladies' waiting room …' Is that the waiting room where you sat down for five minutes or less? —

---

130  Testimony of Louise Masset and Eleanor Eliza Gentle from TNA:PRO HO 144/1540/A61535.

# Masset.

**Louise Masset**

Yes, I sat down close to the door.

Mrs Reece was there? — I cannot say there was an attendant there – at least, not at first. She was not there. I did not see her at first.

The little boy was jumping about on the seats, you say – is that so? I think you said that. — Yes, that is why she came forward.

Lord COLERIDGE: She has detailed the conversation, and she had asked you what the little child was grizzling about. — He was not grizzling at all; he was perfectly happy. What she did say to him was, 'I do not like little boys to jump with muddy boots on the couches'. It was a very wet day and he had muddy boots, I must admit. I spoke then. I said to her, 'I am very sorry but he is but a baby still,' and I drew out my bag and said, 'You can jump over that,' thinking that he would not hurt that anyhow.

That was the Gladstone bag? — Yes, it was down on the floor by the side of the couch, and I drew it forward.

Mr Justice BRUCE: It was on the floor already? — Yes, and the attendant said, 'He looks a big boy'. I said, 'He is about three and a half'. That was all the conversation I had with this attendant.

Lord COLERIDGE: Did you say to her he was fretting for his nurse? — I did not. He was not fretting at all; he was perfectly happy.

Mr Justice BRUCE: You did not say that he was fretting for his nurse? — Not in the least.

Lord COLERIDGE: That is all you recollect of the conversation? — I am perfectly sure that is all the conversation that took place.

Now then, what next took place? — I went out. I did not want to go back to the other waiting room to see whether these ladies had arrived, the one I had made the rendezvous for to see.

Mr Justice BRUCE: You went back to the other waiting room? — No, sir, I did not go back.

You went into the waiting room where you were five minutes, or rather less? — Yes, and I intended to go back to the other waiting room, but I did not go because I met them just outside the general waiting room.

'And I went out, intending to go to the former waiting room where I had been before, and when I got outside the general waiting room –'

Mr MATHEWS: I think the witness said, 'Where I had come for a rendezvous'.

Mr Justice BRUCE: Oh, yes. — It was on the south side where I had given them the rendezvous.

Where you had been at first? — Yes.

That was the waiting room you described yesterday? — Yes.

Lord COLERIDGE: By the parcels office? — Yes, and I met the women outside the general waiting room.

# Fourth Day – Saturday 16 December 1899.

Now, tell us what took place there on the platform before you went in. — I said, 'Well, you have come at last. I have waited long enough.'

Mr Justice BRUCE: Did you notice about what time it was? — No, I cannot say what the exact time was; it was something to three; it might have been 2.45 pm, perhaps. Mrs Browning said, 'I am very sorry, but it has taken us one and a half hours to get here'. Because I said, 'Which way did you come?' because I had no idea of the locality. I had never been there and did not know it at all. Mrs Browning said she came by omnibus to the Bank and from the Bank to London Bridge. It was then that we went in the waiting room – the general waiting room – and crossed right over and sat on the seats right at the back of the room.

Was that the general waiting room where you had been five minutes, or less than five minutes?[131] — Yes. I said, 'It is a great nuisance, because I wanted to go with you'. It had been arranged that I should go with them to Chelsea.

You say you have never been to Chelsea? — No, never.

And you did not know how long it would take to get there from London Bridge? — No, I have no idea. I can only say what they said to me. I have no idea.

Yes? — I went on, saying that I intended going to Brighton by the 4.00 pm train, and I did not see how I could get back in time.

The 4.00 pm train to --? — Brighton. Mrs Browning answered, 'Well, you know he will be all right. You could trust him to us.' They had appeared trustworthy. I did not think they were going to do what they have done.

And then, Miss Masset, you --? — I gave them the money I had promised them in advance.

Mr Justice BRUCE: That was how much? — £12.

And what about the parcel? — I gave them the parcel also.

You mean the brown paper parcel? — Yes.

Lord COLERIDGE: Yes. And what took place after you gave them the money, if anything? — Of course I asked them for a receipt of it.

For a receipt? — She said she had none ready.

Mr Justice BRUCE: Who said? — Mrs Browning. She said she would go to the refreshment room and see if they had pen and ink, and make me one out. She started first, and the sister said, 'Would not this little boy like a cake?' At least, she said Manfred, because she knew his name. She went out of the door on the left, which was almost facing the refreshment room.

Mrs Browning started first, and the younger lady, Miss Browning --?

**Louise Masset**

---

131   Mr Justice Bruce meant the ladies' first class waiting room on the main line.

# Masset.

**Louise Masset**

— She had been playing with the child, and she said would not Manfred like a cake?

When she said that, Mrs Browning went out of the waiting room towards the refreshment room? — Yes, and the child went too, with the sister.

And did the two ladies and the child go into the refreshment room? — I went back to get my Gladstone bag, which I had left.

The two ladies went with the child — Yes.

Do not let me say what is not correct; I only want to get it right. — Yes, that is it.

'I went to look for my gloves.' — No, for my bag. I went to bring it nearer to the window.

The window of the general waiting room? — Yes.

'I went with my bag.' What about the window? — I went nearer the window with the bag to see where they went, to follow their movements, not because I was suspicious of them.

I thought you said something about your gloves. — No, sir. Bag.

Yes? — I did not see them after that. They must have turned down a passage, instead of going into the refreshment room; they must have turned down one of the passages. There are several openings there.

You mean that they must not have gone into the refreshment room? — No, sir.

Lord COLERIDGE: How long did you wait in the waiting room? — A few minutes, just about the time that they would want for making the receipt out.

Then, Miss Masset, what did you do? — I took my bag and went to see where they went.

Mr Justice BRUCE: Into the refreshment room? — Not into it. I only opened the door to see if the women were in there.

To the door of the refreshment room, is that right? — Yes, sir.

And looked in to see if they were there? — Yes. And then I walked down the passage, right down to the side [of the] station, and around again by one of the openings, and back to the waiting room to see whether they had returned there.

Lord COLERIDGE: And you failed to find them? — I did not find them.

At that time, Miss Masset, had you the slightest suspicion of these two persons? — None whatever.

You had their names, you had their addresses. — Yes.

And you had interviewed them on more than one occasion. — That was the third time I had seen them.

Mr Justice BRUCE: I will just ask you this: after they went off with

# Fourth Day – Saturday 16 December 1899.

your £12 without giving you a receipt, did you do anything? — No, I did not do anything. I thought they had gone off with the child because he was happy, and that they had gone off with him because they did not want to bring him near me again, as he was happy. We had arranged with them to write to me on the Monday to let me know they got on.

Lord COLERIDGE: The next train left for Brighton at 4.00 pm? — That was the train I had meant to go by, and I did go by it.

That was the train you meant to go by, and you did go by it. What class did you travel? — First.

What class did you say? — First class.

And it was not a stopping train, is it? It goes straight down to Brighton? — Straight. Yes, it was one of the quick trains.

Was it timed to arrive at Brighton at 5.15 pm? — I cannot say exactly the time. The next time I saw any time was at the Jubilee clock in Brighton.

Mr Justice BRUCE: On the Queens Road, is it? — I think it is at the end of the Queens Road. The Waverley Hotel is about halfway between the station and the Jubilee clock.

We know from the guard that the train did arrive there at 5.19 pm.

Lord COLERIDGE: 5.19 pm, my Lord. You did not go first to the Waverley Hotel? — No, I wanted something to eat. I had had nothing since 12.30 pm, when I started. I had had nothing since. I knew that at the Waverley Hotel they did not –

Now did you pass the Jubilee clock? — Yes, it was 5.50 pm when I passed it.

What did you do with your Gladstone bag? — I put that up in the cloakroom, and I took my waterproof out, which I had strapped at the side, in case I should need it.

Took your waterproof coat, but left your bag? — Yes.

Just describe your movements after leaving the station: where you went, and what you did. — I went straight down the Queens Road. I cannot say the name of the road which continues down to the sea. Queens Road only goes half the way.

Mr Justice BRUCE: After leaving the station --? — I went down Queens Road.

How did you start from the station? How did you go — Along Queens Road, and then there is another road which takes you down to the sea, down into the King's Road, and turned to the left to get to Mutton's, which is a restaurant there.

Does Mutton's face the sea? — Yes.

Lord COLERIDGE: Did you walk there first, or go straight there? — I went straight there. It must have been 6.15 to 6.20. I did not look at the

*Louise Masset*

# Masset.

**Louise Masset**

time. I had no reason for it.

Can you tell me where you went at Mutton's. I do not know Mutton's. — Yes, there is a staircase which takes you up to the first floor.

Mr Justice BRUCE: It is a pastry cook's shop down below? — Yes, the pastry cook's is like to the left, and there is a staircase which goes to the dining room above.

Lord COLERIDGE: That is where people sit down who want to have food? — Yes.

Can you tell us whereabouts in the room you sat? — Near the left. Supposing this was the window, I sat here, at the first table near the window.

Did you eat your meal in haste, or leisurely? — No, I had plenty of time for my meal.

Then, after you had finished, what did you do then? — First of all, I thought I would go to the pier, but it was such a wet evening that I walked up King's Road to West Brighton to look at the shops.

There are some attractive shops that way. — There are beautiful ones, some of them are.

What are they – drapers, jewellers? — Some are drapers and display Indian work and embroideries.

And how long did you walk about looking at the shops? — Well, I really do not know, excepting by that Jubilee clock again.

That would be a very good way of telling. — 9.15 pm when I passed there.

Mr Justice BRUCE: Then you went back to the station? — I was obliged to get my bag and go back to the hotel.

And went from the station to the hotel, did you? — Yes.

When you went to the hotel, did you see the Jubilee clock? — No, I could not.

Then when did you see the Jubilee clock? — As I passed on the way to the station. I then had to pass the hotel to get to the station. It was 9.15 pm when I passed the Jubilee clock.

Was that on your way to the station, or on your way from the station? — To the station; I could not pass the Jubilee clock on the way from it.

Lord COLERIDGE: Then did you get your bag from the station? — Yes.

Mr Justice BRUCE: About how long would it take you to walk from the Jubilee clock to the station? Five minutes? — Ten, I should say. About five minutes between the hotel and the station.

Lord COLERIDGE: The hotel is nearer the station than the clock? — Yes, about halfway.

Then, having got your bag, did you go to the hotel? — Yes.

# Fourth Day – Saturday 16 December 1899.

**Louise Masset**

Did you carry it yourself? — No, I had a boy to take it for me. I took him from the outside before I went into the station, and he went with me to the cloakroom, and he carried it to the hotel.

Mr Justice BRUCE: Was he one of the regular porters? — He was quite a youth, about fourteen or fifteen – one of the boys outside who are quite ready to carry any luggage.

Lord COLERIDGE: Not in uniform? — No.

Mr Justice BRUCE: You found him outside the station and took him in with you to the cloakroom. Is that so? — Yes, he went with me to the cloakroom.

Lord COLERIDGE: Then he went to the hotel. What time, about, was it that you got there? — I cannot say. I did not see any clock after the Jubilee one.

You are not prepared to differ from Mr Findlay? — I beg your pardon? He says it was about 9.45 pm.

Mr Justice BRUCE: Did you meet him on the stairs? — I do not remember it. There is a bell which goes when the door opens and the maid came to open the door.

Lord COLERIDGE: He put it at about 9.45 pm. — It might have been that.

Then, we know, you engaged rooms number 10 --? — I spoke to the maid first and she called up Mr Findlay to see if they were engaged.

You engaged 10 and 11 for the Saturday, and only --? — Only 11 for the Friday evening.

You went under the name of Miss Brooks? — Yes.

Mr Justice BRUCE: That is so, is it? — Yes.

Lord COLERIDGE: Now I will ask you about a little pair of toy scales. — Yes, sir. They were left in my hands when the boy went away. I had been carrying them about from one waiting room to the other.

And you took them down? — I took them down. They were in my pocket the whole time. He had been using them in the waiting room to weigh up biscuits which my sister gave him before we started – little knick-knacks, they were.

These toy scales, we know, were found in one of the drawers. — Yes. I put them there and quite forgot them. I put them there. I was going to give them to him the following Wednesday, when I was to go down and see him.

And there you slept that night? — Yes.

And then, the next morning, how did you occupy yourself? — I went on the pier. I had not breakfasted till about 9.30 am. I started out about 10.30 am, and I was back again about 12.30 am.

Did you breakfast in the public room? — Yes. There were two men

# Masset.

**Louise Masset**

there; two travellers there.

You did not have breakfast in your bedroom? — No, you cannot have anything there except on Sunday, unless you order it beforehand: nothing warm except for dinner.

Except on Sunday? — Then there is general meal for anyone who likes to be there.

What train was Mr Lucas to come by on the following day? — He wrote to say he would be there by 3.20 pm. I cannot say what time he was to start.

That is the train that starts at 2.00 pm and gets down at 3.20 pm. And did you go to meet him, or did you await his arrival? — I went to meet him.

And then you stayed that night with him. The next day you returned? — On the Sunday evening.

Mr Justice BRUCE: You went together, I understand, on the Sunday evening? — Yes.

Lord COLERIDGE: He tells us: when you returned you had your waterproof and were carrying it on your arm. Is that so? — Yes, that was so. I did not know whether it would be fine in London when we reached it.

Where did you leave him, outside 29 Bethune --? — Oh, no, it was not. It was near St Kilda's Road.

Is that a short way off? — That is the first turning from the house.

You have told us that your intimacy with Mr Lucas was unsuspected by your sister and brother-in-law. What reason did you assign to them for your absence from Friday until the Monday – until Sunday? — I said that I was going to France with the child.

That was a tale that you kept up? — Yes.

We know that you wrote to Miss Gentle giving this proposed voyage. — Yes, but I answered her as little as possible so as not to say more than was necessary.

Did you keep up that story? Was your sole object in doing so to keep secret from them the fact that you were going to Brighton with Mr Lucas? — Yes.

Mr Justice BRUCE: Do you say yes? — Yes.

That is, Mr and Mrs Cadisch? — Yes.

Lord COLERIDGE: Your mother lives next door, does she not? — Yes.

And she did not know of this? — That was why I was bound to go on Friday, and Mr Lucas on a Saturday.

I was going to come to that. This story would not fit in with the same story of the visit on Saturday night and return on Sunday. — No. I had

# Fourth Day – Saturday 16 December 1899.

no intention of going to France.

Suppose you had only gone down on the Saturday and returned on the Sunday: there would have been no time for you to have gone to France and back with the boy? — I would not have done, sir.

Mr Justice BRUCE: You said just now that you were bound to go on Friday. — Yes. Mr Lucas was obliged to go on one day and I the other, because otherwise it would have been known that we had gone together.

Known by whom? — My parents and his.

Lord COLERIDGE: He was living next door? — Yes.

And living with your mother? — Yes.

Mr Justice BRUCE: I thought you were in the habit of meeting him frequently. — Yes, but nobody knew of it.

Why did you not meet him on the way to Brighton? — He could not go on Friday.

But why were you bound to go on Friday? — Because if we had gone together it would have been known.

How? — My mother and sister would have guessed it, if I had said I was going to Littlehampton or elsewhere.

Lord COLERIDGE: If you had only gone on the Saturday and returned on the Sunday, you know that you were telling your people that you were going to France. The story you know you told us – delivering the child over? — Yes, delivering it in France.

To its father in France?

Mr MATHEWS: To a cousin of the father, I think.

Lord COLERIDGE: To a cousin of the father. If you had gone on a Saturday only, and returned on Sunday, would that have allowed time to get to the cousin of the father in France and returned again? — Well, I do not quite see how I could have done it. Suppose I had taken the boat on the Saturday, I should have had to start back again to get the boat. I do not know quite what time they start back again.

Mr Justice BRUCE: At any rate, you thought there was not time.

Lord COLERIDGE: When did you first tell them that you were going on the Friday?

Mr Justice BRUCE: Mrs Cadisch? — I told Mrs Cadisch on the twenty-fifth that I was going on the twenty-seventh.

Lord COLERIDGE: You parted with Mr Lucas some little way outside the house? — A few yards from the house.

And you came back, and the next morning was Monday. Had you any lessons on the Monday morning? — Yes – not the Monday morning. I only started from home --

You stayed in to have your luncheon? — Yes.

And did you leave [for] the former two engagements – was it? Or one?

*Louise Masset*

# Masset.

**Louise Masset**

— Two. Yes: at 1.30 pm.

What were they? — One at Mrs Sonnenthal and one at Mrs Haas.

What time was your lesson over with Mrs Haas? — I always left about a quarter, thirteen minutes, twelve minutes to – it just depended – to catch the 1.55 pm train at Loudoun Road Station.

Then how did you travel when you got to Loudoun Road Station? — By train to Dalston Junction.

And from there? — I should have taken the tram home, but did not that day.

That was the ordinary rule? Did you purchase a copy of the *Evening News*? — I did.

Which contained that: just see if that is what you read [handing paper to witness]. — That was it.

Lord COLERIDGE: It is headed, 'Dalston Murder: identification of the poor little victim, the child of a French woman who took him away until the day'.[132] Then it describes the identification: 'The nurse has frequently seen the child's mother whom she believes to be illegitimate'.[133] Did you form an opinion, Miss Masset, in reading that, as to who the child was that was thus described? — That was not the first time I had seen anything of the Dalston murder. I had seen it on the Monday morning. I accompanied my pupil to have a gymnastic lesson, and they provide papers to read while you are waiting, and it was in one of those that I saw what first aroused my suspicion that it might have been my child.

Was that Mrs Sonnenthal? — When I go on Monday afternoon to Mrs Sonnenthal, it is to take her daughter to a gymnasium lesson, and they provide papers there for your amusement while you are waiting for the pupil.

Mr Justice BRUCE: Was it the same paper that you saw, the *Evening News*? — No, and before that I saw, 'Child identified'.

You read a paragraph in the paper as to what effect? — Describing the child.

Then, from the gymnasium, you went on to Mrs Haas? — I went back to Mrs Sonnenthal with her daughter, and then went back to Mrs Haas. That is about ten minutes' walk. I left Mrs Sonnenthal about 5.00 and

---

132  *Sic* in transcript, but nonsensical. Louise Masset's petition, submitted to the Home Office on 30 December 1899, quoted from the same newspaper account: 'Dalston Murder: Identification of the Poor Little Victim. Child of a French Woman who took him away from his Nurse on the day of the Murder.' (TNA:PRO HO 144/1540/A61535/44.)

133  *Sic* in transcript, but, as above, nonsensical. Louise Masset's petition, submitted to the Home Office on 30 December 1899, quoted from the same newspaper account: 'The nurse has frequently seen the child's mother, and has for several years received regular payment for supporting the child, whom she believes to be illegitimate'. (TNA:PRO HO 144/1540/A61535/44.)

# Fourth Day – Saturday 16 December 1899.

then went on to my other lesson.

And from there you went to Dalston Junction and purchased that paper? — Yes, I saw, 'Child identified', and from what I saw in the papers, I thought I would see at once.

Then you bought the *Evening News* and read the paragraph? — Yes.

Lord COLERIDGE: Did either Madame Sonnenthal or Madame Haas know that you were the mother of an illegitimate child? — No, sir.

When you read about --

Mr Justice BRUCE: I understand there was no answer to that question? — I said no. I never told them, and --

Lord COLERIDGE: So far as you knew, they did not know that you were the mother of an illegitimate child? — I never told them.

When you read this, Miss Masset, what conclusion did you arrive at with regard to the identity of the child? — When I read what was in the Evening News?

Yes. — I could only come to one conclusion, sir, but she mentioned that he had been fetched on the Friday.

You thought it was your child? — I thought Mrs Norris had been, as it said, a middle-aged woman.

Mr Justice BRUCE: Were you convinced it was your child? — Yes, because I had seen the description, and I began to suspect in the afternoon as they had disappeared so quickly.

Lord COLERIDGE: When you read it in the *Evening News*, your suspicions ripened into certainty? — Yes, sir.

Do you know, when you read that, that you were the last person seen with the child? — Yes.

Mr Justice BRUCE: What do you say? — Yes.

Lord COLERIDGE: And that you were alone when last seen with the child? — Yes, and that I had told an untruth about taking him away.

Did you come to another opinion as to whether you might or might not be suspected? — I knew that I should be the first person suspected.

We know that, in fact, you did not go home that night. — No, I did not.

You went to your other brother-in-law. — Because I wanted to have his advice. He was an Englishman, and my other brother-in-law was not. I thought he would know more about it than he would.

May I ask whether you -- ... He speaks of you as arriving in a hysterical state. Were you very greatly agitated? — Yes, sir. How could I be else?

And he tells us that you arrived there about 11.00 at night. — I walked to London Bridge. I knew it was 10d to Croydon and I had not enough money. I had only about 11d in my pocket and, instead of taking the omnibus, I walked, so as to have sufficient for my train. When I got to Croydon, I had to wait half an hour for a train, and that was on the South

**Louise Masset**

# Masset.

**Louise Masset**

Eastern line.

And then he tells us of a conversation you had with him, and he said if you would tell him he would befriend you. — Yes, every word he said is true.

Then you made a statement to him, which he has spoken to? — I did. I asked him if possible not to mention Mr Lucas's name.

Then he went off to consult? — He told me to stop with my sister that night, and he would go and remove my sister's anxiety, because she would be anxious at my not returning home.

Then the rest, I think, Miss Masset, is common ground: that the policemen came, and that you very willingly surrendered yourself to them and repeated the statement to them. — Yes, I made the same statement, as far as I can remember.

Let me ask you, Miss Masset, were you attached to your little boy? — I was fond of him, sir.

And is there any truth whatever in the suggestion that you were the author of his death? — No.

*Cross-examined* by Mr Charles MATHEWS.

I think you were not examined on your own behalf before the magistrate, were you, Miss Masset? — Do you mean in the police court?

Yes. — No, I was not examined. You mean I gave no evidence?

Yes, and the statement which you have just concluded is the first statement on oath which you have made in this case? — The first.

You were arrested on 31 October, as we know – on the Tuesday morning? — On the Tuesday morning.

And brought before the magistrate on the next day, was it, or on the same day? — Oh, no, the next day.

That would be 1 November, the Wednesday? — Yes, on the Wednesday.

On that occasion, I think, you were not represented by a solicitor? — I was not.

Some witnesses were called, amongst them Miss Gentle? — Yes.

And Police Sergeant Burch? — Yes.

Being unrepresented, I think that you yourself put questions to them on your own behalf? — The magistrate wished to know if I had anything to ask the witnesses, and I did point out – I did ask a question or two.

I may have to revert to that at a later stage. Take your mind back to the year 1896 and to the May of 1896, when you were arranging for placing the little boy with Miss Gentle. You had references from Miss Gentle? — I had one.

I thought you said yesterday that you had more than one? — No, sir, I did not.

# Fourth Day – Saturday 16 December 1899.

Mr Justice BRUCE: I thought you said you made enquiries of --? — She wished me to make several enquiries, but I only made one.

Mr MATHEWS: Then you are not quite accurate. — She wished me to have some. I wrote to one, to a Mrs Prince.

She was willing to give you more than one reference? She did give you one, and you wrote to the reference that she gave you, and received a reply of a satisfactory character. Did you see Miss Gentle yourself? You did, did you not? — That was the first time I saw her. I only went once to see her.

And was it in Clyde Road that you went? — It was in Clyde Road. I had only known it by an advertisement.

But you went to the Clyde Road? — I went to the Clyde Road.

And saw Miss Gentle, and was favourably impressed by her and having made your enquiry --? — At her request.

And having made your enquiry and had the favourable answer, you allowed the child to go? — Yes.

That was in May 1896? — The date the child went was 22 May.

That was the condition of things under which you were with your child in the May of 1896? — I did not hear the first part. Someone was coughing.

That was the condition of things under which you were with your child in the May of 1896? — Yes.

I suppose, as time went on, you did not get less fond of your child? — Certainly not. As he grows up, you must get more fond of him.

So I should imagine. And I take it that the usual course occurred with you: as he grew up, you grew more and more fond of him? — I can say so, sir.

Now to the next date in the story, as I submit it to you, the August of 1898. It was in that month that you went to live at number 29 Bethune Road? — It was.

It was in that month that the father of the child last ceased to reside in England? — Yes.

Mr Justice BRUCE: That is so, is it? — Yes.

Mr MATHEWS: It was in that month that Eudore Lucas came to reside next door? — That I cannot tell you.

You do not know? You have heard him say so? — He may have done so. My mother and sister would know.

You did not notice him say that in the witness box? That that was the date he came to live at 31 Bethune Road? — He may have done so.

I do not wish to pry at all, as you believe me. When you talk of the child's father ceasing to reside in England in the August of 1898, do you mean by that that, as far as you know, that was the last time that he was

*Louise Masset*

# Masset.

**Louise Masset**

in England? — I am perfectly sure it was the last time.

He has never been here since? — No, he is in the army. He could tell at once when was the last time he was here.

Believe me, I am not disputing that August was the last time. Just this question, so that you may answer it. I think you have already answered it. As from that date, your communication with the father would be by letter addressed by him to you, and by you to him. Do I understand it that his correspondence was addressed to Clyde Road? — It was.

In going to Bethune Road, I think you said yesterday that it had an attraction – that it would be fairly near your work? — Yes.

Not far from your child? — Yes.

And that, I presume, would be an additional advantage in the going to Bethune Road? — I found it a great advantage in going to my lessons then. So long as the child was not out of London, I could always see him.

Do you say that you did not go there because it would be near your child? — No, I do not think so. It was for my lessons.

And the child was secondary? — Yes.

It did not strike you that you would be near your child? — No.

Notwithstanding the increasing affection you had for your child? — You must understand, I am –

Will you answer? Did it strike you as an additional advantage or not? — Not at the time. I do not think it did.

Now the lessons. Mrs Sonnenthal and Mrs Haas were regular employments for many years past? — Yes.

Both before you went to Bethune Road, and after you had left there? — Since 1895.

And, in the August of 1898, was it four times a week that you would be going to those houses? — Sometimes twice, sometimes three, sometimes four. It just depended.

Going by the North London Railway, what would be the nearest station to Mrs Sonnenthal and Mrs Haas? — There are three stations that you could use.

What would be the nearest? — I should say they would be about the same.

You do not agree that Loudoun Road is the nearest? — I do not say which was the nearest.

Was it the one which you generally used? — No. I used Hampstead Heath for two reasons, which I can give you.

Did you tell Mrs Haas that you always used Loudoun Road? — Yes, I did to return.

Then you would use one station to travel there, and when you went back used another station to travel back, and that Loudoun Road was the

# Fourth Day – Saturday 16 December 1899.

station which you used to travel home by? — Yes.

In that way, the Dalston Junction became a most familiar station to you? — Most familiar.

And number 3 platform was one which you would use? — If I came back from Hampstead, or if I went to Loudoun Road.

Do you know number 3 platform? — Certainly.

Do you know the lavatory there? — I have never been there.

You say that? — I say it because I am on oath.

You have never been in that lavatory? — I have never been in that lavatory – or any – at Dalston Junction.

In the time that you have used it, how often do you suppose that you have been at Dalston Junction? — Well, I never go to Dalston Junction except to go to my lessons.

We know: you have told us so. These journeys performed two, three and four times a week, and returning, as you have said, from the Loudoun Road to the Dalston Junction, over a period of time from August 1898 to November 1899 – how often do you think you have been there? — If you take it at an average of three times a week –

Mr Justice BRUCE: 'I was at Dalston Junction at' --?

Mr MATHEWS: On an average of three times a week. You mean three days a week, do not you? — Yes.

Mr Justice BRUCE: Do you mean by that two visits on each day? — Only one. There would be going and returning.

Mr MATHEWS: That would be two visits, then. That would be about six times a week at Dalston, August 1898 to October 1899? — Yes, sir.

But you never went into the lavatory? — Never.

Ever in the ladies' waiting room? — In the general waiting room, which is at the third class, and because I always came third class.

Always third class. I will just take that in passing. Into the waiting room you have been --? — I cannot say I have not been into the general waiting room. I may have been in there. I cannot say I have not.

You cannot say that you have not been into the general waiting room? — No.

Have you ever been in the ladies' waiting room? — No, I have not.

You are serious in telling us that? — Quite.

Mr Justice BRUCE: Is that so? — Certainly.

Mr MATHEWS: They are quite close to each other, these two. Do you know that? One is upon one side, and the other upon the other side, of the ladies' lavatory. — Oh, no. The general waiting room is at one end of the platform, and the ladies' waiting room would be quite at the other, I should imagine.

Let us just see that.

**Louise Masset**

# Masset.

**Louise Masset**

Mr Justice BRUCE: Do you remember the stairs by which you go out? You go down by some stairs --? — It depends if you are at number 3 platform, sir; to go out of the station, you would go up.

Mr MATHEWS: We are dealing with no opening on the platform. We are dealing with the platform itself.

Mr Justice BRUCE: Yes. Do you know the bookstall? — I should say I know that least of any. When I talk about the platform 4, I mean the platform from where I go to my lessons.

Mr MATHEWS: Not the platform 3? — I cannot go to Hampstead by it.

Did not you go to Loudoun Road from number 3 platform? — Scarcely, if ever.

Do you mean that? — I do mean it, for a very good reason.

And I think you said that both going to Hampstead and returning from it that you used number 3 platform? — No, excuse me. I said that both going to Loudoun Road and returning from Hampstead you would use platform 3.

Going to Loudoun Road? — Yes, I know the line well.

You have been in the general waiting room, number 4 platform? — Yes. I have stood inside the door on a cold day, for instance.

You have never been in either waiting room on number 3 platform? — I do not see why I should have been in there. No, I don't think I have.

Never in either waiting room on number 3 platform? — No, I do not think I have.

Between August 1898 and Christmas 1898, you made the acquaintance of Eudore Lucas? — I made his acquaintance last year. December.

Last December? — In December.

He was a lodger of your mother's? — Yes.

And, from that time, used he to pay visits to your sister, Mrs Cadisch? — Oh, often.

Mr Justice BRUCE: He was a lodger of your mother's?

Mr MATHEWS: And may I say a frequent visitor? — No, I should not say a frequent visitor. He would come in and play billiards with my brother-in-law.

And that would be the kind of acquaintanceship between you and him, down to the Easter of this year? — Yes, Whitsun, I think it was.

I was taking it first to Easter. And do you say it was the same degree of intimacy between Easter and Whitsun? — Between Easter --?

Between Easter and Whitsuntide? — I have nothing to point Easter out.

I was taking them in the seasons as we know them. Was that the kind of acquaintanceship? — If you like to put it so. I had never been out with

# Fourth Day – Saturday 16 December 1899.

him before Whitsuntide.

And it was at Whitsuntide that the visit was paid to Brighton? — It was.

When was the public visit? I suppose everybody knew it? — No, they did not. Nobody knew it.

No one knew of it? — Except the lady and gentleman who accompanied us.

It was unknown to the Cadisches? — That was unknown.

And on the return from Brighton, as Eudore Lucas described gradually to us --? — Which time do you mean? At Whitsuntide?

After Whitsuntide. — Yes.

Between Whitsuntide and August of this year, has he described what was the relationship between you? — Yes, it was friendship.

It never became anything warmer upon your side? — Well, I cannot say. In one way it did, but I cannot say it was forever, for any purpose, in any way.

It did not become any warmer between Whitsuntide and August? — I do not know what you mean by warmer.

Don't you? You went out more often? — I said we went out perhaps more often.

Were they secret meetings as between those dates? — Oh, yes, no one knew at the time.

Was your correspondence between these dates --? — The correspondence was one, two letters, perhaps. They were always for appointments, where we should meet.

And appointments which were kept? — Certainly, because they were generally times when I was out, and he could meet me coming back.

Was he right in saying Loudoun Road was a frequent place for meeting you? — I don't know about frequent. Perhaps a dozen times in all.

And travelling back with you to Dalston Junction? — Yes.

Number 3 platform? — No, sir. Number 2.

Not number 3? — Not number 3.

Nor number 4? — They are down lines.

Tell us, then: Eudore Lucas came over to England in the August of 1898, that was so? — I know he was to go back this December; I cannot tell you what he came for: I do not know.

I did not ask you what he came for: I asked you the time he came. — I say I do not know.

Did you say yesterday, or am I incorrect in saying that you said yesterday, that he came here to stay for a year? — I did say so, but in this way: knowing that he came in August, I knew it would make a year, but I did not know at all.

**Louise Masset**

# Masset.

**Louise Masset**

If he came for a year in August 1898, his year would expire in the August of 1899. — I just now said to you that I knew he was to go back in December.

That would be more than a year; can you give me any reason for his staying on longer? — No, unless his father wished it.

You cannot tell me why he stayed here for more than a year? — No.

But he did remain? — Certainly, he is here.

September, October, and at number 31 Bethune Road down to the first week in November? — Yes. His mother came over in August, and it was then that the arrangement was made with her that her son – that he might stop on.

It was an arrangement between the mother and the son? — Yes.

You heard it from Mr Lucas? — No, I heard it from my mother.

Did he mention that his mother had been over in August? — I saw her; I had spoken to her.

Did he mention it to you? — No, I cannot say that he did.

Can you say that he did not? — I should not like to say that he did not. He stayed on.

Mr Justice BRUCE: You heard of this arrangement from your mother? — It was discussed amongst them, his stopping on. It was mostly for him to learn the language a little more – I do not know.

Mr MATHEWS: Now I come to a date mentioned by you yesterday: 8 October. Unless I am mistaken, was that the date when some poetry was passed between the two garden walls? — It was.

You have not preserved it? — No, but I daresay Mr Lucas can give it to you if you wish to see it.

Have you preserved any letters of Eudore Lucas's? — No. I have preserved none of the boy's father's either. I never do keep my letters in any way.

I take the answer as you have given it. You have preserved no letter reaching you from the father of the boy? — No.

What was the date of your forming your intention of going to Brighton on 27 October? — It was between … I cannot say when I formed the intention to go to Brighton, but I had the intention to go somewhere.

With Eudore Lucas? — Oh, yes, but I did not make the arrangement with him.

When did you form the intention? — I said: after having received this piece of poetry.

On 8 October? — On 8 October.

When you formed that intention to go away with Eudore Lucas, were you, or were you not, in love with Eudore Lucas? — No, I was not in love.

# Fourth Day – Saturday 16 December 1899.

You were going away with him, to stay with him and to stay a night with him? — Yes, sir, that was simply arranged on the Saturday.

But you were not in love with him? — I do not know.

When did you first speak to him about the child? — As to time, do you mean?

Yes. — I cannot say.

He fixes it early in September. Do you accept that date as a possible date? — I say I cannot say.

It may have been then? — It might have been. I do not know.

Do you remember his telling you not to speak to him any more about the child? — I do not know that he said, 'Do not speak to me any more about the child'. No, I do not think he said that at all.

What was it he said about not speaking about the child? — Well, the point was this: as we were walking along one day, he expressed the wish for me to go away with him.

Did he say where? — To spend the night with him. I said, 'No, thank you, I have had enough trouble over that.'

When was this? — I cannot fix the date. It might have been in May, or it might have been any time.

Was it before the Whitsuntide visit? — No, after.

The Whitsuntide of this year, unless I am mistaken, was quite at the end of May? — I think it was in June.

I think not. 21 May; it was an early Whitsuntide this year. — It was after that.

When he wanted you to go away with him for the night, he simply --? — He said would I go away with him.

I want you to try and fix how soon after the visit to Brighton at Whitsuntide that this suggestion came from Eudore Lucas. — I have told you, sir, that I cannot fix it. It was simply as we were walking along that he proposed it.

And you said, no, you had had trouble enough? — Yes.

What did he say in regard to the child? — He said, why? In what way have I had trouble? I told him I had had a boy. That was all that passed.

And that was all? — That was all.

Do you really mean that? — I really mean it, sir.

And you made that announcement to him, in those words, and that he made no comment upon it? — He may have said that he was pleased to know I had told him, or something of the kind.

Did he go on to say that it was very fair of you to have told him? — I cannot tell you the words, because it was in French.

Well, you are perfectly capable of saying so. — No, I should say it was 'glad' or 'pleased'.

Louise Masset

# Masset.

**Louise Masset**

Did he go on to say that he did not want to hear anything more about the child? — I do not think so.

Well, you say that he did not? — No, a conversation like that was not to be remembered.

Do you represent that, in a conversation of this kind, there was nothing to be remembered? — I say so, certainly.

A man was pressing you to go away with him for the night? — He suggested it; he did not press it.

You answered him that you had had trouble; had had an illegitimate child? — Yes, so that he should not press it.

And you say that that conversation between you and him is not one --? — Of importance, no.

Simply in passing, an ordinary conversation in passing? — Yes.

You accept that? — Certainly.

Did he renew the request for the night away after this first putting off of it, as you have described it? — He did not.

He renewed no request for the night at Brighton? Was it made or was it --? — The night at Brighton? It was I who thought of it, certainly, owing to this piece of poetry.

Owing to the piece of poetry? — Yes.

And as from the date of the receipt of the piece of poetry, you had determined to go away with him, in your own mind? — No, I had not determined upon going away with him in my own mind. I only thought it would be an occasion.

It was your determination? — Determination? It was my thought.

Are you a woman of some determination, do you consider? — Determination? I don't think so.

Let us take up the story at this important date, on 4 October, visiting the Tottenham Green on that afternoon, with little Manfred. — Yes.

Had you ever been there before? — To the Green, yes.

With the little boy? — Yes, I had been there many a time when it was damp; I said so.

Did Miss Gentle know that you had been there before? — She must have known. We always mentioned where we had been when we came back. We had spoken about the little girl playing with Manfred. Manfred had spoken of it himself.

Then Miss Gentle knew that you had been there before 4 October? — Yes.

Constantly? — I should not say constantly ... Often: it was only in the summer when we went to the Down Hill,[134] because there was grass and it was nicer for the child to play.

---

134  *Sic* in transcript; should be Downhills.

# Fourth Day – Saturday 16 December 1899.

And Miss Gentle knew the little girl, did she? — Yes.

Little Miss Browning? — Millie, I called her.

Little Millie Browning? — I cannot say that she knew the name of Browning.

But she was the little girl? — Yes, but I did not know her under the name of Browning.

But you knew the name of the mother of the girl on 4 October? — Yes.

And we may now, may we, say that the little girl, so far as you can give her name, was Millie Browning, and Millie was the name? — Millie was the name.

The Christian name was the abbreviated Christian name you had known for some time? — Yes.

And so had Miss Gentle? — I cannot say she knew the name of Millie, but it was mentioned that it was the name of the little girl Manfred had played with.

Had she ever seen her? — I cannot say that she did.

She never saw her? — No.

Can you mention any living being who did, except yourself and the two ladies? — I can mention several who had been at the Green at the same time.

Can you mention, or can you call any living person here, who has ever seen that child? — No living person here, no. I should not say that I can.

Now, follow me. — I am doing my best to do so.

Little Manfred, had he not a little girl playmate who was known to Miss Gentle? — One little girl who used to play with him, but never while I have been there.

You knew of her? — A little girl called Ada, I think.

Do you think so? — I swear that, so far as I know, Ada is the name.

You knew that it was the daughter of a publican at the corner? — Yes, Miss Gentle has told me so.

Was she a little playmate of Manfred? — I cannot say that she was a playmate; she had had her in once or twice; it was the only children[135] that she had in.

Is the name, now, Winnie? — Winnie? Ada is the name I knew.

Did not Miss Gentle tell you that the name of your little boy's playmate was Winnie? — I say the name I knew was Ada.

There can be no mistake between those names in their sound. — What names?

The name of Ada and the name of Winnie. — I say the little girl which Miss Gentle has spoken to me about was named Ada.

Whilst you are at the publican's at the corner, do you know where that

**Louise Masset**

---

135  *Sic* in transcript.

# Masset.

**Louise Masset**

publican actually lived? — What I understood it to be was the public house at the corner of Clyde Road at the right from the house.

Follow this. Does it happen that the father of that little girl lives in a public house at the corner, as you say, of Clyde Road, one of the corners of Philip Lane at the other? — I do not know where Philip Lane is; I know the publican is at the corner.

You do not know where Philip Lane is? — No.

And you cannot tell me whether it happened, whether the father of Winnie --? — I am talking about the girl Ada.

You cannot say whether the father of little Winnie lives at the corner of Clyde Road and Philip Lane? — I do not know Philip Lane.

Do you know the name of the public house? — No.

You cannot tell me whether it was the Palmerston public house? — No, I did not like the companionship at all.

You did not? — I did not.

I will not comment upon that. Kindergarten was mentioned by the younger of the ladies? — It was.

The sister-in-law, as I understand, of Mrs Browning? — It was.

Whose name was Browning also, as I understand it? — Of course. I thought it was her husband's sister.

Kindergarten was mentioned by her? — It was.

Do you remember at all being told by Miss Gentle that little Winnie Allam went to a kindergarten? — She might have mentioned it when I spoke of the child's education, but I cannot say Winnie. I said Ada.

She might have mentioned it when you were speaking of Manfred's education? — Yes, because I have said to Miss Gentle that I should have to have his education seen to.

You have said that? — Yes. I never said the kindergarten was attended by Winnie.

Mr Justice BRUCE: It was attended by Ada? — Yes.

Mr MATHEWS: Did you know the surname of the girl? — No, and I do not think the name was given me by Miss Gentle. I think it was Manfred talking which gave me the name Ada.

You had a conversation with Miss Gentle about the education of Manfred? — I cannot say I have had a conversation; it was mentioned. Lots of things come up when you are speaking of a child.

They do. And amongst the things which came up, did it come up that little Ada Allam[136] was going to a kindergarten? — I do not think it was.

Why did you say that you did remember the word 'kindergarten'? — I do not think I did.

---

136   *Sic* in transcript. Mr Mathews knew that the child's name was Winnie, so his use of the name 'Ada' is an anomaly.

# Fourth Day – Saturday 16 December 1899.

Mr Justice BRUCE: You said Miss Browning had mentioned kindergarten. — Ah, Miss Browning did, not Miss Gentle. It was a school, not a kindergarten, I think I should say. I do not think she would have known the word.

Mr MATHEWS: My friend, who is beside me … It may be an inaccurate note, but Miss Gentle might have spoken to you about the education. — I think we can pass that, because it is of no importance.

We can pass it, but I will first call in little Winnie Allam, please. I would like you to see her, and see if there is any likeness between her and the little daughter of Mrs Browning. — I do not think it is necessary to call her up because it is the little girl I should call Ada. I never knew her under any other name.

Mr Justice BRUCE: Is she here, Mr Mathews?

Mr MATHEWS: Yes, my lord, she is coming. [The child was brought in.]

Look at the little girl and tell me --? — I am afraid I cannot recognise her.

Is that the little girl, by any chance, with whom little Manfred so often played in the Green? — Oh, no, never. The only time I ever saw that little girl was once when I went into the house.

Is that the little girl --? — I cannot say. I cannot remember her face at all.

But you cannot say that is the little girl who came to play in the house with Manfred? — I cannot say. I always understood she was called Ada.

Mr Justice BRUCE: That is not the little girl who was playing with Manfred on the Green? — No, certainly not.

Where was the girl you once saw playing in the house? You cannot say? — I cannot say. That little girl would know, for she has never played with Manfred on the Green.

Mr MATHEWS: Before I pass from 4 October, that was the first occasion upon which you saw the strange ladies? — Yes.

Did you meet casually upon Tottenham Green, where they invited you to take a seat beside them? You took off your gloves? — I had them off, I think. I had been playing with the child.

Your gloves were not on? — No.

And one of them, remarking the finger upon your left hand, said or asked, 'Are you married?' or 'You are not married?' — That was not the first point in the conversation.

That occurred during that first conversation, the first time you ever saw these strange ladies? — That was so; the acquaintance was made through the children's meeting

So you have told us. They did not tell you where they were living? — I

*Louise Masset*

# Masset.

**Louise Masset**

told you: I said yesterday that they were living in apartments in one of the roads leading from West Green Road.

They did not mention the road? — They may have, but not so that I catch it.

£12 a year and £6 a year extra for the teaching: £18 a year in all, as you have said. — Yes.

As distinct from the £22 4s which you were paying to Miss Gentle? — Yes.

Have you always remembered that incident – that statement about the £6 a year for the teaching? — Have I always remembered? I do not quite understand what you mean.

Have you always remembered it as forming part of this conversation when the younger of the two ladies said that they would require £6 a year? — No, she said 10 shillings a month.

Well, but you have always remembered this as part of that conversation? — Yes.

You did not mention it in the statement which you made to the police, did you? — I did not. My statement to the police was really questions about the child, questions which I answered, almost.

You did not mention it in the statement that you made to the police. — No. Of course, at the time, I was saying that I had left the child and given up £12 in advance. I did not give up the other money that was to be paid per month.

Now we will go to the eleventh – I pass from the fourth. As between the fourth and the eleventh, you had received those verses. — One verse it was.

And you had, in your own mind, come to a conclusion between the eleventh and the fourteenth? — Yes.

And that was the second occasion on which you saw the two strange ladies? — That was so.

And the same little girl? — Exactly the same.

Little Millie? — Little Millie.

Browning? — Of course, I knew her name.

Were you always there? This was the date that you next saw the two strange ladies? — I was not there on the twenty-seventh or the fourth. That was where I asked to make the remark at the time to Detective Burch – it was the twenty-seventh or fourth, I was not sure. I was always sure that it was the eleventh.

Do not try to meet my question. You were always sure it was the eleventh. You had never any doubt – never any uncertainty in your mind as to whether that second meeting took place on the eleventh or on the eighteenth of October? — Not the slightest doubt.

# Fourth Day – Saturday 16 December 1899.

**Louise Masset**

You had been certain with regard to the date of that second meeting throughout? — Yes, certain of the second, but not of the first. I thought it was a fortnight ago that I had met the ladies first.

Did you put this question to Police Sergeant Burch upon the occasion when you were representing yourself, and before you had Mr Newton to represent you? Did you put this question to Police Sergeant Burch: 'Are you certain that I said I met the women for the first time the next Wednesday, and not two weeks later?'[137] — That is just as I tell you, sir. I do not know whether the first meeting was the fourth or the twenty-seventh, and in that way I do not know whether the eleventh was the first or the second week after.

Did you put the question in the form that I suggest to you? 'Are you certain that I said I met the women for the second time the next Wednesday, and not two weeks later?' — I may have said that, of course, but, as I tell you, it was not the eighteenth. I was sure that it was not.

Mr Justice BRUCE: You may have put the question --?

Mr MATHEWS: To Police Sergeant Burch. 'Are you certain I met the women for the second time the next Wednesday, and not two weeks later?' — I have explained my meaning. I can say no more.

You may have put the question in that form? — Whether it was the twenty-seventh or the fourth. If it had been the twenty-seventh, then the eleventh would have been two weeks after.

What I am upon is as to whether the second meeting with the two women was not, according to your statement, two weeks after your first meeting with the two women? — No, it was not. It was the first week, the eleventh.

Did you hear Lord Coleridge, and in the hearing of the Jury yesterday, cross-examine Burch upon this very point and to this being to the best of his belief, and not a certainty on this point, although he had taken a note of the conversation with you. Did you hear Lord Coleridge yesterday, unless I am mistaken, cross-examine him on that point? — I do not think I noticed it.

You heard Miss Gentle examined in this case, and I doubt not you followed her evidence. — I tried to follow everything as well as possible.

Did you hear Miss Gentle say that, on 11 October, you were away from the Clyde Road about twenty minutes only? — I heard her say so.

Before she met you at the Seven Sisters Station? — You must excuse me; Miss Gentle gave it first as half an hour; then she gave it as twenty minutes, and, since, a quarter.

Did you hear Miss Gentle say that, when she joined you at the Seven Sisters station, that you and she went together on the evening of the

---

137 *Sic* in transcript: references are to Detective Sergeant Burch.

# Masset.

**Louise Masset**

eleventh to Tottenham Green, and stayed there for a considerable time? — Yes.

Did you hear her asked, 'Was the little boy then playing with another child?' Did you hear her answer, 'I never noticed him playing with any other child. I can swear that he did not play with any other child on that day.' — That was not made to any remark of mine.

Did you hear her make that remark? — I did.

Mr Justice BRUCE: What upon that? You have gone a little too fast for me.

Mr MATHEWS: I beg your Lordship's pardon. 'I did not hear –'

Mr Justice BRUCE: I thought the witness said twenty minutes, not half an hour. — She has changed those times. She has said half an hour, and now she says a quarter of an hour.

Mr MATHEWS: Did you hear Miss Gentle say that your child played with no other? — I heard it.

'I can swear that he did not on that day, the eleventh.' — I never said that he did in any way.

Did you hear Miss Gentle go on to say, 'On 18 October, which was the following Wednesday, Miss Masset came to my house; she did not go out that day'? — I did not go out.

'Nor did the child'? — No, I know the day.

The child cried very much? — Very much.

'The mother stopped until 6.00 pm'? — No, it must have been 5.30 pm, about twenty or half past when I always stopped.

But, before the magistrate, were you not anxious, by your question to Sergeant Burch, to fix 18 October as the date of your second meeting with the women? — No, I was not. I have said before: I was only thinking whether it was the twenty-seventh or the fourth when I saw the women first, and I know that it was not.

Mr Justice BRUCE: 'I was not, when before the magistrate, anxious to fix the date on the eighteenth.'

Mr MATHEWS: Your contention was between 27 September and 4 October? — It was scarcely a matter of contention.

Mr Justice BRUCE: 'On the eighteenth, I did not go out. I was not, when before the magistrate, anxious to fix the date of the second meeting on eighteenth.' — I was certainly not anxious to do so.

Did you not add something? — I do not think I meant to say anything.

You did not wish to add to that? — No.

Lord COLERIDGE: She said between the twenty-seventh and the fourth.

Mr Justice BRUCE: Will you suggest it, Lord Coleridge, what she said?

# Fourth Day – Saturday 16 December 1899.

**Lord COLERIDGE:** She was going to explain whether she was in doubt about the women, and finally she was convinced that it was on the twenty-seventh because there was a death.[138]

**Mr Justice BRUCE:** Do you wish to add anything to that? You are not anxious to fix the date on the eighteenth? — I am not.

**Mr MATHEWS:** Was that not that date abandoned when Miss Gentle proved in the witness box that you did not leave the Clyde Road the whole afternoon of Wednesday 18 October? — No, sir, it was not. I knew as well as Miss Gentle that I did not leave the house at any time on the eighteenth.

Before I pass from the incident of Tottenham Green, you say that the child had been there several times with you before, and that Miss Gentle knew that he had been there several times, did you? — I cannot say several times, but I know he has gone home and said that he has played with this little girl.

Do you agree with Miss Gentle that – as far as she knew – that 4 October was the first time that the little boy had gone to Tottenham Green? — She is wrong, certainly.

Did you hear her say so? — I heard her say so.

But she is wrong? — Certainly, in my opinion, she is wrong.

Now the Wednesday, the eleventh. The two strange ladies were still in apartments, were they? — On the what?

On the Wednesday, the eleventh, the two strange ladies were still in apartments? — I suppose so. The question was not raised. I expected so.

You do not know whether they were? — The question was not raised.

And that they told you that they were going to take a house at 45 King's Road, Chelsea? — Yes. They said they had looked at a house and that the house was a very nice one.

Just tell me, what were your occupations at this time? On 11 October, how many pupils had you? — I had Mrs Sonnenthal and Mrs Haas, six lessons a week.

That was all? — I have had that for a long time.

How many times were you going? — I had about six lessons a week.

What days in the week would you go there? — Mondays, Thursdays, Wednesdays and Saturdays.

On four days in the week? — Yes, Mondays and Thursdays were always sure. Wednesdays and Saturdays were the extra days.

Mondays and Thursdays being the settled days? — Yes.

Which left you Tuesday and Friday free? — Yes.

And which left you free to go to your child on each Wednesday afternoon? — Yes.

---

138   The death of Louise Masset's stepfather.

# Masset.

**Louise Masset**

On that afternoon, did you definitely determine that your child should go to the two strange ladies? — Yes, unless they wrote to me, unless there was another alteration in the plan.

So far as any change was concerned, that would rest with them, and not with you? — No.

That was your determination? — If you call it a determination. The arrangement was made.

You say I call it a determination. Did you then decide to leave the child with them? — I decided, as I said, to take the child to London Bridge and go on to Chelsea with them.

Did you then decide to leave the child with them for the £12 a year? — When I mean that I decided that, I mean that I had decided it for that sum.

Did you say, on that Wednesday, that you would come and see the child on the Friday? — Yes, because the child was ill, and I said I would come on the Friday.

That was a free day? — Yes.

You did not go on the Friday? — No. I did not. I think it was because my sister wished to go out and not stop at home, and I stopped at home instead.

I doubt not that the reason was adequate, but you did not go? — I did not.

Nor did you go to Chelsea on the Friday? — No.

Nor to the King's Road, Chelsea, on the Friday? — No.

You have never been in Chelsea in your life? — Never.

No references from the strange ladies? — No, because I had seen them twice and it did not seem necessary. They seemed such nice people.

No visits to the strange ladies' house before you would part with your child to them? — No, sir, there was not.

And yet you were not less fond of him in the October of 1899 than you had been in the May of 1896? — No, but you forget that in May I had an advertisement to answer, and I went to see Miss Gentle because of that.

Have you had no advertisement? — No, I saw the person myself and was perfectly satisfied at the time.

Now before we pass altogether from the eleventh, London Bridge station, was that …? It is a large place: was there anything more definite than that? — Yes, it was Littlehampton side. I said so.

And 2.00 pm? — Yes, I can tell you why I said 2.00 pm. It was because of the train goes to Newhaven. That is why I said it.

You had still that idea in your head? — Yes, I had said so to Miss Gentle.

Now, come to 15 October. I think – correct me if I am wrong – but I

# Fourth Day – Saturday 16 December 1899.

think I heard you say yesterday of that letter that it was all untrue, there was not a true statement in it? — There may be true parts in it. I said the part about the education was true. There might be other things – I cannot remember the whole letter.

It was untrue, of course, we know it now, that you thought you would be able to meet the father on the Friday, the thirteenth, and would go and see Manfred? — Yes.

He came over quite unexpectedly? — Yes. You can prove that for yourself, if you wish, that he never came over.

And I might take it, speaking generally of that letter, that was an untrue letter, except for the education of the child? — There must be other things in it which are true. I cannot say exactly.

'Will bring over the shoes he tried on lately for the house as his clothing will be saved when he has his new home and there is no need for him to carry too much luggage.' Is that true? — Yes, I can quite explain that to you. I would rather explain it, in fact. Miss Gentle knew that I intended putting him into trousers – changing his clothing – and he was to go into them when he got to Miss Browning's, and that was why he was not to take too much.

Not to take too much because he was to change, when he got to Mrs Browning's, into trousers? — Yes, Miss Gentle knew that I intended to change him.

And that was why he was not to take too much luggage? — Yes.

You had not in your mind, at that time, that there was no reason that the child should take away more than one suit of clothes? — No other reason but that.

Mr Justice BRUCE: Do you say you had a reason? — No, no other reason. There was more than one change. I arranged with Miss Gentle what he should take, and the old things were left behind.

Mr MATHEWS: I do not think you had made the arrangement then. — No, I had on the eighteenth – that was the only reason, because I did not wish to carry more than was necessary, because he would have to change his clothing.

Was that part of the arrangement with the two ladies? — What?

That he should be changed into trousers? — Oh, yes, it was spoken of.

You have not spoken of it to us. — If I said everything that passed, it would be very difficult.

The interviews were not very long. Have you ever said that before – that he was to go into trousers – that you had spoken to the ladies about it? — I said he was going to change into trousers.

Have you ever said that you have ever stated before that the arrangement was made with the two ladies that he was going into trousers? — No, I

**Louise Masset**

# Masset.

*Louise Masset*

do not think so. The thought did not strike me then.

That did not occur to you?

*The court adjourned for a short time.*

Mr MATHEWS [resuming]: Miss Masset. On the eighteenth it was that, as we know now, the child was unable to go out. — Yes.

And, on the eighteenth, we heard from you that he was greatly distressed because injudiciously, as you thought, the subject of the parting had in some way been discussed before him? — Yes.

He was very much attached to Miss Gentle? — Mostly to the mother, to Mrs Norris.

At all events, to the household he was in? — Yes, he had been brought up by them.

And he was greatly distressed, the child, at the idea of having to leave them? — Yes.

And then it was that the arrangement had been made in which Miss Gentle was to bring him to London Bridge Station? — On the eighteenth, yes.

Any hour mentioned? — I don't think so, sir, because I was to meet them at the Birdcage and go on with them.

I do not think the Birdcage was mentioned at this time. — On the eighteenth? Yes, it was.

I think she was to go to London Bridge. — Yes, but she would have to pass the Birdcage, and she should go on to London Bridge with me.

But no hour was mentioned? — I do not remember one being mentioned.

And I do not want to use any harsher word than is necessary, but the story with regard to the visit to France, that was, so far as the Norrises were concerned, at the interview on the eighteenth? — It was started for that so that the Norrises should not be broken-hearted at the child going.

It had been started in the letter of 16 October, and it was kept up at the interview on 18 October? — Yes.

And your design was to keep from the Norrises the fact that the child was going into any other hands in England? — Yes.

That was your design? — Yes.

And yet, Miss Masset, the arrangement was that Miss Gentle was to bring the child to the very point where the strange ladies were to take it over? — Yes.

You spoke to Mrs Cadisch on the eighteenth, did not you? — The evening of the eighteenth, yes.

Of the intended journey to France? — Yes, I did, that I thought of

# Fourth Day – Saturday 16 December 1899.

taking the child over there.

Was that the first time that you had told her of the intended journey to France? — Yes.

And that you were going to take the child over, in order that it might be brought up by a cousin of the father, who was living in France? — I cannot say that he was to be brought up by a cousin to Madame Cadisch. I cannot say that those are my words at the time.

You cannot tell us that that is the account you gave her? — No. I would not deny it.

There had been some conversation between you and this very lady, earlier in the year, in regard to this child's education? — To Madame Cadisch?

Yes. — Yes, in May or June.

In regard to the fact that the child was not advancing as you thought he ought, in the manner of education? That was so? — And there was another point I mentioned to Madame Cadisch also: that I thought he required companionship.

On the eighteenth, did you say a single word to Madame Cadisch as to your intention of putting the child into other hands in England? — On the eighteenth, no.

To her, the same deception which you had begun in the letter of 16 October to the Norrises, and which you had kept up? — But for different reasons.

Yes. 24 October, the next date to which I call your attention. — That was a Tuesday.

One of your free days? — Yes, it would be.

Let us just get that after 11 October. 13 October was a free day. 17 October, a free day. 20 October, a free day. 24 October, a free day. Did you go to McIlroy's on 24 October? — No, sir.

You did not? — I did not.

McIlroy's is the draper where the shawl was purchased. — That may be.

You did not go there? — I did not.

You were not the woman seen there by Miss Clifford, about dinner time, on 24 October? — I was certainly not.

Certainly not? — Certainly not. I should not have gone out; if I had gone out on a Tuesday, I should not have gone out before three. I never went out of a morning.

Just confine yourself to answering the question, please.

Lord COLERIDGE: She may give any explanation which she likes.

Mr MATHEWS: Oh, yes. [To the witness] It was not by you that a black shawl was asked for to Miss Clifford? — It was not.

# Masset.

**Louise Masset**

You were in mourning at this time, were you, for your stepfather? — I was, sir.

It was not to you that Miss Clifford sold a shawl, the price of which, she told you, was 1s 6d? — No, I never use shawls in any way.

You never did? — No.

Not by you that the request was made for a longer shawl than the one which she showed you? — No, sir.

Not to you that a larger shawl was shown, which was purchased and paid for, for the sum of 1s 11½d? — It was not.

Miss Clifford is mistaken in her belief that you were the woman who went to the shop on that day? — Yes, sir.

Do you know McIlroy's? — Certainly, I know the shop. I know the name.

Have you been in there? — I think I have been in there once for crochet cotton, but Roberts & Rackstraw's is where I generally go.

But you have been there once? — Yes.

You know where it is? — Oh, yes. I have seen the name lots of times.

It is not far from Bethune Road, is it? — I cannot say how far, no distance ... Ten minutes from the road and ten minutes on.

About twenty minutes, do you say it is? Twenty minutes from the Bethune Road? — No, I would not say so much.

You showed no shawl to anybody because you never wear one? — I never wear one.

The next day, 25 October, a Wednesday again, and there the actual place of parting is determined on as the Birdcage, instead of at London Bridge? — Yes.

That was at Mrs Norris's suggestion? — Yes.

Not your suggestion? — No.

But for that suggestion, which came from Mrs Norris and not from you, the arrangement would have stood that Miss Gentle should have accompanied the child to London Bridge Station, the point where the two strange women were to take it over? — Yes.

The present of the scales was made on that day, as I understand it? — I gave them to him myself. I always took a toy with me.

The little scales, which have been produced here? — Yes, I have seen them. I should know them at any distance.

On the twenty-fifth, with Mrs Cadisch, an interview, was there not? — You can scarcely call it an interview. It was while we were working that the subject came up, and I told her that I should go on the twenty-seventh.

Saying nothing about the letter or any possible change, I think. — No, I did not say anything to her.

# Fourth Day – Saturday 16 December 1899.

And upon that day you told Mrs Cadisch that you were going to Newhaven with the child? — That would be part of the journey if I was going over to France. I could not go any way else from London Bridge if I was going to France.

Leaving London Bridge by the 2.30 pm train? — The 2.00 pm train.

And arriving at Newhaven at 5.00 pm? — I cannot say whether I said 5.00 pm. I do not know what the journey would take.

Is Mrs Cadisch right in saying, 'She said she had to go by the 2.00 pm train, as she had to be at Newhaven by 5.00 pm'? — I cannot say that those are my words; I said as little as possible.

And that you would be back on Sunday or Monday? — Yes.

And, on that same day, the meeting with Lucas at Liverpool Street Station? — Yes.

And the journey taken with him. Did you go by train? — We always came back together, you see.

Back to the Bethune Road? — Yes.

And then you announced to him, for the first time, what had been in your mind since 8 October? — I said to him that probably I could get away from the Friday to the Sunday.

Yes, and that you were going to Brighton on the Friday by the 4.00 pm train from London Bridge? — It was after the conversation that Brighton was settled. I said I could go anywhere.

Is Lucas wrong in saying that you arranged that you should leave by the 4.00 pm train to Brighton? — Yes, we settled it should be Brighton.

On the following Friday? — On the following Friday.

Then he is not wrong? — No.

Was it arranged with him about the same room as you had at Whitsuntide? — Yes, I thought that was my idea, that we should have the two same rooms. I know it was discussed. I cannot say which of us spoke of it.

That you should have the same rooms at the same hotel? — If I could possibly get them.

And he was to come down on the Saturday by the 2.00 pm train from London Bridge? — That he was not sure about.

He was to come if he could? — Yes.

And he was to write to you in the name of Miss Brooks at Brighton, and he was to pass as your brother? — That was so.

Is that the name in which you had last been there, or was that a new name? — No, we went in our own names before.

You had not been in that name before? — No.

Going on Friday, the twenty-seventh … You were at home that morning? — Yes.

Louise Masset

# Masset.

**Louise Masset**

What time did you leave the house? — 12.30 pm, about that time.

Had you been out of the house in the morning, at all? — No, I never went out of the house in the morning, unless it was for a lesson on the Wednesday or Saturday.

Did you know of the existence of that grotto, the rockery in the back garden? — What grotto?

The grotto or rockery to the back garden of your sister's house. — I know there is a border all the way round.

In the back garden ... First of all, did you know of its existence? — I know there was an edging.

Composed of clinker bricks? — Yes.

Did you know that the edging in the front garden also composed --? — Oh, yes. You cannot go into the garden without seeing it, because it is from the gate. You would be bound to see it.

Do you know of some spare bricks that were there in the front garden? — I do not know of any spare bricks at all.

Mr Justice BRUCE: You say you do not know of any spare bricks at all — No, sir.

Mr MATHEWS: Spare, loose bricks which had got away from the edging. You did not see anything of them? They had never caught your attention? — No, never.

Did you pack up your own Gladstone bag – or rather, it was your brother's Gladstone bag – he lent it to you? — I asked him for it.

Did you pack it up yourself? — Certainly.

No one helped you? — No.

Putting into it your night things? — And a dressing jacket; there was a blouse and different things that I might need for a time.

And that was all? — That was all, sir. Shoes and things like that, and anything necessary for toilet, of course.

But within the straps of that did you place your mackintosh? — Yes, it was already rolled up in a strap, and I placed it under the two straps of the Gladstone.

And with that one parcel, as it then became, you went to the Birdcage? — Yes – and my umbrella.

Leaving the house at 12.30 pm? — I had something else – a little purse bag with some money in it. A brown one, just a little one with my initials on it.

Did you carry it in your hand? — Yes.

A purse bag? — A tiny little thing about the size of my hand.

Umbrella: the mackintosh strapped to the Gladstone bag: at 12.30 pm, you set off to the Birdcage on foot and walked there? — Yes.

Taking the omnibus after you had seen Miss Gentle? — Yes. She was

# Fourth Day – Saturday 16 December 1899.

standing in the doorway of one of the shops.

She was there a little before you, as she has told us. — Yes.

And she handed to you, did she, the child? — She put him on my knee.

And the brown paper parcel containing the clothing? — Yes, sir, and a smaller one.

And the little parcel containing the scales? — That was it.

And away you started. Was the child distressed? — I cannot say he was greatly distressed, but he was sobbing hard. He wanted amusing, of course, a great deal to bring him to himself again.

At London Bridge about 1.35 pm – is that about correct? — I cannot say what time I got there, but I must have got there when the omnibus got there, of course.

You do not quarrel with that time? — No, not in the least.

Then to the Littlehampton ladies' waiting room, as we will call it – the place appointed for the meeting with the two strange ladies. — Yes.

Is Mrs Worley right in saying that you were there from 1.45 pm to 2.30 pm? — I must have been there more than that if she changed.

You saw the change of attendants? You saw one attendant go and the other attendant come in? — Yes, one came in about a quarter of an hour before the other went – whatever her name is.

And Mrs Worley is right in saying that you were in that waiting room? — Yes, quite right.

And the conversation she has deposed to here? — Yes.

Is she right in saying that – while you were there – that you were sitting with your head down, and did not look up? — I cannot see how I could do it all that time, considering that I was playing with the child; he was playing with the biscuits and the scales. I might have put my head down.

Looking at the child? — No, I was looking at the things he was playing with.

And when the second attendant came, then you left the waiting room? — Yes.

And after the other attendant went on to duty, you left? — The attendant came some time before the other left.

And then you went to the ladies' waiting room near the refreshment room to see if the women were there? — Yes, to see if they had made a mistake.

They were not there? — They were not.

Had you ever been in that waiting room before? — The second one, never. In the Littlehampton I had been often.

But in the second waiting room, never? — Four years ago, in 1894, I used to go often.[139] I went to school at Littlehampton.

# Masset.

**Louise Masset**

And to the lavatory? — That I cannot say. I went with the little boy.

You did on this occasion? — Yes, certainly.

But to the second of these waiting rooms, this was the first time you had ever been there? — Yes.

There was an attendant there? — I did not see one at first – not when I sat down.

But you did see one? — Yes, she came in afterwards.

You sat down near the door? — Yes, on one of the seats.

And jumping about on one of the seats, the little boy was? — Yes, that is why the attendant came.

Do you say that Mrs Reece is mistaken in saying that you remained in that room twenty-five to thirty minutes? — Yes, she is certainly mistaken. I cannot have stopped more than five.

Is it true that Mrs Reece said, in your hearing, to the boy, 'What are you grizzling about?' — No.

Not true? — No, he was not grizzling; on the contrary, he was jumping up and down.

You say it is not true? — I say she is mistaken. I should not be so rude as to say it is not true.

Is it true that – in your hearing – that to the little boy, Mrs Reece said that, 'What are you grizzling about?' — I say it is quite untrue, if you wish it in that way.

I do wish it in that way. Is it true that she said, 'What is the matter with it?' — No, untrue.

Is it true that you said to her, 'He has just parted with his nurse'? — No, I did not.

Mr Justice BRUCE: Did you use the word 'nurse'? — No, I never spoke of it. I never used the word at all.

Mr MATHEWS: He had just parted with his nurse? — He had, certainly. Well, an hour, I suppose.

Within an hour? — More than that … A quarter to one … Two hours before.

He had been fretting as he came along by the omnibus? — Yes, but not all the way, and Mrs Worley has said herself that he was quite happy in her waiting room.

But you had been making that statement to her at that time? — To whom?

To Mrs Reece. — No.

Can you suggest whence she has got that statement, unless you made

---

139   More than four years had passed since 1894. The defendant was grasping for the chronology, and indicating a rough time period to which her remarks applied: '[About] four years ago, or [some time around] 1894 …'

# Fourth Day – Saturday 16 December 1899.

it to her? — I cannot suggest it.

Did she put the question, 'How old is he?' — I gave the answer, but the question was not put in that way.

You did tell her how old he was? — Yes.

Did you tell her he would be four next April? — No, that he was three and a half.

Not that he would be four? — No.

But to the woman to whom you spoke, you did say that the little boy then with you was three and a half, or about three and a half years of age? — Yes.

Was there any conversation between you as to your taking him to the refreshment room in order to get him a cake? — The conversation was none at all; it would have been absurd, because he had biscuits.

That is untrue? — Certainly.

Mr Justice BRUCE: No conversation about taking the boy to the refreshment room? — No, none whatever.

Mr MATHEWS: Can you suggest, Miss Masset, whence it is that Mrs Reece has got that conversation as to the taking of the boy to the refreshment room for the purpose of giving him a cake? — I cannot suggest anything, unless she got it from my statement. I do not know if she has got it from a paper.

Do you suggest it? — I do not suggest it.

Do you, or not, suggest that Mrs Reece has invented that conversation in so far as it occurred with you?

Lord COLERIDGE: I object, my Lord. A question like that is never allowed.

Mr Justice BRUCE: I do not think you can put it like that, Mr MATHEWS. I never like questions put to one witness as to their view of the evidence.

Mr MATHEWS: Do you say it is untrue, that conversation? — Yes, sir.

You took the little boy out of the waiting room, did you? — I cannot say that he went out with me; I should not have had him by the hand. I had too much to carry. He must have walked out with me, of course.

Taking with you the Gladstone bag and the brown paper parcel? — And the scales which I had with me.

And on the platform you met the two ladies? — Yes.

Mr Justice BRUCE: Do I understand you left the Gladstone bag in the waiting room? — No, sir, I took it with me.

Mr MATHEWS: And the brown paper parcel containing the clothing, and the scales in their little parcel? — Yes, sir. They were no longer in a parcel, the scales.

*Louise Masset*

# Masset.

**Louise Masset**

What had been done with them? — With what?

With the scales. — I had them in my pocket.

And on the platform you met the two ladies, and from the platform you went into the general waiting room? — Yes.

The third waiting room in which you were upon that day? — Yes.

The Littlehampton one, as we will call it. It was familiar to you? — Yes.

The ladies' waiting room near the refreshment room, which you entered for the first time, and the general waiting room, which was the third waiting room which you went into? — Yes.

And you always remembered that you had gone into those three waiting rooms? — I do not know what you mean by 'always remembered'.

But you went into all the waiting rooms, one after the other? — Certainly. I could not do otherwise than do what I did.

And there it was, in the general waiting room, that the child was handed over? — It was so.

The £12 paid mostly in gold? — Yes.

Where did you get it from? — What, the money? It was my own money.

Saved? — Certainly.

Mr Justice BRUCE: £12 of your own savings, was it? — Yes.

Mr MATHEWS: You handed the child to which woman? — It was the sister who took him away; he was handed really to the two, but as they went out the sister had him.

The younger? — Yes.

To whom did you hand the brown paper parcel containing the clothes? — To Mrs Browning, because I was talking to her about the arrangements.

To the mother? — Yes.

Was the child dressed in a little blue serge dress trimmed with white ribbon? — He was dressed exactly as Miss Gentle has said.

That was the colour and the trimming of the dress? — Dark blue, it was.

And the little dark blue coat with the brass buttons? — Yes.

And the fawn turndown collar, and capes and cuffs? — Yes.

And you did not in any way disturb the brown paper parcel? — Not in any way.

You handed that over? — Exactly as it was.

When it was in your care, did you notice any writing outside it? — No, I cannot say that I did. I did not take any notice of it.

And the two women left for the purpose of going to the refreshment room, there to write out a receipt which they were to bring back to you?

# Fourth Day – Saturday 16 December 1899.

**Louise Masset**

— Yes.

And that was the last which you saw of them? — It was.

You went to the refreshment room after waiting a few minutes, and pushed the door open in order to see if they were still there. — Yes.

They were not there? — No.

You walked about to see if they were about? — I thought they might run about as the child was very jovial and larky then.

Was that the child's condition when you parted from him? — He was very jolly. Miss Browning had been playing hide and seek with him in the room whilst I was talking to the mother, and he was in the highest spirits.

And in these high spirits it was that the child left? — It was.

Were you alarmed at the disappearance of the two women who had promised you a receipt? — I was not alarmed in the least. Why should I be? I had seen them twice; there was nothing to be alarmed at. I thought they had taken him off, on the contrary, while he was so gay – and you would not have been alarmed, had you seen the woman, either.

Please just answer for yourself. Did you know London well enough to know of Chelsea that it was no great distance? — I could not tell you where Chelsea was in the least.

And that filled you with no misgiving at all? — I had heard the name, certainly.

But it filled you with no misgiving that you did not know the place where the child --? — No, it had not.

What was your hurry to get to Brighton on this Friday afternoon? — There was no hurry at all.

The women having disappeared, and the child with them, there being no hurry to get to Brighton, why not go to 45 King's Road, Chelsea, and take the next train to Brighton after the 4.00 train? — The thought never came to me in any way; why should I have gone?

You knew the way, did you not? — I knew the way? Which way?

From London Bridge to Broad Street. — Oh, yes, certainly.

From Broad Street --? — I know it from Liverpool Street; that is how I have been to Stoke Newington that way, by omnibus.

You knew the way to Broad Street, and to Liverpool Street? — Yes.

And you knew from Broad Street you could go to Dalston Junction? — Yes, I have been.

Scores of times, I daresay? — I know the line very well.

And you know the way back from Dalston Junction to Broad Street, and so the way back to London Bridge Station? — If you can go one way, I suppose you can go the other.

They were in your mind? — No, they were not.

# Masset.

**Louise Masset**

But they were in your knowledge? — If you had asked me the question which way to go, I might have given you that way.

That is a very fair answer. Were you not back in the second class ladies' waiting room at London Bridge at or about 6.50 pm that same evening? — I am perfectly sure I was not.

Is Mrs Reece speaking truly when she says she saw you in the lavatory attached to the waiting room? — Untruly, if you wish me to say it in that way. I should have said mistaken.

But you say untruly? — Untruly.

Mrs Reece speaks of turning on some water for you to wash your hands. — It was not for me.

She speaks of a parcel untidily done up at the end of the washing slab. — It was not mine.

She speaks of your asking her for a clothes brush. — I did not.

She speaks of giving you a clothes brush. It was not to you? — Oh, no, it was not.

She speaks of your being there until 7.15 pm. — I say she is mistaken.

And of her saying to you, 'You must look sharp if you want to catch the 7.20 pm, because it is past 7.15 pm now'. — I was not there for her to say it to me.

Now, just let us follow this. Mrs Reece did not see you there and did not speak to you there at the times I have mentioned? — I do not say in the afternoon.

Nay, nay, at the times I have last mentioned? — No.

Not you? — No.

You left at 4.00 pm, according to your story? — I did.

Down at Brighton by, as we know, 5.19 pm. You travelled first class on the occasions that you did go down to Brighton? — Yes.

You do not ordinarily travel first class? Ordinarily you travel third class? — For those short journeys, certainly.

For these longer journeys, you travel first class? — I generally do for long journeys.

And you arrived at Brighton at about 5.19 pm? — I cannot say that. It was only by the Jubilee clock I knew the time at all.

You got to Mr Findlay's Hotel about 9.45 pm at night? — As Mr Findlay says so – I should not be sure of the time.

And, down at Brighton, if we take the guard's time as being correct, from about 5.20 pm to 9.45 pm? — Yes, certainly.

A wet night, I think you told me? — It was not so wet down there; it was a fine night down there.

Mr Justice BRUCE: I thought you said it was a wet night? — It was damp, but it was not raining.

# Fourth Day – Saturday 16 December 1899.

Mr MATHEWS: That was the reason you did not go to the pier; it was too wet to go on the pier? — Yes.

And you strolled about looking at the shops? — I did.

After you had been to Mutton's? — Yes.

Had you ever been to Mutton's before? — I think I have been once.

Ever been since? — No, except this time.

After this --? You had been before? — Yes, I think it was about three or four years back.

But not since? — No.

And I take it, Miss Masset, that the three hours and twenty-five minutes – 5.20 pm to 9.45 pm – were occupied by you in Brighton in getting to Mutton's and having something to eat?[140] — I was there about an hour, I should say.

And then going for your walk to the shops? — Yes: going to the station, and getting my luggage out, and going to the hotel.

The temperance hotel is quite near to the station? — About five minutes' walk.

And you passed it, do I understand you, on your way down to Mutton's? — Yes.

And returned past it on your way to the station? — I did.

If you had gone to Brighton by the 4.00 pm train, arriving that day at 5.19 pm, you could have been at the temperance hotel by 5.30 pm? — Yes, if it arrived at 5.19 pm. I ought to have been there about twenty-five past.

You did not get there until 9.45 pm? — Yes, that is the time Mr Findlay says.

If you had travelled by the 7.22 pm train, that arriving that night, if I am not mistaken, at 9.18 pm, at eighteen minutes past nine --? — I ought to have been at the hotel about 9.25 pm then.

And you got there at 9.45 pm? — Yes.

Whenever you did arrive at Brighton upon that day, did you go down to the sea before you went to hotel? — Certainly, I did. I could not have been to Mutton's without going down.

And, on your arrival at the hotel, you had a Gladstone bag with you, had you? — Yes.

And the mackintosh, at that time – was it done up in a separate parcel? — No, not in a separate parcel.

In a separate parcel from the bag? — Quite a separate parcel.

And it was, at the time you arrived at the hotel, in a separate parcel

Louise Masset

---

140  *Sic* in transcript. Mr Mathews's arithmetic had let him down. The period between the arrival of the train at Brighton and Miss Masset's arrival at the hotel was four hours and twenty-five minutes.

# Masset.

**Louise Masset**

from the bag? — Yes, it was.

Mr Justice BRUCE: I am not sure that I understand. Had you it over your arm or in straps? — No, it was in straps. It might be about that size, the length of it strapped up.

Mr MATHEWS: Do I understand that some cakes were bought, or some biscuits were bought, by you for the child? — No, Madame Cadisch gave me some.

Did you take those with you to Brighton? — No, the child ate them in the waiting room. They were little nic-nacs, those hard, dry biscuits.

Mr Justice BRUCE: You left them? — No, sir, he ate them in the waiting room.

Mr MATHEWS: In paper? — No, I had them in my pocket.

Did you hear what the chambermaid said that she had found in a drawer where the scales were found? That she had found some cakes? — Yes, I did. I know where the cakes were from.

Where were they bought? — Mr Lucas brought them down with him on the Saturday.

They were brought by Mr Lucas? — Yes.

Not bought for the child? — No, they were quite a different kind. These were in little fluted papers that he brought down.

Now, on the night of the twenty-seventh, of course, you were alone at Brighton, in the room number 11? — Yes.

And, down to your going to the station to meet Mr Lucas somewhere about 3.00 pm on that afternoon of the twenty-eighth, you were alone at that time? — Well, I was up and down stairs and all.

No one was with you? — No, sir.

What time did you get to the station for the purpose of meeting Mr Lucas? — I started about 3.15 pm, I think.

Can you fix that a little more precisely? — I could not fix it more precisely.

And that walk being about five minutes? — I only go by my dinner time. I ordered dinner for 2.00 pm, but it was not served up till close upon 4.00 pm.

You went to the Brighton Station? — I did.

Arriving there at what hour? — As to its being only five minutes, it was about 3.20 pm.

Was the train in? — No, I cannot say it was. It came in about two minutes after.

Very shortly after? — Very shortly after.

Did you go into any waiting room? — No, there was no necessity for my going inside a waiting room. I had just left the hotel.

As you say, there was no necessity – so you tell me. — Certainly.

# Fourth Day – Saturday 16 December 1899.

There was no natural reason for your going in because you had just left the hotel? — Certainly.

And you did not go into any? — I did not.

Did you know the second class ladies' waiting room at the Brighton Railway Station? — I do not think I have ever been in any waiting room.

You have never been in any waiting room there? — No.

Having met Mr Lucas, you went away from the station with him? — We went straight to the hotel.

You think so, on that occasion? — Yes, for him to put his bag up.

You have been described as perfectly calm, collected and in excellent spirits during the time you were at Brighton – is that a correct description? — Yes, I think so.

The night was spent, as we know, with Mr Lucas, as he has told us. I do not wish to refer further to it. That is correct? — That is so.

And, on the Sunday, there was the return home? — Yes.

Did you see any newspaper in Brighton on the Saturday? — No, I never saw any paper.

On the Saturday? — No.

Any newspaper in Brighton on the Sunday? — No.

Mr Justice BRUCE: Do you say yes or no? — No.

Mr MATHEWS: They are sold in Brighton, are they not? London newspapers are sold in Brighton on Sunday, are they not? — I expect they are.

But you saw none? — I did not pay the slightest attention to any papers.

You saw no papers at all in Brighton – in or out of it?[141] — No.

Did you not know that the *Weekly Dispatch* was taken in there? — No.

You returned home on the Sunday night, bringing the Gladstone bag and the mackintosh back to your sister's house? — Yes.

As to the next morning, Monday, has Mrs Cadisch given us a correct account of the conversation with her? — I think it sounded just the same as had passed.

Did she ask you if the child had been troublesome, and did you reply, 'Only at London Bridge'? — 'Only as far as London Bridge,' would have been my reply.

That is a material difference between you. It was not, 'Only at London Bridge'? — No.

At London Bridge, the child was in high spirits? — Yes, when he saw the ships' masts at London Bridge, he began to be happier – to cheer up.

She asked if you had had a good crossing? — She did.

Did you say that you had had a bad crossing both ways, but that it was

Louise Masset

---

141  That is, in the hotel, or around town.

# Masset.

**Louise Masset**

better coming home – coming back? — I said as little as possible.

But you did say so much as that? — I think I said as much as that.

Still keeping up the deception? — Yes.

There was no word to Mrs Cadisch on Monday 30 October, after your return, as to the two strange woman? — No, of course not, because if I deceived her one way, I should not have raised her doubts.

You did not say anything to her, then, about that? — No.

Upon that morning, you wrote to the Norrises – you sent a testimonial? — It was because they asked me.

And you wrote them the details of your voyage to France? — That was again keeping it up. There was no reason to say any different. It was not Mrs Norris's business, was it?

I will not answer that question. Let me read you this letter:

> Dear Mrs Norris,
>
> I have just returned from my journey and hasten to let you know how we got on.
>
> Our boy would cry till he saw the ships from London Bridge and then he felt better and thought he would like to go into the trains as he could see other men and boys doing. I suppose he was not scared of the engines because they were standing so still and only puffing now and again.
>
> He was scarcely ill on board and the stewardess thought he was a dreadful chatterbox. Poor I was awfully sick both going and returning and I am not having any more just yet, thank you.
>
> I enclose the letter I promised you.
>
> Please thank Miss Norris for all her trouble and tell her how sorry I was not to be able to talk to her on Friday but our young man would certainly have been more upset had she remained. He sent his love to Mummy, Daddy and Nelly[142] and certainly hopes to see them again.
>
> I shall try and be over at the end of the week but not Wednesday as that day I must make up the lessons I lost on Saturday.
>
> Kind regards to all, including Mr Norris.
>
> Yours very sincerely.

That letter was sent in the morning. — I sent it by the 11.00 am post. I simply added it to the other she had asked me for.

Just so – in which you speak truly, do you not, of the great kindness which the little boy had at all times received? — I could not say any different.

---

142 The evidence is not conclusive, but Nellie may have preferred the '-ie' spelling to the '-y' spelling used in the letter.

# Fourth Day – Saturday 16 December 1899.

That was a true description about her kindness? — Certainly.

The letters written, you had to fulfil your duties that afternoon to the families you were teaching? — Yes.

Mrs Sonnenthal's daughter was one. I believe Mrs Sonnenthal's daughter went with you to the gymnasium in Baker Street? — Yes.

And there you saw a newspaper. — I saw more than one.

You saw more than one newspaper? — Yes, several.

Newspapers which announced the discovery of the child's body? — I could not say which one I saw it in. Certainly, I saw some paper with it in.

Describing the child? — Describing the child. There was a description of the child in one of the newspapers I saw.

At what time would you get to the gymnasium? — I left at 1.30 pm – not the 2.00 pm train. 2.30 pm, I was due at the house. If I started immediately it would be about 3.15 pm that we should get to the gymnasium.

How soon after getting to the gymnasium did you see the newspaper description of the child? — About half an hour or three quarters of an hour after.

We may take it, then, that, at 4.00 pm, you had seen a newspaper which contained a description of the child. Did you wait for your pupil and go back with her? — Yes.

And did you go on and see Mrs Haas, as well as her daughter? — I think so. I could not remember that special occasion.

She says she saw you. — If she says so, then I did.

She says further that, when she saw you that evening, you were in your usual health and spirits. Was that so? — I could not say exactly in my usual health.

And spirits? — No.

She says so. — She would not notice. I should not see her more than five minutes.

How long did you stay after you got back? At 7.00 pm --? You left to catch the 6.55 pm at Loudoun Road for Dalston Junction? — The 6.55 pm.

Every journey you made was by that train? — Yes.

As between 4.00 pm, when you were at Baker Street, and 6.55 pm, when you left the Loudoun Road, no effort was made by you to go and trace your child? — But, sir, I only had just a kind of feeling – 'That seems to be like the child' – that was all.

The description of the child?

Lord COLERIDGE: A child. — The description of a child.

Mr MATHEWS: Follow me, please. You arrived at Dalston Junction

*Louise Masset*

# Masset.

**Louise Masset**

between 7.00 pm and 8.00 pm? — Yes.

You go past the bookstall, I suppose, since you saw the placard of a newspaper? — It was outside the station.

And there you saw the placard? — I saw a boy standing there who was holding up a newspaper.

A placard? — Yes.

Was the placard one announcing the identification of the body found at Dalston? — It was a child identified. I do not think it said that.

'Dalston Tragedy: Child Identified'? — I could not swear to what the words were there.

You bought an Evening News? — If that is the paper you have just passed me with that description in it, it was.

Before I go to it, did the paper you had seen at the gymnasium on the Monday afternoon – the first you had seen on that Monday afternoon – contain any reference to the tragedy? — It was the first I had seen.

Did you, at any time, see a newspaper which stated that the two women at Dalston Junction had given the information which had led the authorities to the discovery in the lavatory? — I cannot say that I had seen anything of that.

Can you say you had not? — Yes, I think I can say I had not

You think you can? — I think I can.

You have no recollection of seeing it? — I have no recollection of seeing it.

[Reading the passage from the *Evening News*.] Did you hear Miss Teahan, who was in the box, give her evidence? — I heard her.

Did you hear her say that attention had been called by two women – and that they called the attention of the authorities to it? — I did not catch it.

At all events, you saw no such announcement? — I had never seen it. This was the first paper that I saw.

Containing a description of a child? — Of a child.

This second newspaper that you saw, after you had seen the placard: in that newspaper, did you read that the body was then at the Hackney mortuary? — I could not say whether I read that or not. The only thing that struck me on the Monday afternoon was the description of a child.

That is what struck you on the Monday afternoon, in this evening newspaper? — No, it was in the morning paper.

Then I was wrong. The paper was Monday morning's paper. — I think it must have been that.

Containing a description of a child? — Yes. Of course, it said where the murder had been committed.

Did you, or not, read it? — I did read it, but I could not remember what

# Fourth Day – Saturday 16 December 1899.

I saw – except the one thing.

Did you not notice that the body of the child had been identified at the Hackney mortuary? — I could not say that I read that. I was too much upset.

You did not go to the Hackney mortuary? — I did not.

Did you go home to Bethune Road? — No, I went straight to London Bridge.

Will you just tell us how you returned, the journey that you took that night from Dalston Junction to London Bridge? — As I told you, I walked. I followed the omnibus line and walked to London Bridge Station.

On foot? — On foot.

You arrived at Dalston Junction with the intention of going to Bethune Road? — I had that intention.

But your mind was changed after seeing the placard and the newspaper, and you go to London Bridge? — Because, as I told you, I had not sufficient money to pay the omnibus and the train.

How long did it take you? — Oh, it is a good distance.

How long did it take you, in fact? — I could not say – over an hour.

And then you took the train to Croydon? — I had to wait somewhere.

Eventually you took the train to Croydon? — I took the train to Croydon.

Is it the fact that you came to your brother-in-law, Mr Simes's house, close upon 11.00 at night? — Yes. His house is some distance from the station.

And is it the fact that, when you arrived there, you first saw both him and your sister? — I saw him first.

Did you ask him anything? Do you remember speaking to him? — Yes.

Did you say to him, 'I am being hunted for murder, but I have not done it'? — If Mr Simes said so, I must have said it, but I could not tell you what I said.

I will not pain you further, Miss Masset, except to ask you if the account given by Mr Simes of the interview is a correct one, as far as you know. — Yes, I should say so.

Miss Masset, I must, in spite of my announcement, put one more question to you. With reference to your brother-in-law, first of all: on the night of 30 October, did you mention the name of Browning? — I really cannot say.

To the police, on the morning of 31 October, did you mention the name of Browning? — No, the question was not asked me what the name was. I should have given it had I been asked.

**Louise Masset**

# Masset.

**Louise Masset**

Do you mean you would have given the name if you had been asked? — Certainly.

And that the question was not asked you and therefore you did not give the name? — Certainly.

This case was heard upon three or four different occasions before the magistrates, was it not? — Yes.

Did you ever, to anybody connected with the police or with the prosecution, mention the name of Browning? — I have not seen any one of the police since.

Was yesterday the first announcement you had made with regard to the names of the two ladies to whom you handed the child? — No, I gave it to my solicitor long ago.

The first announcement in public with regard to the ladies to whom you gave the child? — Today is the one in public – at least, yesterday, when I gave it. I have had no opportunity of speaking to anyone.

Mr Justice BRUCE: Or to the police? — I had not seen any. I was not asked any questions from them in any way.

*Re-examined* by Lord COLERIDGE.

You made a statement, Miss Masset, to your brother-in-law? — I made a statement, yes.

That was a short statement? — A very short one. He went almost as soon as I reached his home. I could not remember what I said that night.

Then you made a statement to the police, in the form of answers to questions? — I did.

When the matter was placed in the hands of your solicitor, did you make a full statement of everything that you knew? — Yes, a written statement I gave him.

Did that statement include the name of these two people – Browning? — Yes, it did.

Is this the first day – and yesterday – the first time that you have given evidence in public? — The very first time.

I will ask you just one or two questions to clear up a matter connected with Dalston Junction. You have been asked about number 3 platform. Do you ever use number 3 platform on any occasion? — A very few.

Are those the occasions on which you returned? — Yes, from Hampstead Heath.

From your work? — Yes.

You get in at Loudoun Road, or get out at Loudoun Road? — No, I could not reach number 2 platform from Loudoun Road. Number 3 – number 2 is the one.

What occasions would you use number 3 platform? — I should come

# Fourth Day – Saturday 16 December 1899.

back from Hampstead Heath.

Is the usual round that you make to go to Hampstead Heath, and back from Loudoun Road? — Yes.

And on that round you would not use number 3 platform? — I should not. I should use number 4 and number 2.

Mr Justice BRUCE: When coming from where? — Returning from Hampstead Heath, I should use number 3.

Lord COLERIDGE: Your engagement with Madame Sonnenthal was earlier in the afternoon than that with Madame Haas? — Yes, 2.30 pm I should get there – from that to 5.00 pm.

Madame Sonnenthal's house is nearer Hampstead than Loudoun Road, is it not? — It is about the same, but the road goes downwards, and the trains go every half hour, and Hampstead every quarter.

That was the reason for going more often that way upon your weekly rounds? — Yes.

Mr Justice BRUCE: Did you use the Hampstead Heath Station or the other station in coming home? — I always used the Loudoun Road in coming home. I went to Hampstead because it is downhill to the house. If I used Loudoun Road I should have to walk up the hill to the house.

Lord COLERIDGE: You go to Dalston Junction, and not to Hampstead Heath? — Yes.

And you use number 2 platform? — Number 4.

You then pay your visits? — To Madame Sonnenthal.

Getting in at Loudoun Road? — Afterwards, when I have been to Mrs Haas.

Mr Justice BRUCE: Will you repeat that? — I go to Hampstead Heath Station, and then to Loudoun Road.

What platform do you use? — Number 4.

Lord COLERIDGE: Then you discharge your duties with Madame Sonnenthal and you go on to Madame Haas. Which is the nearest station to Madame Haas? — The Loudoun Road.

You get in at --? — Loudoun Road.

And, coming to Dalston Junction, you arrive at number 2? — At number 2.

How many times in your life do you suppose you have been at number 3 platform? — Fifty or sixty, I might have been.

You have been at number 3? — Yes, I should go from Hampstead on a Wednesday – I mean on a Saturday morning, not Wednesday, because I go on to Tottenham.

Do you ever wait at Dalston Junction? — I never had time. I started from home at 1.30 and took the train. It was ten minutes to the station, or a quarter of an hour to get my ticket and all.

**Louise Masset**

# Masset.

**Louise Masset**

At Dalston Station, did you ever wait? — No.

Mr Justice BRUCE: Do you change carriages at Dalston? — No, there is no necessity to do so.

Mr MATHEWS: Did you leave the carriage at Dalston? — No.

Lord COLERIDGE: There was no occasion to use the waiting room or lavatory? — No, none whatever. I have the ladies' houses to go to, and I always use them there, in preference.

You have been asked a question about what you asked Inspector Burch. As I understand, you were in doubt as to whether the first time that you met the Brownings was on 27 September or 4 October? — The fourth, yes.

Were you always sure you met them on 11 October? — Yes.

Speaking of the interval of time between the first and second visit, it would be a matter of a week or a fortnight, whether it was on 27 September or 4 October? — Yes.

Speaking of the interval between the visits? — Yes.

Mr Justice BRUCE: Then you say, 'I was always sure that I met the ladies on the fourth'. — No, my Lord, on the eleventh.

Lord COLERIDGE: But you are not sure as to whether the meeting prior to the eleventh was the Wednesday before, or two Wednesdays before, is that it? — Yes.

Were you in doubt as to whether it was the Wednesday before 11 October, or the Wednesday before that, when you put the question to Inspector Burch? — That was why I put the question.

As to which Wednesday it was? — Yes, that was why I put the question.

Have you discovered anything to enable you now to fix 4 October, and not 27 September? — Yes.

What is it? — My stepfather died on that day.

Mr Justice BRUCE: What day?

Lord COLERIDGE: 27 September, my Lord. — Yes.

Mr Justice BRUCE: Therefore you know it was not the twenty-seventh that you had seen those women? — That is so.

Lord COLERIDGE: My learned friend has alluded to the fact that, until it was suggested by Mrs Norris that they should part with you at the Birdcage, until then the arrangement was that they should accompany you to London Bridge Station. — It was so, sir.

In the ordinary course of events, what time would they arrive at London Bridge Station, starting as they did as you came by that bus, 1.20 pm? What time would you arrive at London Bridge? — Oh, I should arrive there in about three quarters of an hour from the Birdcage. I should arrive at London Bridge Station.

You therefore arrived at London Bridge Station half an hour before the

# Fourth Day – Saturday 16 December 1899.

appointment with the Brownings? — Yes.

You did not wish the Norrises to meet the Brownings? — Of course not.

Did you think you satisfactorily arranged that you should not? — Yes, of course. I should say goodbye to her at the station.

You mentioned to your sister, Mrs Cadisch, as long ago as May – as early as February – that you were thinking of making a change in the custody of your child? — Yes. When I took him to Mrs Norris, it was on the understanding that he was to remain three years at the most with her.

Mr Justice BRUCE: There is one question I wish to ask you. You told us that what Mr Simes said was correct, that he gave a true account of the interview; and he told us that you had told Mrs Simes that the child was going to France. — Not Mrs Simes. Mrs Cadisch.

Mr Justice BRUCE: 'My wife said that the child was going to France.' — Yes, but she might have heard it from my mother, or sister, or anyone – not from me.

You had not told her? — No.

Because he says, 'She told her the story. The story that was told was untrue.' And I asked him how he came to know that, and he said, 'Because my wife heard that the child was going to France'. — Yes, he did ask me that question, if it was true, that night. I did not tell him the fact at the time.

A Juror: I should like to know whether Miss Masset mentioned to the two women to whom she gave the child the fact that she was going to Brighton. — Yes, sir, I stated so in my evidence.

Has that come out? — Yes, that was the reason I could not go with them, because I was going by the 4.00 pm train to Brighton.

The two women to whom you gave the child knew you were going to Brighton? — Yes, by the 4.00 pm train.

Mr Justice BRUCE: Is there any other evidence, Lord Coleridge?

Lord COLERIDGE: No other evidence, my Lord.

Mr MATHEWS: Perhaps, with your Lordship's sanction, I may recall Miss Gentle?

Mr Justice BRUCE: Is it upon matters upon which she has not been cross-examined?

Mr MATHEWS: It is as to the statement as to the little child, and the name of the little child mentioned to Miss Gentle by Miss Masset herself.

Mr Justice BRUCE: Miss Gentle was asked whether the boy ever played with any child on the Green, and she said not.

Mr MATHEWS: That question was in my learned friend's cross-examination of Miss Gentle. Perhaps I may recall Miss Gentle in order

# Masset.

**Louise Masset**

that she could tell the jury what her version is as to the Christian name of the little child, and what she told the prisoner as to whence the little child came, and where the little child was in the habit of going to school.

Lord COLERIDGE: I cannot conceive upon what ground this application is made, when it is rebutting evidence, and when the case is more than finished. First of all, it is a matter of extreme rarity; and, in the next place, it is wholly novel, it has never arisen before, and it is immaterial to the issue.

Mr MATHEWS: My submission is that it becomes very material to the issue as to who the little child was playing with on Tottenham Green.

Mr Justice BRUCE: According to the evidence of Miss Gentle, the child was playing on Tottenham Green.

Lord COLERIDGE: The prisoner never said the child playing on Tottenham Green was Ada, or Winnie, to whom Miss Gentle was going to speak. She never suggested it, and, with regard to the time at which this is fixed specifically – that is, 11 October, on which date admittedly Miss Gentle, by her own testimony, was not at Tottenham Green – she would not be precise as to which day it was.

Mr MATHEWS: With regard to 11 October, my friend is inaccurate. She was there.

Lord COLERIDGE: She was not there at the time deposed to by the prisoner, as to when the little child was there.

Mr Justice BRUCE: I do not quite see what point Lord Coleridge made of that in his cross-examination.

Mr MATHEWS: Yes, he did make a point of it.

Mr Justice BRUCE: The fact of children playing in the presence of Miss Gentle ... but she denied it.

Lord COLERIDGE: My friend took an erroneous view of what the facts were, but it transpired, and it is quite clear, that Miss Gentle by her own evidence and testimony said that she was not present with the prisoner at Tottenham Green at the time the prisoner alleges the girl was there.

Mr MATHEWS: My submission is that, the prisoner having come and said this for the first time, that I should be allowed, with regard to this little girl, who was seen at Tottenham Green before 4 October, to show that on 11 October she said to the prisoner that that was a child known to Miss Gentle and spoken of by the little boy, Manfred, to Miss Gentle.

Mr Justice BRUCE: With reference to that, Lord Coleridge, I think the question in cross-examination was whether any girl had ever been spoken to. That was the matter in cross-examination, but Miss Gentle would not deny that.

Lord COLERIDGE: What was the allegation?

# Fourth Day – Saturday 16 December 1899.

Mr Justice BRUCE: I will look at my note as to what Miss Gentle was told.

Mr MATHEWS: She knew of it. She always said it, and she knew of the little girl, Millie.

Mr Justice BRUCE: Miss Gentle knew of the little girl, Millie. Miss Gentle never saw the little girl, but she knew of the little girl. I think, Mr MATHEWS, all that you are entitled to ask is whether Miss Gentle knew this little girl, Millie.

Lord COLERIDGE: She was never mentioned.

Mr MATHEWS: Then, my Lord, I would like to recall Miss Gentle, and ask that question.

Mr Justice BRUCE: You can ask that question; but, so as to dispose of this, is there no other question you are entitled to ask?

[Miss Gentle, who had been called in, was requested to leave the court, and did so.]

Mr MATHEWS: My submission, my Lord, is that I should be entitled to ask her whether she did not know a little girl whose first name was Winnie, and whether she did not mention that first name to the prisoner, and whether they had not a conversation as to that little girl attending kindergarten, and whether, in the course of that conversation, it was not suggested that Manfred should attend as well.

Mr Justice BRUCE: We are only concerned with the little girl with these ladies. That little girl, according to the prisoner, was not the little girl with the lady, and you are not entitled to contradict that. You are entitled to cross-examine, but not to contradict. You are entitled to ask her the question: whether Miss Gentle knew.

ELEANOR ELIZA GENTLE, recalled and examined.

Mr MATHEWS: Miss Gentle, will you answer the question I put to you simply? Is it the fact that you knew of the existence of any little girl called Millie? — No, sir, not Millie – Winifred.

Not Millie? — No.

Mr Justice BRUCE: You say, 'I knew of no little girl called Millie'? — No, sir.

Mr MATHEWS: May I submit this question?

Mr Justice BRUCE: Yes.

Mr MATHEWS: Had Miss Masset, or the little boy, ever told Miss Gentle that any little girl named Millie had played with him on Tottenham Green?

Lord COLERIDGE: I submit that any answer would be rebuttal, and the matter would have to be gone into again.

Mr Justice BRUCE: No, I think you must be content with the fact that

# Masset.

**Eleanor Gentle** she knew of no little girl called Millie.

*Cross-examined* by Lord COLERIDGE.

You knew that the little boy played at Tottenham Green? — Only on that afternoon – one afternoon, 4 October, when Miss Masset took him out – only on that occasion.

Will you tell me whether or not you knew that the little boy played at Tottenham Green? — On the one occasion I went to Tottenham Green, he played while his mother and I were sitting down. That was the only time that I had ever been to Tottenham.

How do you know? — Because I was there, and I know –

Mr Justice BRUCE: The learned counsel wants to know whether the boy played there on other occasions. — Whether he did the time his mother took him out on other occasions?

Do you know that? — If I was not there, I could not know.

Lord COLERIDGE: I will not ask you any more.

Mr Justice BRUCE: Do you know from the boy himself, or anything the mother told you, except on this occasion, that he played at Tottenham? — When he came back, he said he had been to the Green.

Do you know that he played there on any other occasion except this one? — No.

Is this the only occasion you ever heard of the boy playing at Tottenham? — That is so.

Never before? — No, sir, never. I wish to be quite truthful in what I say.

The court adjourned.

*******

# Fifth Day – Monday 18 December 1899.

## Closing Speech for the Prosecution.[143]

Mr MATHEWS summed up the case on the part of the prosecution. The prisoner had given evidence for her defence, but no other witness had been called on her behalf to corroborate her statement. The prisoner had, he submitted, shown herself a woman of enormous strength of will and strength of purpose. Would she stoop to falsehood in carrying out a design which she had formed? The case was one of great importance and of great human interest. He suggested that when they came to consider the case the jury should start with the question: Yes or no, did the prisoner travel to Brighton from London Bridge Station on the afternoon of Friday 27 October, by the train which was timed to leave at 4.00 pm, and which did leave at 4.01 pm, and which reached Brighton, according to the evidence, at 5.19 pm? Did she go by that train? If she did, she was falsely accused of this crime. If she did not go by that train he contended that she was in London between 4.00 pm and 6.00 pm on that afternoon, and that she was the authoress of this terrible crime. Was it by the 7.22 pm train on that evening that she travelled to Brighton? The learned counsel proceeded to refer to the evidence in the case given by the witnesses for the prosecution and to the prisoner's evidence. The two women to whom the prisoner said she handed over the child had never been seen by any mortal eye but hers. The two women and the little girl must have existed to the knowledge of someone, but no human eye saw them except the prisoner's. With regard to the clinker brick found near the dead body of the child, it might, no doubt, be truly said that it was like a great many other clinker bricks, but it was also true to say that it was similar to the clinker bricks in the front and back garden at number 29 Bethune Road, where the prisoner lived. The body of the child was found loosely covered with a black shawl. There was nothing unique about that shawl, and there were doubtless very many others like it. The assistant at the draper's shop at Stoke Newington stated that to the best of her belief the prisoner purchased a black shawl at that shop

**Mr Mathews**

---

143　This account of Mathews's closing statement is taken from *The Times*, 19 December 1899. The article was clipped by the governor of Holloway prison, Lieutenant-Colonel E. S. Milman, and retained by the Home Office in what is now TNA:PRO HO 144/1540/A61535/2.

# Masset.

**Mr Mathews** on 24 October. The learned counsel referred to the fact of the brown paper parcel containing the blue frock and coat worn by the child being found in the waiting room at Brighton Station between 3.00 and 3.30 on the afternoon of Saturday 28 October, and pointed out that the prisoner was at Brighton Station on that afternoon waiting for the train by which Mr Lucas was travelling and which was timed to arrive at 3.20 pm. The prisoner said that, when at a gymnasium in London on the afternoon of Monday 30 October, she saw a paragraph in a newspaper which made her suspect that the child whose body had been found was her child. He contended that if the prisoner was innocent she would, on seeing that paragraph, have at once gone to the address given by the two women at Chelsea and that she would afterwards have gone to the police and told them that she had handed her child to two women named Browning. The prisoner, however, did not do that, but went to give lessons to some of her pupils, and she was then in her usual spirits. In concluding his address, the learned counsel suggested that the motive for the alleged commission of the crime by the prisoner might have been that she was desirous of being married to Mr Lucas.

## Speech for the Defence.[144]

**Lord Coleridge** Lord COLERIDGE addressed the jury for the defence. He said that at last the opportunity had arrived for him to present the case for the prisoner to the jury. He should make no appeal to their passions. He should appeal to their calm, sober judgement. The case which he was going to present to the jury on behalf of the prisoner could be stated in a single sentence, and that was this – he asked them to believe her story. At the outset the case as presented by the Crown contained two grave and inherent improbabilities. The crime which the prosecution alleged that the prisoner committed showed by the nature of it that if she was the author of it she was a monster, inhuman, unnatural, cruel, and pitiless. Was that the character of the prisoner? The evidence of those who knew her was that she was a kind, sympathetic, affectionate woman. She was attached to children, and her attachment to them was specially demonstrated in her love for her own child. Many a woman had an illegitimate child and did not want to see any more of it. That was not the case here. The prisoner paid visits to the child increasing

---

[144] This account of Lord Coleridge's closing statement is taken from *The Times*, 19 December 1899. The article was clipped by the governor of Holloway prison, Lieutenant-Colonel E. S. Milman, and retained by the Home Office in what is now TNA:PRO HO 144/1540/A61535/2.

# Fifth Day – Monday 18 December 1899.

in frequency as the months and years rolled on – visits which it was not incumbent on her to pay. No one would have found fault with her if they had not been paid, and they could only have been prompted by maternal affection. Those were facts. One of the inherent improbabilities with which the case for the prosecution started was the sudden conversion of a kind and affectionate woman into a fiend and a monster without pity. The second of the grave improbabilities was that counsel for the prosecution attempted to fashion out of his own brain what he conceived might be a more or less adequate motive. There were many objects for which women might destroy their offspring, and first and foremost would be the desire to conceal their shame. That was not the case here. The fact that the prisoner was the mother of the child was known to her family, and she had been pardoned for her slip from virtue. The motive suggested by counsel for the prosecution was that the prisoner desired to marry Mr Lucas. But what evidence was there of that? Mr Lucas denied it. Mr Lucas was a young man, nineteen years of age, a Frenchman who was only residing in England temporarily – and the consent of his parents must be obtained before he could marry. The prisoner repudiated the suggestion and said that not for one moment did she think of matrimony. She told Mr Lucas of the existence of the child, and, if her object had been to destroy the child for the purpose of matrimony, did the jury think that she would have informed the person she desired to marry of the existence of the child, she, as the prosecution alleged, intending secretly to destroy its life? That suggested motive was the coinage of the brain of counsel for the prosecution and did not rest on any evidence. There was no motive connected with money. Money came regularly from the child's father. The prisoner paid Miss Gentle £1 17s a month regularly for taking care of the child. There was no evidence that there was the slightest difficulty with regard to money. There was no evidence that the money supplied by the child's father had come or was to come to a termination. He thought he had said enough to show that the motives which were usual for the commission of a crime of this nature were absent in this case. Lord Coleridge went on to point out that as long ago as February the prisoner expressed the opinion that a change in the custody of the child was desirable for the two reasons that the child had not adequate companionship and had not adequate education. Counsel for the prosecution discredited the existence of the two women to whom the prisoner said she handed over the child on the afternoon of 27 October at London Bridge Station. The jury must be well aware that there did exist in the metropolis and had existed baby farmers to whom in all innocence mothers handed over their children. The story was not an incredible one if in its main outlines experience told them it was

**Lord Coleridge**

# Masset.

**Lord Coleridge**

true. With regard to the purchase of a shawl by a woman on 24 October, he pointed out that the assistant at the draper's shop said she would not swear that the prisoner was the woman who purchased it. Similar shawls were sold by wholesale by hundreds and thousands. There was no evidence that the Gladstone bag contained a clinker brick. There was no evidence that the prisoner was at Dalston Junction on the afternoon of 27 October, or that she travelled by the 7.22 pm train to Brighton. He contended that Mrs Rees[145] was mistaken in identifying the prisoner as the woman she saw in the waiting room at London Bridge Station shortly before 7.00 on that evening. The prisoner and the child were never seen at Dalston Junction. There was no evidence that the prisoner was the person who deposited the brown paper parcel containing the child's clothes in the waiting room at Brighton Station. If the prisoner was the person who committed the crime, was it likely that she would have deposited the parcel in a place where it must be discovered? There were a hundred ways in which it might have been got rid of. If the object of the persons who committed the murder was to throw suspicion on the mother of the child, how could they do it better than by placing the parcel in the waiting room of the railway station at Brighton, they knowing that she had gone to Brighton? The jury had heard the prisoner give evidence for her defence, and there was not a single inaccuracy or inconsistency in her evidence. Mr Mathews, with all his art in cross-examination, was not only unable to shake her evidence, but she brought in continually fresh little matters which showed the probability of her story. The jury must only act on proof, and if they did that the prisoner would await their verdict without fear.

## Judge's Summing-Up.[146]

**Mr Justice Bruce**

Mr Justice BRUCE: Gentlemen of the Jury. This case is of the greatest importance – the greatest importance to the prisoner at the bar, and of the greatest importance to the public. You have given great attention to this case and I shall give you best assistance not by reading over the whole of the evidence to you, but giving you those points which most deserve your attention.

I shall begin by calling your attention to the evidence with reference to what occurred about 6.18 pm on the night of 22 October.[147] It was at 6.18

---

145  *Sic* in article. Should read 'Reece'.
146  Mr Justice Bruce's summing-up from TNA:PRO HO 144/1540/A61535.
147  *Sic* in transcript. A mishearing by the shorthand writer, or a mistake on the judge's part – should read '27 October'.

# Fifth Day – Monday 18 December 1899.

pm, according to the evidence, that the train, with Miss Teahan and Miss Biggs, arrived at Dalston Junction and, soon after the arrival of the train, they both went to the waiting room. Miss Teahan went to the passage leading to the water closet; she opened the door of the first water closet and, just as she was in the act of closing it, she saw a dark object on the floor, and then she saw a child's face.

Naturally she was shocked. She closed the door; she went into the waiting room and spoke to her companion, and then she spoke to a porter.[148] The ladies then left the station and they say they arrived at the lecture room, which they say is about five minutes from the station, about 6.30 pm. Therefore, we have it that the body was discovered a little after 6.18 pm and a little before 6.30 pm. Standing, the porter, fetched the inspector. The Inspector says he arrived there at 6.42 pm, and he says the body was slightly warm. Then the police were sent for; and Dr Fennell was sent for, but did not arrive there till nearly seven. He said the extremities were cold but the trunk was warm.

Now, questions were put to him and the other doctors in order to guide us as to when death occurred. Dr Fennell says that he thought death occurred within 1/2 an hour of his coming there. That we know could not have been; the ladies saw the body dead a little after 6.00 pm – or 6.18 pm. The doctor now states that he thinks he is mistaken in the statement he gave before the coroner.

Dr Jackman says that it is exceedingly difficult to form any opinion as to the time that death occurred, but within two hours; but we have the evidence of Mr Bond, who is a Fellow of the Royal College of Surgeons.

I am sure I do not wish to speak disrespectfully of the experience of general medical practitioners; they are a most adequate body of men, and, when they are called in to attend us or our children, they seldom fail to relieve our sufferings.

They are not in their ordinary experience accustomed to deal with questions of this kind, relating to appearances and conditions after death, and therefore Mr Bond said that he thought he was more competent to form an opinion on a question of this kind than Dr Fennell, and he said it is very difficult to say between one and four hours. From the evidence of Dr Bond, who, I venture to think, in your opinion will be the most trustworthy witness on this point – does not assist us[149] – it may have been one hour, or four.

Now, it is clear from the prisoner's own statement that the boy and she were at the London and Brighton Railway Station and that she did not

**Mr Justice Bruce**

---

148  In fact, it was Margaret Biggs who alerted the porter.
149  There is an omission in the transcript – this remark should probably read something like, 'the evidence of the other doctors, though given honestly, does not assist us'.

# Masset.

**Mr Justice Bruce**

leave until after the change of attendants. The change of attendants took place about 2.30 pm, and it was after the change of attendants that she went into the second waiting room, where she stayed about five minutes. After that, she said, she met the ladies, and then she waited for a few minutes, but found that they were gone. So she must have been with the boy some little time after 2.30 pm.

The time occupied from Dalston Station to London Bridge Station is just under half an hour – about twenty minutes – and therefore it means that the boy could not have been taken so as to arrive there before 3.00 pm: probably after 3.00 pm. Therefore the murder – because I do not think you can doubt that the murder took place – must have taken place after 3.00 pm and probably before 6.00 pm.

If you believe Mrs Reece's evidence – I shall have to call your attention to her evidence on another point – Mrs Reece says that she saw the boy at the London Bridge Station with his mother about 3.10 pm, and, if so, it is difficult to suppose that they could arrive at Dalston Junction, or that the boy could have arrived at Dalston Junction, at 3.30 pm at the earliest.

Now, in the first water closet, on the floor, there was found the body of the child – as I have said – at 6.18 pm, or near that. The body was stripped of every vestige of clothing which the child had worn when at the London and Brighton Station which was left upon him.[150] He had been suffocated. Death had been caused by suffocation, and, as one of the medical men who made the post mortem said, there were marks on the mouth and nose as if there had been pressure over the mouth and nose. The face was so battered as to be beyond recognition. You will remember Miss Gentle's evidence. She said, 'I identified the body, but not by the face'.

According to the evidence that was given us in great detail by one of the medical men who conducted the post mortem examination, there were five wounds on the head and face, and four bruises. Now, it is difficult – I venture to think you will find it difficult – to avoid coming to the conclusion that the clothing had all been scrupulously removed and the face battered in the way it was in order to escape identification. The murderer, whoever the murderer was, had taken away the clothes and had battered in the face in the hope that the body might not be identified. There was, by the body, on the floor, a brick which was produced, and you probably will have little doubt that that brick was used by the murderer to inflict the wounds and the bruises on the face and head. That violence had been used was, I think, apparent from the fact that the brick had a piece broken off it, the larger portion of the brick lying on one side

---

150    *Sic* in transcript.

Mr Justice Bruce
*Author's collection*

# Fifth Day – Monday 18 December 1899.

of the child's head, and the smaller portion of the brick lying on the other side of the child's head.

There is one other matter I should mention with reference to the body. Hard and depraved as the heart of the person must have been who committed that murder, whoever it was, yet at the last moment there was, I think, [had] some touch of human feeling. It seems to have been repellent to the murderer to leave that little child lying stark, and so a shawl was thrown over its body. A brick, a shawl, and the body – those are the three matters we have to deal with. No bit of clothing, save the shawl, to assist in identification.

I think you will probably be of opinion – and now I have used it once I shall probably have to use it frequently – just let me remind you that all questions of fact you will have to deal with, and remember you are the judges of fact. With you alone rests the decision of fact, and it is my duty, presiding in this court, to rule that, on questions of fact, you are the supreme judges, and that I am endeavouring simply to put the case to you, and am pointing out to you the various matters of fact. If I express any opinion on questions of fact to you, you must come to your own opinion on the questions of fact.

That brick was used, I think you will say, for inflicting those wounds and I think you will also say that the brick was brought there by the murderer.

The evidence is that there are no bricks about the railway station. You would not expect to find that brick in a waiting room or in a water closet. It must have been brought by the murderer, and for the purpose of using it, and so the shawl was laid over the body by the person who committed the murder. The body was stripped of all its clothing, and, somehow, the clothing must have been disposed of. I venture to think that you will think for the purpose of avoiding identification.

The brick – I think you will be of the opinion – was brought there to be used. Where does a brick come from? A clinker brick is not a very uncommon thing. No doubt there are many places in London where clinker bricks are to be found, but still one cannot avoid attaching some significance to the evidence that at 29 Bethune Road there were clinker bricks like the clinker brick which was found in the lavatory. No evidence to show that it was taken from that place; but there is the coincidence, and when you come to deal with matters of coincidence, you must not look at it by itself but with other coincidences.

The shawl – it had no distinctive mark on it. If it had a distinctive mark on it, it would not have been used by the person who took away the clothing in order to avoid identification. But it was a black shawl – according to Mr Mooney, who sold the shawl, and who carries on

**Mr Justice Bruce**

# Masset.

**Mr Justice Bruce**

McIlroy's business – not an ordinary patterned shawl. A person going to the wholesale warehouse could get one like it, but at the same time not an ordinary shawl.

Miss Maud Clifford says that she sold a shawl – not the shawl, because it is a black one, but one like that – on 24 October, at McIlroy's shop, at 161 High Street, Stoke Newington. Is she correct in that? That the shawl was sold on 24 October, I venture to think, you will have no doubt, because the copy invoice [shows] that a shawl answering the description of this shawl was sold on 24 October. To whom was that sold? Miss Clifford says, 'I am nearly certain the prisoner was the woman'. Now, the question of identity. It is always difficult to judge of the accuracy of the evidence of witnesses simply by the expression she uses. I think it was said by one of the counsel who addressed you that it is the persons who are most positive get most wrong. Miss Clifford says she is nearly certain. You may judge of the accuracy of her evidence not merely by the expression, but more by her conduct. 'Would you know the woman?' She is taken on 4 November, ten days after she sold the shawl, and there she is shown fourteen women, and she is asked if she can pick out the woman to whom she sold the shawl. She does pick out the person, and she says, 'That is the woman'. Of course, for all matters of identification, it is important that the test should be fairly applied – that there should be no help from the police – but there is this to be said about the various questions put about the help in identification.

Mrs Worley was called in. She was unable to identify the prisoner. Although the police were fair, at all events, in the way in which they conducted the test, Mrs Worley was not able to identify the prisoner. Miss Maud Clifford says she did identify the prisoner, and she said she is the woman to whom she sold the shawl. Now, if she is the person who sold the shawl, it is not conclusive evidence, because it is only like the shawl she sold. If it stood alone, you might regard it with some doubts – but it does not stand alone.

Now I come to the fact that the child was stripped, and that the clothing was gone. It must have taken some little time to have stripped the child of its clothing. Some of its clothing was spoken to. The red cap, the necktie, and all the smaller articles of underclothing – we have no trace. We do not know what became of them. They were disposed of in some way or other, but they left no clue. We can only trace the coat and the frock worn on 27 October.

On the following day, 28 October, a brown paper parcel was found in the ladies' waiting room at 3.30 in the afternoon. It was not there at 3.00 pm. How did it get there? No one was seen to put it there. Now, the remarkable thing about this parcel is that it is the same piece of paper

# Fifth Day – Monday 18 December 1899.

**Mr Justice Bruce**

– or a portion of the piece of paper – in which a change of clothing was wrapped up by Miss Gentle on 27 October; but the underclothing had all gone, and there is wrapped up – in the same piece of paper – the coat and the frock that the child wore when last seen at the London-Brighton station. The contents had been removed. The coat and frock had been put inside and wrapped up in the same piece of paper.

The prisoner was at the Brighton Station, London and Brighton line, between 3.00 pm and 3.30 pm. She went to meet the train, and it was due at 3.20, and it was about that time that the parcel mysteriously disappeared[151] at the London and Brighton station.

Now, let me deal with the contents of this. It contains the frock and the coat, but the frock is altered. The band of the frock was gone; the braid was gone; the collar and the cuffs were gone. The turndown collar was gone. I think it was a fawn turndown collar. The cuffs were gone, the brass buttons were gone. For what purpose were these taken off? You will probably be of opinion that they were taken off to destroy identity. It was suggested – and one must attend to every suggestion that is made – that those strange ladies who took the child away, in order to divert suspicion from themselves, may have sent or got this parcel off to Brighton because they heard she was going to Brighton, or they may have got some friend to place it in the waiting room at this critical period. If those ladies had sent this parcel for the purpose of attracting suspicion to the mother, why did they take off the buttons? If sent for the purpose of putting suspicion on the mother, I think the buttons would have been left on. There again, I am only anxious to put before you matters for you to consider. But do not you think that the buttons would have been left on?

It would have taken some little time to have removed the buttons, and cuffs, and the collar. I fail to see, if the object was to attract attention to the mother, why the person would place these articles of clothing at the Brighton rooms.

If, on the other hand, the prisoner herself had taken those things to Brighton, she may have been able to dispose of the small articles of clothing, and, having destroyed their identity, these things might safely be left in the waiting room.

It is said by Lord Coleridge, 'Might not she have thrown them into the sea, or done a hundred things?' That, gentlemen, might always be said, but in these cases people do not always do the wisest things. It constantly happens that persons act foolishly, and that it is by reason of their acting foolishly that they give themselves away.

---

151  *Sic* in transcript. Probably the shorthand writer's error – the word must have been 'appeared'.

# Masset.

**Mr Justice Bruce**

Now, gentlemen, I have dealt with those three things – the brick, the shawl, the clothing. Those are the three questions in this case to which you must give your careful attention. Now comes the question – at what time did the prisoner go down to Brighton? She says she went down by the 4.00 pm train. Mrs Reece says she saw her in the refreshment room[152] at 7.00 pm, or about 7.00 pm, and she was there until about 7.15 pm on the Friday. Now, Mrs Reece's evidence is important, and I will call your attention to a portion of it. She saw the prisoner, you know, on two occasions, according to her evidence. She saw her about 2.40 pm at first – I do not know that the exact time is admitted – but the prisoner does not deny speaking to and seeing Mrs Reece on that afternoon, although she says Mrs Reece is wrong in saying that she was so long as Mrs Reece says she was. She says she was only there five minutes. Mrs Reece says she first observed the little boy at 2.55 pm. Then she looked at the prisoner to see what the prisoner was doing to the little boy. 'I noticed the little boy going backwards. That attracted my attention to the prisoner. I saw him again going sideways. About a quarter of an hour afterwards, I spoke to him. During the whole of that time the prisoner and the boy remained in the waiting room.' Then: 'As I put the key in the cupboard, he looked at me. I said, "What are you grizzling about?" I said, "There is nothing here for little boys". He looked up to me, and I said to the prisoner, "He is a fine little fellow. How old?" She said, "Four next April". I said to the prisoner, "What is he fretting about?" The prisoner answered, "His nurse". I looked intently at the prisoner. She looked at me. She said, "Perhaps he is hungry. I will get him a cake." She said, "Have you a refreshment bar?" I said, "Yes, to the left as you go out". She took up something in her hand and went out of the bar[153]. That, I think, was between 3.05 pm and 3.10 pm.'

The prisoner does not deny that, but she denies altogether that she said anything about the nurse – but that does not become very material. The prisoner was there in the afternoon, and, beyond question, she [Mrs Reece] was right in saying that the prisoner was there. She had a conversation with her, and with the boy.

Now comes a matter which is in dispute with Mrs Reece's evidence. 'I saw the prisoner again about 6.54 the same evening, in the lavatory. She washed in the middle basin opposite the looking glass. She was drawing up her sleeves. I turned on the tap for her. I saw her reflection in the glass, and I recognised the lady who had been there with the boy in the afternoon. I gave her a towel and went out to make my tea. I returned to get some sugar from the cupboard, and she asked me when the next

---

152  *Sic* in transcript. Mr Justice Bruce meant the waiting room, not the refreshment room.
153  *Sic* in transcript. Again, Mr Justice Bruce meant the waiting room.

# Fifth Day – Monday 18 December 1899.

train for Brighton was. She said, "Have you a clothes brush?" I said, "Yes. Can I brush you down?" She said, "No". I did not see if she used it. I saw her go out of the waiting room door. That was about 7.18 pm. She had a brown paper parcel – not a tidy looking parcel – and she went out.' If it be true that at that time the underclothing of the child had been taken out of the parcel – the frock and the coat put in – it may have been an untidy looking parcel.

Mr Justice Bruce

Now, Mrs Reece had seen her in the afternoon, and, beyond all doubt, Mrs Reece is right in saying that she saw her in the afternoon. Is she right in saying that she saw her in the evening? Lord Coleridge suggests that she picked her out as the woman she saw in the afternoon, not in the evening; but Mrs Reece said at the time that she recognised her as the same woman she saw in the afternoon. If Mrs Reece is right, it is important because it shows that the prisoner was in London after the time the murder was committed, and that her statement that she went down to Brighton by the 4.00 pm train was untrue.

Now, when does she arrive in Brighton? The 7.00 pm train[154] arrives at Brighton at 9.18 pm, I think – shortly after 9.00 pm – and she arrived at Brighton with two packages. It is quite true nobody sees the brown paper parcel. She has her Gladstone bag and a package which Alice Riall, the chambermaid at the hotel, describes as a plaid. 'When she came, she had two packages. That was all I saw – a little plaid bound round with leather.'

According to the prisoner's own statement, that seems to have been a mackintosh – but there was every opportunity for a brown paper parcel being placed inside. Whether that was so, we do not know. She had a Gladstone bag and this mackintosh. She had opportunities in the train of putting the brown paper parcel inside the mackintosh, wrapping the mackintosh round the brown paper parcel. We do not know how it was done.

Mr Findlay spoke to her coming in with two parcels and coming in just about 9.45 pm, which would be right – the hotel was about five minutes' walk from the station, and, if she went to the sea before going to the hotel, she would have time to go to the sea and come back by 9.45 pm. She said she went down by the 4.00 pm train. She booked her bag; she went to Mutton's and had food there; and then went about looking at shops, and then went back to the station, getting to the hotel about 9.45 pm.

Now, one important question will be, you know – what was she doing between the hours of 3.00 pm and 6.00 pm? No one saw her. She gives no account of what became of her between 3.00 pm and 6.00 pm, or

---

154   *Sic* in transcript. Should read: '7.22 pm train'.

# Masset.

**Mr Justice Bruce**

between 3.00 pm and 7.00 pm.

Now I want to direct attention to the prisoner's conduct before and after the time when the child's death occurred. Beyond all question, she represented that she was going to take him abroad. She says that is an excuse made to spare Mrs Norris and Miss Gentle pain, because Miss Gentle was very fond of the boy and she would have been distressed if he had been removed to another nurse in England. Representations were made to Mrs Cadisch, her own sister, that she was going to take the boy to a cousin of its father in France; and also Mrs Simes, her sister, said that she had declared that the child was going to France, and indeed she said that the prisoner had taken it to France: so that all her relations, so far as we know, Miss Gentle, Mrs Norris, and her sister and Mrs Cadisch both believed that the child was gone there.[155]

Now, she says that the representations made to Mrs Cadisch were made in order that she might go to Brighton with Lucas; but she had gone the previous Whitsuntide to Brighton with Lucas. apparently without Mrs Cadisch knowing anything about it.

The Prisoner: My Lord, I did. I said I had been to Littlehampton and Mr Lucas to Brighton at Whitsuntide.

Mr Justice BRUCE: Well, that may explain it. but her statement now is that she made the statement to her sister, Mrs Cadisch, that Mrs Cadisch might not know that she was going to Brighton with Lucas and that her sole object was to keep the secret that she was going with Lucas. Were these representations made for that reason alone? You have to ask yourselves – was the story one which would account for the absence of the child? If the body had not been identified, would the falsehoods have ever been discovered?

The Prisoner: Yes, my Lord. The father and his friends knew all about it, and his friends would have asked questions about it.

Mr Justice BRUCE: That is a matter for you, gentlemen, to consider.

A Juror: We have no evidence, my Lord, upon it.

Mr Justice BRUCE: We have no evidence upon it at all. So far as we know, all the prisoner's friends thought it was going to France. You will remember there was a conversation on the Monday morning with her sister, Mrs Cadisch, who asked what sort of a passage they had had. The prisoner said that they had had a passage better one way than the other. Mrs Cadisch forgot which way it was. And the prisoner wrote a letter to Mrs Norris in which she said that she had had a bad passage. Eudore Lucas was the only person who knew the truth, and he knew nothing of the place of residence of the child; and I suppose Eudore Lucas might be trusted to keep the secret.

---

155 A muddled sentence, but sic in transcript.

# Fifth Day – Monday 18 December 1899.

Now, I do not propose to enter into her relations with Lucas. It seems that it only supplies the possible motive if she committed the crime; but it seems to me vain to seek for any motive. No motive was sufficient. It is enough for us to enquire what she did it for.

Now I propose to deal with the account given by herself on 4 October. On that day she met two strange ladies in Tottenham Green; perhaps I had better give her own account of it.

'There were two perfect ladies sitting on the seat; the first thing they said was, "Is this the little boy my daughter has spoken so many times about?" They made a movement and I sat down beside them. They saw I had no wedding ring; they said, "Are you married?" I said, "No". One of the next things they said was how was it they had not met me before, as I had seen their little girl. I explained I was only there on Wednesdays; they explained that they had brought the little girl from Philip Lane, where they lived, and used to leave her to play. They enquired where my child was living. I said it was a nurse child. The manner in which the child spoke showed that his education was not attended to. I had mentioned that more than once to my sister, Mrs Cadisch. The ladies spoke very nicely; they began talking about themselves; the older lady was about forty-five, not dressed in weeds, but she told me she had been a widow about six months. The younger was about twenty-seven or twenty-eight. They told me their name was Browning. They thought of taking a house; they were then under terms and would like to have two children to bring up with their little girl. The young lady was to have a kind of kindergarten, but it was not decided where they would go. People were rather difficult to get who would pay. I said, "What about terms?" They said £12 a year – it was to be paid in advance because they wanted money. I said I could not make up my mind in a hurry like that. They were to look about and see what house they could get, and let me know next time. I did not mention this to Miss Gentle. It would have been a sore point with her.

'On the following Wednesday, I went to Tottenham Green as I had an extra lesson in the morning and my afternoon was free. I took the train and omnibus from Dalston Junction to Seven Sisters Corner: that was about ten minutes' walk from Miss Gentle's and three minutes from Tottenham Green. I waited till the boy was dressed and then went out with him. I went down Clyde Road with the boy and met the ladies; the older lady told me she was looking out for a house at Chelsea. I thought it was rather far off. She asked me if I had decided if I would let her have the boy. I then made arrangements to meet her if there was no change in her plans. She wanted time to move in, and I wanted time to give notice to Miss Gentle. The child would not go in the train – we can get

Mr Justice Bruce

# Masset.

**Mr Justice Bruce**

to London Bridge without going by the train. I was in the Clyde Road and turned into the West Green Road – or West Grove Road[156] – and met Miss Gentle.'

No other person was with her when she saw the ladies, except the little boy. She met them alone. She says she arranged with these ladies that they should meet her at London Bridge Station.

She made no arrangement to go and see their house; she was content with the ladies' statement; she said they were attractive people; she was content and had no suspicion.

On the twenty-seventh she went to London Bridge. Now, the question has been put once or twice, why at London Bridge? It is very difficult to say why they should meet at London Bridge. These ladies were coming from Chelsea; but they did meet at London Bridge and the prisoner was there. 2.00 was the time appointed for meeting; she was there some time before, and she went to London Bridge and there, she said, she met the ladies. She waited for them for some time, and waited till 2.30, when the change of attendants in the waiting room took place.

When the second attendant came, she left that waiting room and went into the other waiting room, where, she says, she went to see if the ladies were there; and they were not there; and then she met them on the platform. 'I met them outside the general waiting room on the platform. I said, "Well, I have waited long enough". Mrs Browning said, "It has taken us one and a half hours to get here". She said she had no knowledge of the locality. We then went into the general waiting room near the waiting room where we had last been. I said, "It is a great nuisance your coming so late". It had been arranged that I should go with them to Chelsea. I had no idea how long it would take to go to Chelsea.'

Now, that seems not unimportant. She is arranging for a place for the boy to go to. She meets the ladies at London Bridge, and it was arranged that she should go to Chelsea. One would think the very first thing she would have done would be to go with them. That was why she was annoyed at their being late. Why did she not still go with them to Chelsea? Why should she be obliged to go by the 4.00 train? She had the evening before her; if it had been arranged, why did she not go?

'I went on, saying I intended going to Brighton by the 4.00 train; I did not see how I could get back in time. Mrs Browning said, "Well, you know he will be all right – you can trust him to us". They appeared trustworthy. I did not think they were going --.[157] I gave them £12. I

---

156 Mr Justice Bruce had difficulty deciphering his own handwriting. He had correctly written 'West Green Road' in his notes.

157 The defendant's testimony had been, 'I did not think they were going to do what they have done'. Mr Justice Bruce, keeping his notes, recorded, 'I did not think they were going -- [fit of sobbing]'.

# Fifth Day – Monday 18 December 1899.

**Mr Justice Bruce**

asked for a receipt. Mrs Browning said she had none ready, but she would go to the refreshment room and see if they would let her have a pen and ink. Miss Browning said would not he have a cake? The two ladies went with the child in the direction of the refreshment room. I went for my bag; I went nearer the window to follow their movements. They must have turned down one of the passages and not gone into the refreshment room. I waited a few minutes. I took my bag to the door of the refreshment room; then I walked round outside the station and back to the refreshment room to see if they had returned, but did not see them. I had not the slightest suspicion at that time. I had their names and addresses. It was the third time I had seen them.'

Well, now, let us consider that, gentlemen. These were ladies to whom she paid £12. She knew nothing of their address, except what they told her. They left her without giving her an opportunity of saying goodbye to her boy when he left to go into the refreshment room, and when, in a few minutes, she returned, they were gone. It was said by the learned counsel – who addressed you with great ability on behalf of the prisoner – that that was just the thing a baby farmer would do. But is there no suspicion in the mind of the mother at that time? However, she says £12 was paid, and she says, 'My boy was taken away without my having the opportunity of saying goodbye to him'.

She knows the address – 45 King's Road, Chelsea – and yet she is perfectly happy and contented, and goes down to Brighton, as she says, by the 4.00 pm train, with no suspicions of these people whatever, and without the opportunity of saying goodbye to the boy.

Then, she says, she goes by the 4.00 pm train. It has been said by the learned counsel who addressed you on behalf of the prisoner – with reference to the prosecution – that there is absence of information to show if the prisoner went to Dalston Junction, how she went there, and how she came back. In these crowded thoroughfares, there is so much traffic that we lose sight of her altogether from the time she leaves the refreshment room at London Bridge Station until 7.00 pm. Miss Worley[158] says she comes back, but she is lost sight of again until she is seen at Brighton, at the hotel, at 9.45 pm.

Now, gentlemen, I want you to follow what took place at Brighton. She spends the evening at Brighton. She spends the Saturday and Sunday at Brighton, and she comes up on the Sunday evening, and, on the Monday, she first of all writes a letter giving an account of her voyage to Mrs Cadisch's sister. She tells her about the voyage, and then she goes out in the course of the afternoon to her pupils. Then she takes one of the pupils

---

158   *Sic* in transcript. Mrs Reece was the witness whose sighting of the defendant was being referred to.

# Masset.

**Mr Justice Bruce**

to a gymnasium at Baker Street in the afternoon. While there, she saw a paragraph relating to the child. She says, 'I went to the gymnasium at Baker Street. I first saw a paragraph in the papers describing the child.' That must be a paragraph describing a dead child. What did she do? Did she enquire if it was her own child?

The Prisoner: I did not know it was my child.

Mr HUTTON: The prisoner said, 'describing a child', and the newspaper said, 'a child'.

Mr Justice BRUCE: 'A child?' My note is, 'describing the child'. She went back with her pupil to the house. She went to Dalston Junction where she saw a placard announcing that the child's body had been identified, and she bought the *Evening News,* which she read. Now, the paragraph in the *Evening News* from which she read was this:

'Dalston Murder. Identification of the Poor Little Victim. Child of a French Woman who took him away from his Nurse on the day of the Murder. The victim of the Dalston murder was identified today and the police now have an important clue. Shortly before noon a middle-aged woman, respectably dressed, walked into the mortuary at Hackney, where half a dozen bodies were lying, and said she might be able to identify the five year old boy who was so foully murdered last Friday evening. The woman explained that for about five years she had nursed and reared a fair haired child, brought to her by a French lady.'

I need not read the rest. Her suspicions, before roused, were now reduced to a certainty that it was her child when she read that – whatever suspicions she had before. What does she do? Having regard to her conduct, is she innocent or guilty? What would be the conduct of an innocent person? What would be the conduct of a guilty person? If innocent, I venture to think that her emotions would impel her to seek justice for the foul outrage done to her child. If guilty, her security would be the motive to her conduct. She left her child, according to her own account, on the Friday with two ladies in whom she had confidence. She knew their names; she knew their address: Brownings, 45 King's Road, Chelsea.

On the Monday afternoon, or on the Monday evening, she finds information which makes her certain that her child had been brutally murdered. Surely the first impulse would have been at once to inform the police that she had given the child over to Brownings of 45 King's Road, Chelsea, and to demand that justice should be done, the person arrested, or enquiries made at once. How does she act? She does not go home? She says this: 'When I read what was in the *Evening News*, I was convinced it was my child. I began to suspect in the afternoon. From what I read in the *Evening News*, my suspicions ripened into certainty.

# Fifth Day – Monday 18 December 1899.

**Mr Justice Bruce**

I knew I was the last person who had seen the child until he was taken away. I knew I was the person to be suspected. I had told an untruth. I did not go home. I went to Mr Simes to ask his advice, because he was English. I walked to London Bridge and took [the] train to Croydon.'

'I was the last person who had seen the child.' 'I knew I should be suspected.' 'I had told an untruth.'

If the last person seen with the child, the more reason was there, perhaps, for giving information to the police with a description of the persons she had handed over the child to; if the Misses Brownings were the persons to whom she handed the child, the police should know. And we are dealing, gentlemen, with the prisoner as not an unintelligent person but one who must have known that the only way of deepening the suspicion upon the last person who had seen the child was not to give information to the police of the persons into whose hands the child had fallen.

She does not go home. She walks to London Bridge. She then takes the train to Croydon. She sees Mr Simes, her brother-in-law. 'She said, "Can I speak to you?" I said, "Yes, what is it?" She said, "I am being hunted for murder, but I have not done it". I said, "The child found at Dalston is not yours, is it?" She said, "Yes".'

The expression 'I am being hunted for murder, but I have not done it' is hers. I do not know what there was in the paragraph which led her to suppose that she was hunted for murder. She might suppose she was a suspected person. One would have thought that the first thing she would have said to her brother would have been, 'My poor child has been murdered; I want you to help me to find out the person, and to bring to justice the persons who have taken over the child and deceived me. I had given over the child to them. Let not one moment be lost, so that these persons may be traced and not escape justice.'

But her own thought apparently was first for her own safety. 'I am being hunted for murder; I have not done it.' She said she bought a paper giving a description from which she was sure it was her child.

'Then she made a statement to me [Mr Simes] that she handed the child over to two women at London Bridge Station, and afterwards that she went in the 4.00 pm train to Brighton, where she arrived a little before 6.00 pm and went to a restaurant --' Mutton's, I think '-- for something to eat, and that afterwards she went to the Temperance Hotel --' Lucas's '-- and stayed on the Friday and Saturday nights.'[159]

She spoke of the night before her visit to Brighton. With regard to the morning, the witness says, 'I left my residence early on the morning of

---

159    Mr Justice Bruce had forgotten that the hotel was Findlay's, not Lucas's

# Masset.

**Mr Justice Bruce**

the thirty-first --' that is, Cadisch's, 39 Bethune Road[160] '-- leaving the prisoner with my wife.'

In cross-examination, the witness [Mr Simes] said, 'I told her, "If you tell me the truth about it," whatever it was, I would do my best for her. She said, "How do you think I could murder my own child?" She told me they had found out from her it was a nurse child, that they were setting up a house in the King's Road, Chelsea.' Then she said that they agreed to take £12 a year, and that she agreed to hand over the child to them at London Bridge Station on the Brighton railway.

Then there is this curious fact in her own evidence. She says, 'To Mr Simes I did not mention the names of Browning on 30 October'. Mr Simes was her own relation. She went to him because he was an Englishman, having married her sister. He was a businessman – an auctioneer, a capable person, and yet she does not mention a word about the name of Browning or give him any clue beyond mentioning the King's Road, Chelsea. Nothing was done in the way of informing the police that these ladies were the people who had been living at 45 King's Road, Chelsea. It is very difficult to suppose – if she at that time had informed Mr Simes that these ladies were named Browning, and where they lived, at 45 King's Road, Chelsea, knowing that address – that means would not have been at once taken to inform the police. Nothing of the kind was done. Therefore, it is, gentlemen, I invite you to consider her conduct before, at the time, and after the murder was committed.

Now we have Inspector Forth, who was at the police station when she was charged, after she had made the statement, which is in substance what I have read from the evidence of Mr Simes. The charge was read to her. 'She said, "Cannot I say something to clear myself?" I said, "Yes, if you like". Mr Simes said, "You had better not say anything now".' And the prisoner said no more. Probably it was good advice as far as she was concerned. Where an accused is charged with crime, it is the practice of the police generally, and it is a wise practice, not to invite them to make a statement, because they may thoughtlessly and carelessly make statements which afterwards may prejudice their case. But where the case is a case of this kind – where the person charged with the crime was last seen with the child, and she has handed over the child to other persons, it is reasonable to suppose that a statement might be made.

But no statement is made to the police. The importance of it at the time is this – that if there was any truth in the story, the police could have been put upon the track of these persons. But no information was given to the police. That is one of the matters which you must consider in coming to

---

160 Mr Justice Bruce has confused the address; the witness leaves Stretton Road in Croydon, and the Cadisches lived at 29 Bethune Road.

# Fifth Day – Monday 18 December 1899.

a conclusion upon which side your verdict ought to be given.

Mr HUTTON: There was a statement made to Burch.

Mr Justice BRUCE: Yes, but not the name of the person.

Mr MATHEWS: Not the name, but the address.

Mr Justice BRUCE: Not the name. I will read the statement, if you like, which she did make to Burch. Burch said to her this: 'We are police officers. I said, "You have a child which you took away from the nurse last Friday. Can you account for it to me?" She said, "I last saw my child, Manfred Louis Masset, aged three and a half, on Friday at London Bridge Railway Station waiting room. On that occasion two women gave me the address 45 King's Road, Chelsea. I gave them £12, most of it in gold, to take care of it. I had seen them at Tottenham Green four Wednesdays back. I had the child with me then. They first spoke to me. By their conversation, they found out it was a nurse child. They said they were setting up a home – would I mind letting them have him for £12 a year? At first, I did not agree with it. I met them there again next Wednesday – I had the child with me then. I decided then to leave it with them for that sum. I then arranged to meet them at London Bridge at 2.00 pm on Friday last at the Brighton Railway refreshment room, and I left. I met them there. Before going there, I went into another waiting room ..."' And so on. '"There was one attendant there. Another one came and relieved her while I was there. We left to go to the refreshment room. They took the boy with them ... I waited two or three minutes. They never came back. I have not seen my child since."' She then said to Burch that the ladies gave the address 45 King's Road, Chelsea, though she does not state the name of the person.

Now, gentlemen, I have called your attention to the main facts of this case. I now leave the case in your hands. It is for you to say what verdict you arrive at; you will not, I am sure, come to an opinion without carefully weighing the whole of the evidence to which you have already given attention. You will agree with me, I am sure, that the matter is one which requires your careful and anxious attention. Important as I have said it is in the interest of the public; important as it is in the interest of the prisoner; it is for the prosecution to make out the case against the prisoner to satisfy you that the prisoner is guilty of the crime with which she is charged, and not for the prisoner to prove her innocence.

On the other hand, when I say 'prove the crime', of course, there is no such thing as certainty in human disputes, but the crime must be proved with that reasonable certainty that you would agree upon in the affairs of life; and, however painful the duty may be, if you come to the conclusion, having regard to the whole of the facts, as men of the world and reasonable men, looking at the facts fairly and impartially – if you

**Mr Justice Bruce**

# Masset.

**Mr Justice Bruce** can come to no other conclusion than that she committed the crime, it will be your duty to say so, however painful it may be.

If on the other hand you come to the conclusion, after hearing the facts of the case, that the case is not proved against the prisoner, then it will be your pleasing duty to say, 'Not guilty'.[161]

A Juror: The jury have requested me to ask if the prisoner will state why, if she was going to this hotel, she went to Mutton's restaurant. She brings no evidence as to that.[162]

Mr Justice BRUCE: I would rather not put the question. The practice of interrogating prisoners, until recently, was not allowed, and I would rather we did not interrogate her now because she has given her statement, and she has been cross-examined. I should prefer, gentlemen, that you should find your verdict on the evidence already given and not interrogate her further.

A Juror: It struck me that there might be something on the Gladstone bag which traces its having been in the luggage office. Is there a label?

Mr Justice BRUCE: If you like, you can look at it.

A Juror: There may be something stuck on – a gummed label, or a check on the bag.

Mr Justice BRUCE: You can look at the Gladstone bag – that is in evidence – but further evidence I should not like to ask the prisoner to adduce.

# The Verdict.

[At 4.54 pm, the jury retired. They returned into court at 5.23 pm.]

The Clerk of Arraigns (Mr Read): Gentlemen, have you agreed upon your verdict?

The Foreman of the Jury: Yes.

The Clerk: Do you find Louise Masset guilty or not guilty?

The Foreman: Guilty.

The Clerk: You say that she is guilty, and that is the verdict of you all?

The Foreman: Yes.

The Clerk: Louise Masset – you stand convicted of the crime of wilful murder. Have you anything to say for yourself why the court should not give you judgement of death according to law?

The Prisoner: I am quite innocent of the charge.

---

161  Mr Justice Bruce concluded his summing-up at 4.52 pm.
162  The defendant had already stated that – with the exception of Sundays – it was only possible to get hot food at Findlay's Hotel by ordering it in advance.

# Fifth Day – Monday 18 December 1899.

[After the usual command for silence.]

Mr Justice BRUCE: Louise Masset – after a most careful trial, the jury have found you guilty of the crime of which you are charged. I will not harry your feelings by making observations upon that verdict. I will content myself with passing upon you the sentence of the law, which is that you be taken from here to the place whence you came, and from thence to a place of execution, and that you be there hanged by the neck till you are dead, and that your body be buried within the precincts of the place within which you were last confined; and may the Lord have mercy on your soul. [Amen.]

The Clerk: Louise Masset – you stand convicted of the crime of wilful murder. Have you anything to say why there should be any stay of execution of your sentence?

[The prisoner slowly shook her head after this had been repeated to her by a wardress.]

# Appendices.

# APPENDIX I.

## The Testimonial Letter.[163]

---

Ivy House,<br>
29 Bethune Road,<br>
Stoke Newington, N.<br>
<br>
Oct 30th 1899.

Dear Mrs Norris,

I felt so sorry at withdrawing Manfred from your kind care.

He has been so lovingly & thoroughly taken care of, that should you think of taking another nurse child I shall be most pleased to answer any enquiries the parents or guardians may wish to make.

You treated my son in every way as you would have treated your own child and I again take this opportunity of thanking you for 3½ years kindness.

Yours ever sincerely,

    L. Mason.

---

[163] TNA:PRO CRIM 1/58/5. Punctuation and grammar are, throughout, Louise Masset's own.

# APPENDIX II.

## The Humble Petition of Louise Josephine Jemima Masset.[164]

---

To

    Her Majesty's Principal Secretary of State for the Home Department,
    Home Office,
    Whitehall, S.W.

The Humble Petition of Louise Josephine Jemima Masset, Spinster, now a Prisoner under sentence of Death at Her Majesty's Prison Newgate, Old Bailey, in the County of Middlesex

Sheweth as follows:-

1    Your Petitioner is an Unmarried Woman, aged 36, the Daughter of a French Gentleman, of old and respected French Family, by his Marriage with an English Lady, her two sisters, Mrs Simes and Mrs Cadisch being married to Gentlemen of respectable position in London. Your Petitioner, at the time of the occurrences more particularly hereinafter set forth living with her sister Mrs Cadisch, having with credit to herself and her family employed her talents as a good musician and linguist, by keeping herself since a young girl of the age of 18 by her profession of a governess, from which she received substantial remuneration – it being testified by many witnesses, and freely admitted by the Prosecution, that she was always of a kind, considerate, patient, loving disposition, especially towards little children, and particularly so towards her little illegitimate son Manfred Louis Masset who was 3½ years of age at the time of the occurrence hereinafter mentioned, and whose birth had been long since freely forgiven by all her family, and whom she had visited regularly nearly every week since his birth, at the house of Miss Gentle, the nurse into whose care he was entrusted when a few weeks old, your Petitioner having invariably paid regularly £1 17s 0d a month for his keep, the money being sometimes paid in advance, and it being given in evidence by Witnesses called for the Prosecution that she always had plenty of money in her possession and at her disposal.

---

164    TNA:PRO HO 144/1540/A61535/44. This petition was originally sent to the Home Office on Saturday 30 December 1899.

# Masset.

2   On the 3rd day of November 1899 Your Petitioner was arrested at 'Quinta', Streatham Road,[165] Croydon by Detective Serjeant[166] William Burch, the place in question being the house of her brother-in-law Mr Simes, to whom she had immediately gone to seek advice directly she saw in the *Evening News* of October the 30th; that the child found in the Ladies' Lavatory, No. 3 Platform of the Dalston Junction Railway Station on Friday the 27th day of October 1899 about 6.20 pm had been identified as hers by the following description:-

## DALSTON MURDER
### Identification of the Poor Little Victim

---

## CHILD OF A FRENCH WOMAN
### Who took him away from his Nurse on the day of the Murder.

---

The Victim of the Dalston Murder was identified to-day and the police now have an important clue.

Shortly before noon a middle-aged woman, respectably dressed, walked in to the mortuary at Hackney, where half a dozen dead bodies were lying, and said she might be able to identify the five-year-old boy who was so foully murdered last Friday evening. The woman explained that for about five years she had nursed and reared a fair haired child, brought to her by a French lady.

Last Friday afternoon the mother called upon her and asked for her boy, saying that she wanted to take him over to Paris. The little lad, nicely dressed, was handed over to the parent, and the nurse saw nothing more of him until to-day.

'I could identify him from a bruise on one of his thighs,' she said, just before entering the mortuary: 'he fell down the other day when playing about the house'. The cloth covering the body had scarcely been removed when the nurse exclaimed, 'There he is!' and immediately swooned away.

The woman was assisted into one of the rooms at the mortuary, and remained there until the arrival of the chief of police, who had been telephoned for by Detective-Inspector Forth, in charge of the case. The

---

165   *Sic* in petition; should read, 'Stretton Road'.
166   *Sic* in petition.

# Appendix II.

nurse was evidently very fond of the child, who was brought to her when only a week old.

Between her sobs she could be heard exclaiming, 'Poor child! My poor little boy!' until she was taken away.

The nurse has frequently seen the child's mother, and has for several years received regular payment for supporting the child whom she believes to be illegitimate.

3   Your Petitioner was on the following day – the 4th day of November 1899 brought up in custody before Edward Snow Fordham Esquire, one of the Magistrates of the Police Courts of the Metropolis, sitting at the Police Court, North London and after the said Detective Serjeant Burch had given evidence as follows:-

WILLIAM BURCH, Detective Sergeant, J Division on oath saith as follows:-

Since Monday last I have been keeping observation with other Officers in Bethune Road, Stoke Newington. Yesterday about 8 am I saw two Gentlemen leave No. 29. I followed them with P. C. Allen to London Bridge Station. On the Platform one of them made a statement in consequence I went to Streatham Road,[167] Croydon. In a house named 'Quinta' there I saw the Prisoner. I said we were Police Officers and said, 'You had a child which you took away from its nurse last Friday. Can you account for it to me?'

She said, 'I last saw my child Manfred Louis Masset, age 3½, on Friday at London Bridge Railway Station in the waiting room. I gave it to two women who gave me the address of 45 King's Road, Chelsea, with £12, mostly gold, to take care of it for a whole 12 months. I had seen them at Tottenham Green from Wednesday back.[168] I had the child with me then. They spoke to me[169] and by their conversation they found out it was a nurse child[;] they said they were setting up a home and would I mind letting them have mine for £12 a[170] year[;] at first I did not agree with it. I met them there again the next Wednesday[;] I had the child with me then[.] I decided then to leave it with them for that sum – I then arranged to meet them at London Bridge at 2 pm Friday last in the waiting room London and Brighton where the refreshment room is on the left. I met them there but before going there I went into another waiting room[,] the

167   *Sic* in petition; should read, 'Stretton Road'.
168   Burch's original statement reads, 'from four Wednesdays back'. A manuscript annotation adds, '4 Oct'.
169   The original statement gives, 'They first spoke to me'.
170   The original statement gives, 'per'.

# Masset.

one near where the parcels come out. There was a woman attendant there [who] had a cap on[;] another one came to relieve her while I was there. They left to go to the Refreshment Room and took the Boy with them as they asked him if he would like a cake. They were to come back and bring me a receipt for the money.

'I waited there two or three minutes but they never came back[.] I have not seen my child since.'

I told her that she would have to accompany me to Dalston Police Station. She said, 'I'll go there willingly'.

I then took her to the Police Station where she was charged by Inspector Forth. I wrote her statement down as she said it.

By PRISONER:-[171]

To the best of my belief, you said you met the women for the second time the next Wednesday and not two weeks later.

(Signed) WILLIAM BURCH.

(Recalled)[172]

I received the pair of Scales produced from Mr Finday[173] at Brighton on the 1st ulto. I had them in my custody till they were given up in Court.

I took a journey on the 28th ult from Dalston Junction No 1 Platform to Broad Street and thence by omnibus to London Bridge. I left Dalston Junction about 18 minutes to 6[,] waited 5 minutes for a 'bus at Broad Street and reached London Bridge at 6.17.

By PRISONER'S SOLICITOR:-

I was told to go 5 minutes before I started.

(Signed) WILLIAM BURCH.

was (your Petitioner then being unrepresented by either Counsel or Solicitor) remanded in custody for 7 days.

4   On the 11th day of November, Your Petitioner was again brought up at the said Police Court before the said Magistrate[,] the Prosecution being conducted by Mr Richard David Muir of Counsel[174] on behalf of the Director of Public Prosecutions, your Petitioner being defended by Mr Arthur

---

171  That is, cross-examined by the prisoner.
172  On 1 December 1899.
173  *Sic* in petition; should read 'Mr Findlay'.
174  *Sic* in petition.

# Appendix II.

Newton, Solicitor, of Great Marlborough Street, W, when the Learned Counsel for the Prosecution opened the case at length, a shorthand note of which is annexed hereto, to which your Petitioner craves leave to refer – which statement is inaccurate in saying that your Petitioner did not mention to her Brother-in-law about the two ladies, [but] as his sworn evidence clearly proves, she did say so at the time.

5  The Case against your Petitioner was subsequently remanded to the 24th of November and the 1st day of December on which latter day she was committed by the said Magistrate to take her Trial at the December Sessions at the Central Criminal Court for the alleged wilful murder of her said illegitimate son Manfred Louis Masset on the 27th day of October 1899 at Dalston Railway Station[175] as above more particularly hereinbefore set forth.

6  Pending the enquiry before the said Learned Magistrate at the said Police Court, an Inquest was held at the Coroner's Court, in the Parish of Hackney in the County of London before William Wynne[176] Westcott Esquire, one of Her Majesty's Coroners for the said County[,] to ascertain the cause of death of the said Manfred Louis Masset on the 2nd, 9th and 16th days of November 1899.

7  Your Petitioner duly attended on the said 2nd day of November and at her request and by the permission of the said Coroner saw the dead body of her little son, and according to the evidence of the Prosecution was greatly affected and distressed to see the manner in which he had been disfigured by terrible blows upon his face.

8  Your petitioner duly again attended the said Inquest at the aforesaid Court on the said 9th day of November but owing to the disgraceful scenes enacted by a crowd of about 500 persons, mostly composed of low class women, who had assembled in the vicinity and who nearly succeeded in overturning the Cab, in which your Petitioner was conveyed to the said Coroner's Court, and made use of the most filthy and threatening language towards her, she did not attend at the final hearing of the said Inquest on the said 16th day of November, being unwilling to again subject herself to such unfair and cruel prejudice, and on the said date, she was duly committed upon the Coroner's Warrant upon the said charge above mentioned.

9  No further evidence was adduced at her trial against your Petitioner beyond that foreshadowed by the Counsel for the Prosecution on the said 11th day of November at the said Police Court, beyond that of a Mrs Rees,[177] an attendant at one of the Waiting Rooms at the London Bridge Railway Station

---

175  *Sic* in petition.
176  *Sic* in petition; should read 'Wynn'.
177  *Sic* in transcript; should read, 'Reece'. The same error is repeated almost immediately.

# Masset.

of the L. B. & S. C. Rly Company whose evidence was as follows and to whose cross-examination by her Solicitor Mr Arthur Newton, your Petitioner humbly craves most particularly and earnestly to refer as clearly proving that the evidence of this Witness is in no way conclusive or certain in any way against her, and is absolutely and entirely uncorroborated.

ELLEN REES on oath saith as follows:-[178]

I am a widow living at 8 Raul Road[,] Peckham.

P. S.[179] Nursey took a Statement from me last Tuesday – I am attendant at the First Class Ladies['] Waiting Room main line section London Bridge Station – On 27th October I was in charge there from 2.30 pm till midnight. This morning I was shewn[180] a number (about 19) of women in the yard of this Court[;] all were dressed in black and I picked out the Prisoner – On 27th October I saw her about 2.40 pm sitting on the Couch in my waiting room[;] a little boy was with her. The Photograph (4)[181] is very like the child but he had his hat on. It was a red hat[182] – She remained until after 3 o'clock. I noticed the child didn't want to go to her. He was fretting[;] I said, 'What are you grizzling about[?]'

I was putting away my bonnet and he came and looked at the cupboard[.] I said[,] '[T]here is nothing here for little boys[;] it[']s all paper parcels[.]' I asked prisoner what was the matter with him[;] she said[,] 'He's fretting for his nurse'.

I said, 'He's a fine little fellow, how old is he[?]' [S]he said[,] 'Four next April[.]' [S]he said[,] '[P]erhaps he's hungry, I'll get him a cake. Have you a Refreshment bar on the Station[?]' I said[,] '[O]n the left'[.] [S]he picked up something with her hand[183] and went out with the child.

That was about 5 or 10 minutes past 3[.] I next saw her at 6.50 pm in the Lavatory in my waiting room[.] [S]he came to the door and asked for a towel and said she would like a wash[.] I drew the water[;] she asked when the next train went for Brighton[.] I said[,] '7.20'[.] She washed and she asked for a clothes brush[;] I gave her one and told her she would have to hurry up as it was a quarter past 7[.] [S]he took up a brown paper parcel

178 Here Newton copies a very slightly abridged version of Mrs Reece's statement to the police court to the Home Office – who had the original copy. The Home Office also held the original statement of William Burch, previously given, and that of Maud Clifford, which follows shortly.
179 That is, Police Sergeant. As discussed above, Nursey was a detective sergeant, not a police sergeant.
180 The original statement gives 'shown'.
181 A misreading on Newton's part; should read, 'A' (that is, exhibit 'A').
182 This sentence, present in the original statement, was omitted by Newton at this point: 'There was a little fair, curly hair round his hat'.
183 The original statement specifies the 'right hand'.

# Appendix II.

and her gloves and hurried away. No child was with her then. I did not see if she had a bag with her.

By PRISONER'S SOLICITOR:-

I did not relieve Mrs Warley[184] – sometimes 400 or 500[,] sometimes 600[185] use my waiting room during one period of duty – my waiting room is the one where the Refreshment Room is on the left – It is a busy one – I do not know what persons were in that Room between 2.30 and 3 on that day.

Amongst the 400 or 500 persons who came,[186] there are sometimes a great number of children.

I have read about this case in the papers more than once – I have read about it every time it has been in both before the Coroner and the Magistrate. I have read it in the *Daily Mail*[,] *Telegraph*[,] the *People*.

I can't say if I read an account of the Inquest in the *People*[.] I have the *People* every Sunday. I do not remember reading an exact description of the Prisoner and the child[,] how they were dressed &c.[;] I saw a picture of the Prisoner without her hat – I think it was three Sundays ago. I do not remember seeing a description of the child[.] [W]hen I read about the Dalston Murder[,] I wondered if this was the child from the description I saw – I never said that to the Police – I did not communicate with the Police because I did not want to have anything to do with it – I did not consider it any part of my duty till I was forced to it.

When the Police Officer came to me he showed me nothing – of the 400 or 500 persons who came[187] in an afternoon[,] a great many are dressed in black. I will swear Prisoner is the woman who had the little boy and whom I saw again at 7. I could not be positive till I saw her[.] [S]he was put among 20 other persons this morning. I should think she was not at the end or[188] yet exactly in the middle. She was dressed entirely in black on the 27th October – If she had any colours I did not observe them.

Of the people I saw this morning several were dressed in black – I can't say if the others somewhat resembled prisoner in appearance and height. Some did in age and general appearance. I haven't heard Prisoner's voice to-day – Prisoner was the only one I recognised as having seen before. I can't indicate any single peculiarity by which I distinguished her from the

---

184 *Sic* in petition; should read, 'Worley'.
185 The original statement says, 'and sometimes 600'.
186 *Sic* in petition; should read, 'come'.
187 *Sic* in petition; should read, 'come'.
188 The original statement says 'nor'.

others – I have never seen the photograph (H) before[.] I have never been asked to pick it out.

*Re-examined:-*

The Police came to me[;] I have not communicated with them at all.

I am not at all desirous of giving evidence in this case.

By the MAGISTRATE:-

The Police first communicated with me on the 21st inst[.] I am quite satisfied Prisoner is the woman as far as my conscience and ability.

I fix the time I was there[189] by the time I resumed[190] my duties – I fix the later time because I was finishing some crochet work and thinking I had[191] no tea[.] I looked up and saw it was 6.50 pm.

I was putting the kettle on when prisoner came back – I said nothing to her earlier in the day.[192]

I did not enquire after the child.

(Signed) Ellen Rees[193]

and at the Trial of your Petitioner Mrs Rees admitted that nothing unusual occurred to attract her attention to the person she believes was your Petitioner, whom she alleges she saw shortly before 7 pm on the said 27th day of October – the date of the alleged murder – and also was constrained to admit that sometimes 1000 people visited her waiting room in one day and that she could not described any other person who had called there, even a day or two before she gave evidence at your Petitioner's Trial.

10  Your Petitioner was subsequently indicted upon the said charge of wilful murder at the December Sessions of the Central Criminal Court and tried before Mr Justice Bruce on the 13th, 14th, 15th, 16th, and 18th days of December, the Prosecution being conducted by Mr Charles Willis Matthews[194] and Mr Richard David Muir, of Counsel, instructed by the Director of Public Prosecutions and your Petitioner's defence being entrusted to the Rt. Hon. Lord Coleridge Q. C., and Mr Arthur Hutton of

---

189  A misreading of 'I fix the time I saw them'.
190  In the original statement, 'resume'.
191  In the original statement, quite properly, 'had had'.
192  A telling mistake. Far from disclaiming her previous evidence about talking to Louise Masset in the afternoon, Mrs Reece actually told the magistrate that 'I said nothing to her about having seen her earlier in the day'.
193  *Sic* in petition; the signature, of course, reads 'Ellen Reece'.
194  *Sic* in petition; should read 'Charles Willie Mathews'.

# Appendix II.

Counsel, instructed by Mr Arthur Newton, your Petitioner being found guilty upon the said indictment and sentenced to death.

11  From first to last no motive for the committing of the said crime was ever really seriously put forward or suggested either by the Counsel who conducted the Case before the Magistrate, or by the Coroner who held the Inquest, or by the Counsel who conducted the Prosecution at our Petitioner's Trial, or by the learned Judge who tried the Case on Indictment at the said Central Criminal Court, but the Jury were invited to practically convict the Prisoner by great and elaborate stress being laid upon the fact of her committing the act of immorality of staying 2 days at an Hotel at Brighton with a young Frenchman of 19 and writing letters to Miss Gentle – and telling her relatives – untruths in some detail obviously to hide such immorality from them – It was also suggested to the Jury that (1) the fact of a clinker brick similar to those in Mrs Cadisch's garden, where your Petitioner lived, being found close to the dead body of the child, should tell against her, although it was admitted by all the witnesses that exactly similar bricks can be found in hundreds of gardens in London – and also admitted that no trace remained in the garden of any brick having been removed therefrom, nor of your Petitioner ever having been seen with such a brick either by Miss Gentle, or her Mother, who met her on the said 27th day of October, nor were there any traces of a single spot of dirt or mould from such a brick in the prisoner's bag or on her clothing, nor in fact was any evidence brought to shew that she ever went to Dalston Station[195] on the day in question, although she has regularly travelled 3 or 4 times a week from that station for many years past going to her pupils at Hampstead, and being consequently known to all the employes[196] at the said Station.

(2) The fact that a common ordinary black shawl which cost 1s 11½d at a Drapers in High Street[,] Dalston,[197] was found round the child's body, which an Assistant at such Drapers stated she believed was purchased by the Prisoner on the 24th day of October – although – like Mrs Rees this witness' evidence was absolutely uncorroborated and she frankly said she would not swear to the identity of the Prisoner – this witness' evidence Miss Clifford was as follows[198] - and your Petitioner again craves leave to refer to the cross-examination of this witness before the Magistrate as clearly shewing that this evidence is most unreliable, especially as at the Trial Mr Newton produced exactly similar shawls, which he had purchased without difficulty at other retail Drapers.

---

195  *Sic* in petition; should read, 'Dalston Junction station'.
196  *Sic* in petition; should read, 'employees'.
197  *Sic* in petition; should read, 'Stoke Newington'.
198  The syntax of the petition is no longer the servant of its vocabulary or its semantics, but not for the first time in this passionate, rambling document.

# Masset.

MAUD CLIFFORD on oath saith as follows:-

I am single and live at 161 High Street Stoke Newington a Drapers owned by Mr McIlroy[.] I am his Assistant – This shawl[199] is one I sold to a lady on Tuesday 24th October. It was before dinner I sold it. I showed the lady a smaller one and she said she wanted one a little larger[.] She also said she wanted it black. I made out a duplicate bill. This is it (K). We had only had those[200] particular shawls about a week. This was the first black one of that lot I had sold[.] I have sold none since.

On Saturday 4th inst I went to North London Police Court and saw a number of women in a row[:] over a dozen[,] some dressed in black and some in colours. I was asked to pick out the lady to whom I had sold the shawl. I picked out the prisoner. When I sold her the shawl as far as I remember she was dressed in black as she is now. I think she is the same person.

By PRISONER'S SOLICITOR:-

I have been about 2 years in the business. There are about 25 young ladies there – It is a busy shop.

The shawl is a very ordinary line which could be bought anywhere.

The selling of the shawl had quite passed from my mind till the 3rd November when the detective came. The shop walker brought out[201] this shawl alone and I was asked if I had sold it. I recognised it as one of the same line I had for sale. On the 4th inst[,] there were several other people there for the purpose of identifying the prisoner. I saw nobody else identify her – I was called out of a room[.] [A]fter I saw prisoner among others I said to a Police Officer[,] 'I think that's the woman'. At the inquest I said, 'I won't swear positively she's the woman. I won't swear that now.'[202]

By the MAGISTRATE:-

I believe Prisoner is the woman but I can't swear it – I am sure I did sell a black shawl[.] [T]o the best of my belief this is the shawl.

*(Recalled)*

---

199   The original statement notes that the shawl was exhibit 'K1'.
200   The original statement gives, 'these'.
201   A misreading; should read, 'me'.
202   Newton's petition presents these comments as if they were both made at once at the inquest: 'I won't swear positively she's the woman. I won't swear that now.' In fact, Miss Clifford's statement at the police court places the first comment at the inquest ('I won't swear positively she's the woman'), and the second within her evidence before the magistrate (as in, I know that I said at the inquest that I wouldn't swear to her identity, and 'I won't swear that now').

# Appendix II.

I produce two of the parcel of 3 shawls of which I sold one – I compare (K)[203] with the two I produce – It is just the same.

By PRISONER'S SOLICITOR:-

There is nothing to identify the shawl (K)[204] beyond the manufacture.

(Signed) Maud Clifford

(3) Mrs Rees' evidence which has already been fully dealt with under paragraph 9 of this Petition.

(4) The fact that some of the dead child's clothing – a small dress and coat – were found mutilated in a waiting room at Brighton in a portion of the same paper in which the child's change of clothing had been given to your Petitioner by Miss Gentle – although no evidence was brought to show that your Petitioner was ever seen in the waiting room in question, or that any scrap of the child's clothing had ever been traced into the possession of your Petitioner since, as she alleged, she handed the child to Mrs and Miss Browning about 3 o'clock at the rendez-vous made at London Bridge Station on the said 27th day of October – it being therefore apparent that here again the matter remains in the greatest possible doubt and obscurity.

(5) The fact that your Petitioner left openly in an unlocked drawer in her room in the Hotel at Brighton where she stayed a small pair of scales, which she kept, on handing over the child to Mrs and Miss Browning as aforesaid –

(6) The fact that directly she saw the identification of the child, she did not that instant rush off to the Police or the Mortuary, but went at once to ask the advice of her brother-in-law – Mr Simes – frankly told him all her movements at Brighton and elsewhere, and authorised him to tell the Police, without which they had absolutely no clue to her movements, and remained at his house – when – if guilty – she could easily have escaped – and waited for the Police, saying – that if suspicion rested on her she was prepared to meet it – all this being, it is earnestly submitted, the actions of innocence and not of guilt.

(7) The fact that she removed the child from Miss Gentle with whom he was admittedly happy – although your Petitioner explained in evidence – and was corroborated by Miss Gentle and Mrs Cadisch that the child was spoilt – gave way to violent temper, and spoke in a common unrefined way, and that in February last your Petitioner had mentioned to Mrs Cadisch that she thought of making a change and only wrote the letters of the 16th and 30th of October so as not to hurt the feelings of Miss Gentle, who had been so kind

---

203  A misreading; the original statement gives, 'K¹'.
204  As above; should read, 'K¹'.

# Masset.

to the child, by letting her think, he was going to another nurse in England and not abroad.

(8) The fact that Mrs and Miss Browning obviously gave a false address and cannot be now traced – although it is within the knowledge of nearly all Lawyers of experience and many members of the Police Force that the circumstances of the manner in which your Petitioner states she gave her child to the Ladies in question are similar to those in which many innocent Mothers have given over their child to apparently respectable people who have murdered them for much less than, as in this case, £12 – so as to keep the money and not have the expense or trouble of the child, and your Petitioner craves leave to refer to the copy reports of such cases the facts of which the learned Judge refused, as your Petitioner most respectfully submits, improperly, to allow her leading Counsel Lord Coleridge to elicit in Cross-examination of the Police, with the result that the most important features of corroboration of her statement was absent from the minds of the Jury.

(9) The fact that your Petitioner never rectified the address of Mrs and Miss Browning – although it was shewn that her experience with Miss Gentle, whom she heard of simply through an advertisement, had been a good one and therefore left no doubt in her mind as to the bona fides of persons of better manners and education than Miss Gentle –

Your Petitioner most humbly submits upon the above mentioned facts that it was the duty of the Judge who tried her case to have pointed out to the Jury that in all Criminal Cases – and especially in a charge of Murder – where the evidence is of a purely circumstantial character – that they ought not to convict the accused upon any general impression or opinion upon the whole case but that – especially as in this case where absolutely and literally no motive whatever was shewn why your Petitioner should murder her little boy, to whom admittedly she was devoted – they ought to look critically to see whether in fact the Prosecution had not many links altogether missing in the chain of evidence, and that he ought to have pointed out to the Jury that all the above mentioned points urged against the accused, each and every one of them when carefully analysed, failed to form either individually or collectively such a clear case against the Prisoner to shew that she, and no-one else, must have committed the alleged murder, instead of which the learned Judge simply called the attention of the Jury to these points against the Prisoner, saying that they were 'coincidences' from which they must draw their conclusions as reasonable men of business as to whether your Petitioner was guilty or not.

Your Petitioner therefore humbly prays that you will be pleased to advise Her Most Gracious Majesty that there is a serious and reasonable doubt as to her guilt in this case and that the sentence upon your Petitioner be commuted accordingly

# Appendix II.

AND YOUR PETITIONER WILL EVER PRAY &C.

This Petition is Presented by Messrs Arthur Newton & Co of 23 Great Marlborough St., Regent St, W

Solicitors for the Petitioner[205]

---

[205] One page of signatures follows; a note on the Home Office docket in which the petition is stored states, 'Other signatures detached'. It was also noted by Charles Murdoch, assistant undersecretary to the Home Office, that 'many of the signatures' were 'in the same handwriting'. The covering letter from Newton clarifies – if this is the right word – that 'some of the signatures are not in the handwriting of the persons themselves; but in each of those cases we have received letters from the persons in question stating that they cannot attend personally at our office for the purpose, but requesting and authorising us to sign their names to the petition, which we have accordingly done' (TNA:PRO HO 144/1540/A61535/31).

# APPENDIX III.

## *Daily Chronicle*, 4 January 1900.

---

### MISS MASSET AND THE NURSE.

Among the applicants to Mr Fordham at North London Police Court yesterday was Miss Gentle, the nurse who had charge of the child for whose murder Miss Masset is lying under sentence of death. Miss Gentle asked what she was to do with reference to the disposal of a few belongings of the child. Mr Simes, Miss Masset's brother-in-law, demanded the things, and she did not know whether she would be right in giving them up. They consisted of a few articles of clothing and a mail cart. They were not worth much – probably not more than 10s.

Mr Fordham: They really belong to Miss Masset?

Miss Gentle: They do.

Mr Fordham: The things belong to the mother at present. If she makes a will she can leave them to whom she chooses. I should advise you to keep them for a fortnight or so; then, if you gave them up to Mr Simes I don't think you would be far wrong.

Miss Gentle went on to say that for all her attendances at this court and the Old Bailey she had only received £1 12s. The shock of the murder had so upset her that she had been under medical treatment ever since, and the amount she had received would not pay her doctor's bill. Moreover her living was gone, she had had to part with her piano to meet her expenses, and her character as a nurse was gone.

Mr Fordham could not do anything with regard to the expenses, but he could assure the applicant her character stood higher than ever.

Miss Gentle broke down, and sobbed out that Miss Masset had made allegations in the witness box. She said that she (Miss Gentle) did not bring up the child properly. It was the first stain on her character, and since it had been published she had not been able to get another nurse child.

Mr Fordham said from what he knew of the case Miss Gentle's character stood higher than ever. It had been proved she had behaved most properly towards the child, and if she wished for a private reference she could refer to him (the magistrate). She was not, however, to use the reference as an advertisement.

# Masset.

Miss Gentle: Thank you, sir, but Miss Masset swore it in the witness box.

Mr Fordham: My good woman, Miss Masset's word goes for nothing. The jury did not believe her. Nobody believes her.

---

# APPENDIX IV.

## *Daily Chronicle*, 6 January 1900.

---

LOUISE MASSET'S CASE.
MORE WITNESSES MAKE STARTLING STATEMENTS.
TWO WOMEN SEEN AT DALSTON.
DAILY CHRONICLE SPECIAL.

Some fresh chapters have been added to the strange story of Louise Masset and her murdered child. Mr Arthur Newton yesterday forwarded to the Home Office two signed statements, to which he attaches no little importance, as tending to corroborate the story told by the accused woman.

Two Strange Women.

It will be remembered that the body of the child was first discovered by two young women who happened to be at Dalston Junction on the night of Oct. 27. Both gave evidence at the trial, and yesterday one of these – Miss Mary Tehan,[206] a governess residing at Isleworth – made a further statement.

'When I left the lavatory after discovering the body I noticed two ladies dressed in black who were sitting close by, and when I heard Miss Masset giving evidence on the Saturday it struck me that her description of the two women to whom she handed the child exactly tallied with the appearance of the persons I had noticed on the platform. I mentioned this to the Treasury solicitor, but heard nothing more of it.'

To Mr Newton yesterday Miss Tehan expressed surprise that the matter was not referred to at the trial. Her statement was forwarded to the Home Secretary yesterday.

Last night Mr J. Hughes-Ellis, of 128 Westminster Bridge Road, was shown a photograph of the child, taken on the day before it was murdered. The photograph was taken on the initiative of Miss Gentle, who wished to have a memento of the little one she had tended so long. After examination Mr Hughes-Ellis expressed his belief that it was a portrait of the child he saw in the omnibus, an incident we referred to yesterday. It was not until he saw a report of the trial, with Miss

---

206  *Sic* in article. Should read, 'Teahan'.

# Masset.

Masset's cross-examination, that he felt impelled to state what he had seen.

He went to the Stones End Police Station, whence he was referred to Inspector Forth, who was in charge of the case. He told the officer he believed he could identify the child, but he was not shown any photograph. Mr Hughes-Ellis's statement was forwarded to the Home Secretary last night. Extracts from this statement are given below.

### MR HUGHES-ELLIS'S STATEMENT.

The following is a copy of the extracts from the statement made by Mr John Hughes-Ellis: —

I left home on Oct. 27 last about three o'clock and went by tram to the Elephant and Castle, and then went by bus to Cornhill or the Monument (am not sure which) on my way to 90 Leadenhall Street, on business, and afterwards went by train (sixteen minutes past four) to Benfleet. From a quarter to half-past three our bus stopped opposite the 'rest' in the centre of the road facing the London Bridge approach. I sat with my back to the 'rest'. I happened to turn my head round and caught sight of two women and a child standing on the 'rest'. The elder of the two women hurriedly walked across to where the bus conductor was standing, spoke to him, and then beckoned to the younger woman to come across, which she did, but the child seemed very unwilling to come with her, and appeared as if he wanted to go towards the station (the reverse way), so she picked the child up and carried him across.

The younger woman, still holding the child in her arms, got into the bus, being helped by the conductor, and sat opposite me with the child on her knee. The elder woman then got into the bus and sat beside the other. I do not know to what place they took a ticket. The elder woman paid the fare. While in the bus and crossing London Bridge the child (a boy apparently about four years of age) seemed very uneasy, and struggled to get down off the woman's knee; but she held him tight with her arms round his waist, and kept whispering to him, but he seemed to treat her as a stranger. I got out of the bus, as stated before, either at Eastcheap or the Monument,[207] and the bus went on with the two women and child inside. The older woman appeared to me to be about sixty to sixty-five years old, and the younger about half that age. The older woman was stout and of medium height, the younger shorter and slighter built. The appearance of the women and also from the way the younger one spoke to the child in the bus gave me the impression that they were not of the educated class.

From my having been for some years missionary in Lambeth and other places in South London, I am well able to judge of the type of woman, and I was much struck with the fact that the two women should have such a child, apparently

---

207 *Sic* in article. The correct reading is probably 'Cornhill or the Monument'.

# Appendix IV.

well brought up and of refined features, in their possession. There was nothing peculiar or attractive in the dress of the child that I can recollect.

[The remainder of the statement is irrelevant.][208]

### THE PETITION FROM FRANCE.

The Press Association says the editress of the French journal 'La Fronde', who has arrived in London bearing a petition to the Queen in favour of Louise Masset, writes as follows: —

It is in response to the desire expressed by many governesses that 'La Fronde' has taken the initiative in this petition. They addressed themselves to the 'Fronde' because the journal has many readers among the teaching body, and also because its attitude at the time of the shameful attacks of a section of the Press on the British Government, and even on the person of her Majesty the Queen, has won for it real sympathies in England.

Several English papers have reproduced articles in which we have tried to recall certain of our compatriots, first to a sense of respect for international politeness, next, and above all, to respect for a lady, the most venerable, and also the most lovable of Sovereigns. I add that the 'Fronde' being the only paper in the world directed, administered, edited, and printed exclusively by women, has taken the initiative without wishing to arouse national susceptibilities on one side or the other, and without raising diplomatic difficulties.

It is, in fact, to avoid these latter that we have not transmitted our petition through the official channel, and that I have been charged to convey it. It is from women who ask from a woman, a Queen, pardon for a woman, and our only argument is an appeal to clemency and pity.

### THE EDITOR OF THE DAILY CHRONICLE.

Monsieur le Rédacteur, — Je me borne à observer que Louise Masset n'a pas fait d'aveux, qu'un doute peut subsister sur sa culpabilité, et que des temoignages postérieurs à la condamnation viennent préciser ce donte. Je n'y vois qu'un argument de plus, qui peut militer en faveur de cette malheureuse. Sous ces reserves, je pense qu'il nous et permis de l'invoquer. S'il y a doute, il est juste que la condamnée en bénéficie. C'est un principe que tous les legislatures s'accordent à reconnaître.

    Andrée Téry,
    Rédactrice à la Fronde.
    Hôtel Cecil, Strand, W.C., Janvier 5.

---

[208] This editorial remark sic in article.

# Masset.

### THE EDITOR OF THE DAILY CHRONICLE.

Sir, — The further evidence in connection with this most lamentable case leads one to assert that, in the present system of conducting Treasury prosecutions there is something wrong somewhere. Lord Coleridge administered a necessary and dignified rebuke to Mr C. Mathews at the trial, and one now wonders what the Treasury will have to say to that gentleman. As Lord Coleridge said, his address was full of prejudice and passion. I affirm that it was more: it was vindictive, harsh, and characterised by the absence of that restraint and judicial fairness which ought to adorn the speeches of all prosecuting counsel. The suggestion that vital evidence was suppressed recalls to us the trial of Captain Dreyfus, when all the clericalism and militarism of France were hounding down an innocent man.

    Yours faithfully,
    W. O. F.
    Jan. 5.

### THE EDITOR OF THE DAILY CHRONICLE.

Sir, — Miss Masset stated that she went to Brighton by the four o'clock train, and dined at Mutton's Hotel soon after her arrival. This, if true, would establish her innocence. It is plain that if she was not at the hotel on that day she could not have known that a lady whose general description accorded with hers had dined there, and that this lady was alone – for the gentleman who dined there did not come or go with her. It was a remarkably lucky guess on her part if she was not the person who dined there. A young lady coming in alone about the time that she mentioned, dining at the hotel, waiting for a time, but going away again without sleeping there, was a very strange incident, especially as there was but one other person dining there on that day. If she had said that she dined at a large restaurant, where fifty or 100 persons sat down to dinner, it would have been different. Her absence could hardly be proved. But she names a hotel where only two persons dined on that one day, and one of these answered in many respects to the description of the prisoner.

    Truly yours,
    A Barrister.
    Jan. 5.

The following letter has been addressed by the Humanitarian League to the Right Hon. Sir Matthew White Ridley, M. P., her Majesty's Secretary of State for the Home Department: —

Sir. — With regard to the sentence of death passed on Louise Masset, and the fact that she was condemned on purely circumstantial evidence, I am instructed by my committee to express our earnest hope that you will give due weight to the

# Appendix IV.

element of doubt that exists in her case.

I am, Sir, yours truly,
Joseph Collinson
Hon. Secretary, Prison Reform Department,
Humanitarian League, 53 Chancery Lane, Jan. 4.

# APPENDIX V.

## A Mysterious Letter.[209]

---

Home Office No. A61535/31.

Date: 3 Jan 1900.

Louise Josephine Jemima Masset.

Governor of Newgate Prison forwards letter which has been addressed to the convict, but which he thinks should be kept from her.

Minutes: The above was referred to Mr Anderson whose report is placed within.

Enquiry shows no truth in the anonymous communication. Sir K. Digby to see. CM, 3 Decr 1900.[210]

    K. E. D. Jan 4 1900.[211]

---

3 Jany '00

Dear Murdoch,

The enclosed will explain itself.

Yours sincy,

R. Anderson.

---

[209] TNA:PRO HO 144/1540/A61535/31.
[210] Initials of Charles Murdoch, assistant undersecretary to the Home Office. Date sic in minute (and '1800' overwritten with '1900'); should read, '3 Jan 1900'.
[211] Initials of Sir Kenelm E. Digby, permanent undersecretary to the Home Office.

# Masset.

METROPOLITAN POLICE.
Bethnal Green Station.
J Division.
1st day of January 1900.

Referring to attached Home Office letter and anonymous letter addressed to Louise Masset, Newgate Prison.

I beg to report that on the night of the murder, viz 27th October last, every Porter who was on duty at Dalston Junction Railway Station between the hours of 2 pm and 12 night were interviewed by Police and asked if they had seen any person (male or female) with a child answering the deceased. These porters and also the ticket collectors were again seen after the body had been identified and each one of them in the presence of P.S. Burch C.I.D. and Police Inspr Perks, North London Railway, said they had not noticed any person with a child that day that would in any way resemble the deceased.

On the receipt of this correspondence we have again interviewed the three porters who were on duty on No. 3 Platform on day of murder (this includes John Standing, the porter who gave evidence at the trial[212]) and also all other porters who were on duty at the Station that day with the exception of two who have rejoined their Regiments and proceeded to South Africa. Those interviewed deny having noticed any female or females at the Station on the day of murder with a child or that they have stated to any person that they had done so.

These porters would undoubtedly render any assistance to us if they could do so in this matter & I am of opinion there is no truth in this anonymous letter.

Rich. Nursey, Act. L. Inspector[213]
F. Weston, Supt[214]

---

[212] Incorrectly named in this report. Should read, 'Joseph John Standing'.
[213] Richard Nursey, Acting Local Inspector, Metropolitan Police, J Division (Bethnal Green).
[214] Frederick Weston, Superintendent, Metropolitan Police, J Division (Bethnal Green).

# Appendix V.

Home Office,<br>
Whitehall,<br>
SW.<br>
3 Jan 1900.

Sir Kenelm Digby,

I believe this a mere try on, but shall I send it to Mr Anderson[?]

You will remember that Masset never told the Police the name of the Chelsea women till her actual trial – then said they were Mrs & Miss Browning. The address 45 King's Road turned out to be dairy man's. CM, 30 Decr 1899.

Seen by Sir K. Digby, 30.12.99.

---

HM Prison Newgate,<br>
29 Dec 1899.

Dear Mr Murdoch,

LOUISE MASSET.<br>
Under Capital Sentence.

I venture to send you the enclosed anonymous letter addressed to the above, which I do not consider well to give her. Her Solr. Arthur Newton visited her yesty and told her he was sending a petition to the S. of State which I suggest has somewhat unsettled her.

Yours sincerely,
Everard S. Milman
Governor.

---

# Masset.

[Envelope stamped London E. C., 6.45 pm, Dec 27 99]
Miss Louise Masset
Newgate Prison
E. C.
<u>Deliver to Prisoner</u>

26th Dec. 1899

Miss Louise Masset

The women of Chelsea must keep out of sight – but they are not anxious to hang you. If the porter (a porter) at D. junction would speak he could tell who he saw at 4.45 there. Anyhow put this in your lawyers[215] hands – it may save you.

Love children's trade must be kept up – we defy the police & send this – make the best of it

---

215  The author of the letter spelled 'anxious' in the elegantly-structured first sentence without difficulty, but omitted the possessive apostrophe from 'lawyer's'.

# APPENDIX VI.

## Louise Masset's Relatives Send a Petition to the Home Secretary.[216]

---

Home Office No. A61535/80.
Date: 8th Jan 1900.

### Louise Masset.

Messrs A. Newton & Co. forward petition from relatives of above.

Minutes: This petition is founded on the double lines of belief in her innocence, & insanity in the family, if she did commit the crime.

Mr Newton in his letter expresses the hope that from the facts disclosed in the petition it will be obvious that if the prisoner did commit the murder as is practically admitted without motive she did so in a state of mental aberration.

As to motive the letters to the father unfortunately supply it, & curiously enough in these the sum of £12 is mentioned which is the sum she said she gave the women.

Insanity is negatived by her actions, her defence, the report of Dr Scott, and lastly by Mr Ramsey (the chaplain) as to her recent frame of mind. CM, 8 Jan 1900.[217]

K. E. D. Jan 8.
S of S MWR.[218]

Wrote 8/1 copy herewith.

Ackd.[219] C. 8.1.00.

---

216 TNA:PRO HO 144/1540/A61535/80.
217 *Sic* in original. Should read: 'Ramsay'.
218 Initials of Sir Matthew White Ridley Bt M.P., Secretary of State for the Home Department.
219 Acknowledged.

# Masset.

Whitehall.
8th January, 1900.

Copy

Gentlemen,

I am directed by the Secretary of State to inform you that he has fully considered the Petition from the relatives of the prisoner Louise Masset which you forwarded to him in your letter of this morning; but that he regrets that he must adhere to the decision which has already been communicated to you in this case, namely, that he would not be justified in recommending any interference with the due course of Law.

I am,
    Gentlemen,
        Your obedient Servant,[220]

Messrs Arthur Newton & Co.,
    Solicitors,
        23 Great Marlborough Street, W.

---

[220] The copy of this letter in the Home Office files is unsigned.

# Appendix VI.

Telegraphic Address,
'Litigation, London'.
Arthur Newton & Co.
Solicitors.

Telephone No. 35468.

                                  23 Great Marlborough Street,
                                              Regent Street, W.
                                                        London.
                                                    8th January 1900.

Recd. 12.35, 8/1/00.[221]

Sir,

                          Re – Louise Masset.

We beg to acknowledge the receipt of your letter of Saturday, which you were courteous enough to send up by special messenger; but regret that you cannot see your way to advise Her Majesty to commute the sentence passed upon our client.

We are instructed by our client's relatives to send you the enclosed short Petition setting out the history of family insanity,[222] and venture to hope that from the facts disclosed therein, it will be obvious that if in fact our client did commit the murder – as is practically admitted, without motive – she did so under some sudden mental aberration, such as unfortunately from the history above-mentioned, has overtaken other members of her family.

We have the honour to be, Sir,

Your Obt Servants,

Arthur Newton Co.


The Under Secretary of State
Home Office
Whitehall, SW.[223]

---

221   Manuscript annotation added upon receipt of the letter and petition at the Home Office.
222   This word lavishly underlined at the Home Office.
223   Recipient's address.

# Masset.

To Her Majesty's Principal Secretary of State for the Home Department
>  Home Office
>  Whitehall, S. W.

The humble petition of GEORGE SIMES of 'Quinta', Streatham[224] Road, Croydon, in the County of Surrey, Auctioneer and Surveyor, and Mathilde Simes his wife, Richard Cadisch of 29 Bethune Road, Stoke Newington in the County of Middlesex, Merchant, and Leonie[225] Cadisch his Wife, and Elizabeth Armstrong (formerly Masset) Widow, of Bethune Road aforesaid, the Brothers-in-law, Sisters, and Mother of

>  LOUISA JOSEPHINE JEMIMA MASSET

now confined at Her Majesty's Prison, Newgate, Old Bailey, E. C., under sentence of Death for the alleged murder of her son Manfred Louis Masset on the 27th day of October 1899.

>  Sheweth as follows:-

1  Your Petitioners crave leave to refer to the Petition already presented on behalf of their above mentioned relative, praying for a remission of the sentence of death passed upon her by Mr Justice Bruce at the Central Criminal Court on the 18th day of December 1899, as disclosing all facts material to be considered upon the Present Petition, without again recapitulating the circumstances in the said Petition so clearly in detail therein set forth –

2  The said Louise Josephine Jemima Masset has from first to last most emphatically protested to your present Petitioners and to her Solicitor Mr Arthur Newton her entire innocence of the terrible charge preferred against her, namely of deliberately murdering her little son, to whom it has been admitted on all hands she has been devoted for 3½ years – since his birth – absolutely without reason or motive –

3  Your Petitioners feel that, notwithstanding her absolute denial of guilt – and whilst entirely and implicitly believing in their relative's most solemn assurance of innocence – the following facts may not inappropriately be brought before Her Majesty's Principal Secretary of State for the Home Department in the difficult task which now lies before him in advising Her Most Gracious Majesty as to what course ought to be ultimately adopted with reference to this most extraordinary and inexplicable case in the History of alleged Crime, the accuracy of which statements your Petitioners

---

224  *Sic* in petition. Should read, 'Stretton'.
225  *Sic* in petition. Léonie preferred to spell her name with an acute accent over the first 'e'.

# Appendix VI.

can personally vouch as being correct –

4    Mr Albert H. G. Burchatt of 8 Holly Villas, Clarendon Road, South Woodford, Essex, - a gentleman occupying an important and responsible position in a large firm in the West End of London has, as a blood relation of the above named Louise Josephine Jemima Masset, voluntarily written to Mr Arthur Newton her Solicitor a letter in which he makes the following clear and precise statement of the family history, which your Petitioners most humbly submit is an unfortunate and terrible family record, which throws light upon the present case and calls for sympathy instead of retribution upon the alleged conduct of their unfortunate relative.

8 Holly Villas,<br>
Clarendon Road,<br>
South Woodford,<br>
Essex,<br>
December 24th, 1899.

Dear Sirs,

I received your letter of the 22nd inst., and yesterday I conveyed to Mr Simes the cover of a family bible containing a record of the names and dates of birth of my father and his brothers and sisters. With this I sent some notes in further elucidation of the instances of insanity, suicide, and attempted suicide among the members of that family, some particulars of which I had already furnished. To make clear my relationship to Louise Masset let me repeat that my father and her maternal grandmother were brother and sister.

I classify these cases thus:- (1) An authentic case of suicide – My Aunt Maria. (2) An authentic case of insanity – My Aunt Susan. (3) A rumoured, but doubtful, case of suicide – my Aunt Charlotte. (4) An authentic case of attempted suicide and undoubted insanity – my Uncle Thomas. (5) A credibly reported case of suicide – my Uncle Edward – all these cases occurring in one generation.

In the next generation it will be seen by my notes that the list was increased by (6) An authentic case of permanent insanity – my first cousin Alfred Houghton. (7) An authentic case of permanent insanity – my first cousin Mary Anne Burchatt. (8) An authentic case of temporary insanity and detention in an asylum – my first cousin Elizabeth Wyeth (sister of the last named).

In the third generation we find (9) the idiotic son of Mrs Wyeth – Daniel is I think his baptismal name – and (10) Louise Masset.

These last two cases present widely differing characteristics, yet in my opinion both have their origin in the same obscure physiological trait which is so strikingly apparent in the two preceding generations. I have not seen Daniel Wyeth since he was a child some few years old, but at that time he had scarcely any control over

# Masset.

the action of his limbs, and he had hardly any power of speech. He is now a man, and I am told that he has to some extent improved in both these respects, and also in his mental powers. Louise Masset, on the other hand, is of good physique, with strong and little-controlled passions, a quick but most short-sighted intelligence and a rudimentary or non-existent moral sense so abnormal as to permit of her committing the cruel and unnatural act of which she has been pronounced guilty, without altering her equanimity or disturbing her in the slightest degree in the pursuit either of her pleasures or her ordinary avocations; and in my humble opinion the soundness of her mental condition is, to say the least, so doubtful that she ought not to be subjected to the extreme penalty of the law.

I am, dear Sirs,

    Yours faithfully,

        Albert H. G. Burchatt.


To Messrs Newton & Co.

The following is the detailed list referred to in the said Albert H. G. Burchatt's letter to Mr Arthur Newton:-

    Detailed List of all brothers and sisters of Miss Masset's Grandmother.

    <u>Born</u>

| | |
|---|---|
| 17th Septr. 1800 | Elizabeth died unmarried. |
| 13th Mch. 1802 | John was my father. He had one other son, my elder brother, who is living and whose address I have given to Mr Simes. |
| 7th Novr. 1803 | Mary Ann married a Mr Othen, and died not long afterwards, leaving no family. |
| 31st Octr. 1805 | Thomas was the man who, somewhere about the year 1855 or '6, attempted suicide by cutting his throat, was found to be insane, and was removed to an asylum, where he died. |
| 7th Novr. 1807 | Rebecca married a Mr Reffell. Her eldest daughter is Mrs Armstrong (whose first husband was Mr Masset). She was therefore the grandmother of Louise Masset. |
| 8th Jany. 1810 | Susannah became insane when a young woman and never recovered her reason. She was confined for many years in Hanwell Asylum, where she died. |
| 13th Jany. 1812 | Charlotte died unmarried in Australia. I have heard that there was some doubt whether she did not commit suicide. I have heard that she lived alone and was found dead in her house. |

# Appendix VI.

| | |
|---|---|
| 28th Novr. 1814 | Maria committed suicide by taking poison when a young woman. I have heard that it was through some love affair. |
| 27th Jany. 1816 | Charles married and had two sons (both dead – the 2 sons unmarried) and two daughters. Of the two daughters one (Mary Anne) became permanently insane when a young woman. I am not sure whether she still lives. The other daughter (Elizabeth) married, and had a family.1 She was temporarily insane and under restraint. One of her sons is mentally and physically deficient – idiotic, or semi-idiotic. |
| 27th August 1818 | Matilda married a Mr Houghton and had two sons. One is dead and the other became incurably insane and was placed in an asylum in America, to which country he had emigrated. I am not sure whether he is living or dead. |
| 24th Decr. 1820 | Edward, the youngest, and the last survivor of the family, was a Warrant Office2 in the Royal Navy. He died recently. I remember hearing my Father say that he (Edward) had once attempted suicide, but I never was told any details, my father being rather reserved upon these matters. I think he was on foreign service at the time, and it is quite possible that my father was the only person who knew about it. Edward was a posthumous child and my father was 18 years his senior, and would have been the natural confidant of his younger brother; between them there was great affection. |

The last two names on the list are those of my elder brother and myself and we can both of us testify as to what is above written.

    A. H. G. Burchatt,

      8 Holly Villas,
        Clarendon Road,
          South Woodford,
            Essex.

Decr. 22nd 1898.    All of them were born at Godalming.
A. H. G. B.

# Masset.

The following is a further list setting out further details in respect of the above insane relations of the said Louise Josephine Jemima Masset.

### Sisters of Maternal Grandmother.

i   Susan Burchatt became insane when a young woman and was in Hanwell Asylum from about 1848 until her death some 20 years later.

ii  Maria Burchatt committed suicide by taking poison at her house in Church Street, Godalming.

iii Matilda Burchatt married Houghton[226] and the youngest son of this marriage, Alfred Houghton, is known to have become insane and an occupant of an asylum in San Francisco in the '70's.

### Brothers of Maternal Grandmother.

i   Thomas Burchatt, resided at Bermondsey, attempted suicide, died in an asylum between 1860 and 1870.

ii  Charles Burchatt of Godalming (who never exhibited any signs of insanity) married and had two daughters.

   1 Mary Ann Burchatt who became insane in July 1886 recovering in October 1867.[227] She relapsed in 1879 since when she has been an occupant of Dr Paul's private asylum, Peckham Road, Camberwell.

   2 Her sister, married and residing at Godalming, was temporarily insane and in Bethlehem Hospital for about 9 months in 1880.

5  On the 27th day of September 1899 the Step-father of the said Louise Josephine Jemima Masset died somewhat unexpectedly, and during his illness she was, to use the expression of her own Mother, 'exquisitely kind' and devoted to him and in the opinion of your Petitioners his death had a great effect upon her – coming as a great shock.

6  In addition to the shock received by their relative as in paragraph 5 of this Petition above set forth,[228] your Petitioners have ascertained through the efforts of Mr Arthur Newton who has been to France and seen the Father of the deceased child that ever since the 29th day of December 1895 up to the 6th day of October 1899 – that is to say only 10 days before the important letter of the 16th day of October 1899 written by their relative to Miss Gentle, that a regular correspondence had been kept up being full of pathetic and loving details written by their relative with reference to her love and affection for her little son and her pride in his growing beauty and affection for her – his

---

226  Lacuna present in original.
227  *Sic* in original, but the dates are unworkable. 'July 1886' is presumably meant to read, 'July 1866'.
228  In the context of this statement, it is ironic that this paragraph was numbered '4'.

# Appendix VI.

mother – but that suddenly without rhyme or reason the Father ceased to write so regularly and then – a week after the sending by him of a loving and affectionate letter – he wrote saying he had found another woman to love. Mr Newton has the whole of these original letters in his possession, 2 dated respectively the 30th day of September 1899 and the 6th day of Octr. 1899 are as follows:-

Saturday Morning,<br>30th September 1899.

My dear little Husband,

I am really astonished not to have received any news from you. For mercy's sake write to me!!! you know how unhappy I am and unhappily placed for the present you would help me for I know your heart. I can only suppose that you are not receiving my letters or that you are travelling and that thus you do not know how unhappy I am, but however you had promised me to let me know the result of the revision. Were you taken – yes or no? Will you help me – yes or no?

They are wondering in the family that I do not buy black things and I answer that I will think of it during the week. What will they say when they see me one day come back with Manfred – Or rather I do not think I shall ever have courage to bring the child to the house, then we will have to stop without shelter that is all, for I have promised not to speak about you and if I bring back the child they will force me to say your name I was not thinking a year ago, that I should be so frightfully unhappy, I had faith in your heart and love for us and when I read over again your last letter it shows that you still love us; then why this complete silence? If your father interferes let me at least know it, do not leave me in my frightful despair for I am at the last extremity.

Your little Loulou – who beseeches you to help her.

*

# Masset.

219 Clyde Road[229],
South Tottenham,
Middlesex,
October 6th 1899.

My dear Maurice,

In receiving the few lines you sent me on Wednesday I felt as if stunned, the shock was too great especially after your last letter still full of love. But to-day I am awake and I accept for me the fate destined to me. I do not find you a coward to have loved another but a coward to leave me just at the time of my greatest misery for you know as well as I that your son will never be received in my family. They have told me often enough. I ask nothing for myself, it was your kisses I wanted, because I loved you and will always love you but having had advice outside the family I tell you that your son cannot and must not be thoroughly as dirty linen. I ask you then to assure him a shelter to send him an annual sum of 12 pounds, it is very little for a father who comes from a wealthy family. In that case I swear that you will never be bothered in any way. At the age of 15, that is in 12 years[230] time, the annual sum can cease as Manfred, your flesh, will have then I hope a fairly good education and health to work himself – Answer me on that subject and all correspondence will end between us but do not let me wait long for your answer. Your heart is your master but remember my own is a mother's heart and it also speaks.

Your well-wisher,

Louise.

Mrs Mason.[231]

and your Petitioners most earnestly beg careful and exact reference being made to the terms of these letters from which it will be seen that their unfortunate relative – in her devotion to the Father of her little son – and to him – to use her own words 'felt as if stunned' – the shock being too great.

7   Your Petitioners crave leave if necessary to refer to Mr Arthur Newton who can strictly corroborate the above statements with regard to the authenticity of the letters in question and as to his interview with the Father of the said child in France as shewing the terrible mental effect such shocks tend to have under such circumstances upon the mental balance and impulse.

---

229  *Sic* in petition; in fact, the Norrises lived at 210 Clyde Road.
230  *Sic* in original.
231  These letters appear in transcript in the petition, so the handwriting cannot be judged (samples of Louise Masset's exist and could be used to compare to them). There must be some doubt about whether they were genuine, or whether they were concocted by Arthur Newton.

# Appendix VI.

YOUR PETITIONERS therefore humbly pray and submit that under all the circumstances hereinbefore set forth there is a very grave and serious doubt in the whole case which may reasonably justify you in advising Her Most Gracious Majesty to commute the sentence of death passed upon the said Louise Josephine Jemima Masset and

YOUR PETITIONERS WILL EVER PRAY &C.

Dated 8th Januy, 1900.[232]

| Name of Person Signing. | Address. | Occupation. |
|---|---|---|
| Elizabeth R. Armstrong | 31 Bethune Road | |
| R. Cadisch | 29 Bethune Road | Merchant |
| Léonie Cadisch | 29 Bethune Road | |
| Geo R Simes | 'Quinta', Stretton Rd, Croydon | Auctioneer |
| Mathilde Simes | 'Quinta', Stretton Road | |
| Susan Matilda Reffell | Burwood, Caterham, Surrey | |
| Albert H. G. Burchatt | 8 Holly Villas, Clarendon Rd, South Woodford, Essex | Manager to Limited Company |

---

[232] 'Januy' sic in original.

# APPENDIX VII.

## *Daily News*, 10 January 1900.

---

### CIRCUMSTANTIAL EVIDENCE.

It will be a great satisfaction to many worthy people that the unhappy woman who was executed yesterday morning for the murder of her child confessed her guilt before she died. Even the mind of the Home Secretary, who deserves none of the abuse which has been showered upon him, will be relieved. A deeply-rooted instinct of human nature suggests doubt of unacknowledged crime. And in this case the motive seemed to be wholly inadequate for the commission of so cruel and unnatural an act. Whatever the motive may have been, it was probably not disclosed, and is not likely to be disclosed now. The circumstantial evidence was clear and strong. People who say that there is 'only circumstantial evidence,' do not seem to know what they are talking about. Murders are not as a rule committed in public. Privacy is always desired, and usually obtained. If nobody could be punished for an offence which nobody saw him commit, one gaol would hold all the prisoners in England. But that very desirable consummation must be reached by other and more legitimate means. The prisoner was the last person seen with the child. The railway station where the body was found is a station she knew and frequented. On the day of his death she took him from the family with whom he boarded, and gave them false reasons for doing so. The child's clothes were found at Brighton, where she went immediately after the murder. When she read in a newspaper that the body of a little boy had been discovered at Dalston Junction she went to her brother-in-law, and told them she was being 'hunted for the murder of her son,' which was untrue. Certain allegations made after the trial, and not worth discussing now, deserved inquiry, and we have no doubt that they received it. Some of them might have been, and were not, brought forward at the trial. The others were vague and inconclusive. The prisoner gave evidence on her own behalf, and told an ingenious story to explain away the evidence against her. It was wildly improbable, and unsupported by any testimony except her own. Her admissibility as a witness aided the cause of justice, because it showed that there was no valid defence. All executions are horrible, and especially the execution of a woman. But if ever a woman deserved to be hanged, it was this one.

---

# INDEX.

Ada (Manfred's playmate) *see* Allam, Winnie
Adkins, Eliza, 56
Allam, Winnie, 22, 153–5, 183–4, 185
Allen, Detective Constable Frederick, 7–8, 111
Armstrong, Elizabeth (*née* Reffell; then Masset; Louise's mother): background, 1&n; takes in Eudore Lucas as lodger, 2; petitions for reprieve, 33, 242
Armstrong, Peter William (Louise's stepfather), 1n, 78, 120, 246

baby-farming, 1n, 23–4, 29, 50, 55, 189, 224 *see also* infanticide
Baker, Sergeant Horace: evidence at trial, 113–14
Ballard, Eliza, 1n, 73
Bartlett, Adelaide, 1n
Berry, James, 47n
Bethnal Green Police Station, 42
Bethune Road (No 29), Stoke Newington, 1, 4, 7, 78, 108, 111, 166
Bigge, Sir Arthur, 39
Biggs, Margaret Ellen, 4, 16, 191; evidence at trial, 100
Billington, James, 47, 48
Birdcage (public house), Stamford Hill, 3, 74, 75, 81, 113
Bond, Dr Thomas, 18, 191; evidence at trial, 117
Bonner, Thomas, 53; evidence at trial, 81
Boucher, Eliza, 56
Bowers, William: evidence at trial, 112
boys, haircutting, 3n
brick clue *see* clinker brick
Brighton, 21, 137–8, 172–3, 175 *see also* Findlay's Hotel; Mutton's Restaurant
Brighton Railway Station, 6, 30, 52, 106, 137, 139, 174–5, 194–5
Brown, William James: evidence at trial, 106
brown paper parcel, 6–7, 30, 52, 76, 106–7, 130, 170, 194–5, 197, 223
Browning, Millie, 20, 22, 120–1, 152–3, 156, 183–6
Browning women: Louise concocts story about, 8, 20–1, 22, 29, 50–1, 205; supposed meetings with Louise, 120–3, 124–6, 155–61, 182, 199–200; alleged hand-over of Manfred, 20–1, 131–3, 134–7, 170–1, 200–1; seen on omnibus, 42–4, 229–31; seen at Dalston Junction, 45, 56–7, 229; as baby farmers, 224
Bruce, Sir Gainsford (Mr Justice): tries Masset case, 11; delayed attending fourth day of trial, 20; brushes aside jury complaints, 22–3; hears arguments for recall of witness, 183–5; summing-up, 25–7, 190–206; disallows further questions from jury, 27, 206; passes sentence of death, 207; trial notes, 85n; criticised by Newton, 224; writes to Home Office, 53n, 54
Bucknill and Co. (Brighton solicitors), 40, 41
Bunday, David, 4; evidence at trial, 101–2
Burch, Detective Sergeant William: at crime scene, 111–12; circulates description of body, 5; takes statement from Nellie Gentle, 76; keeps watch on 29 Bethune Road, 7, 111; pursues Simes and Cadisch, 7; takes statement from Louise Masset, 8, 111, 205; arrests Louise, 8; takes possession of clinker brick, 102; takes possession of toy scales, 216; evidence at police court, 215–16; questioned by Louise, 157; evidence at trial, 111–12
Burchatt, Albert H.G., 33–4, 243–6

Cadisch, Léonie (*née* Masset; Louise's sister): Louise moves in with, 1, 36, 119; acts as guarantor, 54, 118; attitude to Manfred's illegitimacy, 9, 54–5; Louise lies to about going to France, 70–1, 78, 162–3, 164–5, 175–6, 198; evidence at trial, 77–9; as witness, 13, 51; petitions for reprieve, 33, 242
Cadisch, Richard (Louise's brother-in-law): pursued by police, 7; evidence at inquest, 16n; evidence at trial, 108; petitions for reprieve, 33, 242
child murder, 37n, 54, 56 *see also* baby-farming
Clifford, Maud: evidence at police court, 221–3; evidence at trial, 79–80; as witness, 13, 163–4, 194
clinker brick: found at crime scene, 100, 102, 111; used to inflict Manfred's injuries, 18, 114, 192–3; similar bricks at Bethune Road, 13, 78, 79; possibly carried in

253

# Index.

Gladstone bag, 29, 130; police enquiries, 113; Louise Masset's evidence, 166; petition arguments, 221
clues *see* brown paper parcel; clinker brick; shawl; toy scales
Clyde Road (No 210), Tottenham, 72–3, 145
Coleridge, Lord: defence counsel, 11; cross-examinations: Léonie Cadisch, 13, 79; Ellen Reece, 15, 87–97; Nellie Gentle, 186; examinations: Louise Masset, 118–44; re-examinations: Dr Fennell, 117; Louise Masset, 180–3; opposes recall of Nellie Gentle, 184–5; closing speech for the defence, 23–4, 25, 26, 188–90; letter to Home Office, 36–7
Collinson, Joseph, 232–3
committal hearings, North London Police Court: Louise unrepresented, 144; evidence of Detective Inspector Forth, 10; evidence of Detective Sergeant Burch, 157, 215–16; evidence of Ellen Reece, 88–9, 217–20; evidence of Maud Clifford, 221–3; Louise warranted for trial, 9, 217
coroner's court *see* Hackney coroner's court
Court, Henry: evidence at trial, 106
criminal appeal system, 46
Criminal Evidence Act 1898, 28–9
Crippen, Hawley Harvey, 38

*Daily Chronicle*: on Masset trial, 31–2; petition from France, 39, 231; public opinion on case, 39–40, 232–3; publicises new witness evidence, 40–1, 229–31; calls for reconsideration of case, 44–5; claims Teahan evidence kept back at trial, 45, 56–7; 'Miss Masset and the Nurse' (4 January 1900), 227–8
*Daily Mail*, 4–5
*Daily News* (London), 32, 45–6, 48–9, 251
*Daily Telegraph*, 14, 16, 17, 19, 22
Dalston Junction Railway Station: ladies' waiting room and closets, 18, 101–2, 117; Manfred's body found, 4, 16, 99–101, 191; murder scene, 17, 114–15; Browning women seen at, 45, 56–7, 229; police enquiries, 236; route from London Bridge to Dalston, 171; train and travel times, 100, 101, 102, 107, 113, 192; use of station by Louise Masset, 51, 147–8, 171, 180–2
Dalston Police Station: Louise Masset charged, 8–9, 111, 113; identification parade, 15, 87, 94–6, 98, 107, 112–14
*Derby Daily Telegraph*, 44
Digby, Sir Kenelm, 235
Dougal, Samuel Herbert, 38
Drake, Sarah, 56
Dyer, Amelia, 24n

*Echo* (newspaper), 46–8
Edmunds, Christiana, 33n
*Evening News* (London), 7, 76–7, 142–3, 178, 202; 'Dalston Murder' (30 October 1899), 214–15
*Evening Standard* (London), 7, 11, 13, 28–30

Felstead, S. T., *Sir Richard Muir: A Memoir of a Public Prosecutor*, 53–4, 56
Fennell, Dr James: examines body at scene, 4, 17, 114–15; post mortem on Manfred, 17–18, 115–16; evidence at trial, 114–16, 117; as witness, 191
Findlay, John, 12; evidence at trial, 106
Findlay's Hotel, Brighton, 3–4, 12, 21, 103, 104, 105–6, 139–40, 173–4, 197
Fitzgerald, Marion, 97; evidence at trial, 114
Fordham, Mr Edward (magistrate), 9, 32–3, 227–8
Forth, Detective Inspector Frederick: circulates description of body, 5; keeps watch on 29 Bethune Road, 7, 107; accompanies Louise Masset to mortuary, 10, 113; at identification parade, 15, 95–6; crime scene experiments, 18, 117; brought into court to be identified, 95; evidence at trial, 112–13, 117; and Hughes-Ellis witness evidence, 42, 43, 230
*Fronde, La* (journal), 38, 231

Gentle, Eleanor Eliza ('Nellie'): takes Manfred as nurse-child, 2, 73, 118, 144–5; visits from his mother, 2, 73–4, 77, 119–20, 124, 125–6, 128; and Manfred's playmates, 153, 154, 183–6; given notice of Manfred leaving, 2–3, 127–8, 161; final parting from Manfred, 3, 74–5; reads of discovery of child's body, 4–5, 76–7; identifies Manfred at mortuary, 5, 43, 76, 214–15; statement to police, 6, 76; testimonial letter from Louise, 5, 75–6, 176–7, 211; evidence at trial, 72–7, 185–6; as witness, 9, 12–13, 157–8, 159; survivor guilt, 9–10; applicant at police court, 32–3, 227–8; returns to

# Index.

childcare work, 33
*Globe, The*, 30
Gould, Lucy, 37 & n, 56
Gull, Sir William, 33n
Gurney Winter, W., 40–1, 43–4

Haas, Clara, 15, 36, 142–3, 146, 159, 177; evidence at trial, 99
Hackney coroner's court, 9, 10, 11, 217
Hackney mortuary, 5, 10, 13, 43, 76, 113, 179, 214–15
haircuts for infant boys, 3n
Hall, Thomas: evidence at trial, 100
Highgate Hill (No. 17), Holloway, 1&n
Home Office: letter from Lord Coleridge, 36–7; petitions against Masset verdict, 33, 39, 44, 225n, 239–41; and new witness evidence, 41, 44, 57–9; called to reconsider case, 44–5; mysterious letter addressed to Louise Masset, 235, 237
Hughes-Ellis, John, 42–4, 45, 58, 229–31
Humphreys, Sergeant Frederick: evidence at trial, 72
Hutton, Arthur, 11, 202, 205

infanticide, 37 & n, 54, 56 *see also* baby-farming
inquest (into death of Manfred Masset), 9–11, 16n, 217

Jackman, Charles Howard, 17–18, 19n; evidence at trial, 116–17

King's Road (No 45), Chelsea, 112

Lee, John, 47n
Lewis, William, 57, 58, 59
life expectancy of working men, 58
*Lincolnshire Chronicle*, 23–4
*Lloyd's Weekly Newspaper*, 9–10, 22–3, 26–8, 54
London Bridge Railway Station: lost property office, 106; number of people using lavatory and closets, 51, 91–2; refreshment room, 97, 114, 135–6; route to Dalston Junction, 171; train times, 112; waiting rooms and lavatory facilities, 81n, 90–1
Loudoun Road Railway Station, 146–7
Lucas, Eudore: takes lodgings in Bethune Road, 2, 145; appearance and character, 16; relationship with Louise, 12, 16–17, 21–2, 102–3, 127, 129, 148–52; delays return to France, 149–50; weekend with Louise in Brighton, 3–4, 16, 104–5, 165, 174; evidence at trial, 102–5; as witness, 198

magistrates' hearings *see* committal hearings
Mansfield, Percival James, 33
Mason, Maurice (Manfred's father): shadowy figure, 1; financial commitments to Louise, 36, 38, 54; returns to France, 145–6; letters apparently from Louise, 34–5, 38, 247–8; Louise makes excuses about, 2, 128; interviewed by Newton, 246–7, 248
Masset, Elizabeth (Louise's mother) *see* Armstrong, Elizabeth
Masset, Ernest Etienne (Louise's father), 1n
Masset, Léonie (Louise's sister) *see* Cadisch, Léonie
**MASSET, LOUISE:**
**Before the trial:** family history of insanity, 33, 243–6; family background, 1n; as governess, 1, 36, 99, 108, 118, 146, 159; birth of Manfred, 1; family's shame and embarrassment, 9, 54–5; places Manfred under care of Nellie Gentle, 2, 73, 118, 144–5; moves in with sister Léonie, 1, 36, 119; visits Manfred, 2, 73–4, 77, 119–20, 124, 125–6, 128, 152; relationship with Eudore Lucas, 12, 16–17, 21–2, 102–3, 127, 129, 148–52; illness and death of stepfather, 78, 120, 246; relationship with Manfred's father, 246–7; letters apparently sent to Manfred's father, 34–5, 38, 247–8; supposed meetings with Browning women, 120–3, 124–6, 155–61, 182, 199–200; and Manfred's playmates, 152–5, 184; writes to Mrs Norris terminating care arrangement, 2–3, 127–8, 161; departure arrangements, 3, 128, 162, 164, 182–3; buys shawl, 13, 79–80, 163–4; plans trip to Brighton with Lucas, 165; makes up story of going to France, 70–1, 78, 140–1, 162–3, 164–5, 183, 198; leaves house on morning of murder, 166; travels with Manfred to London Bridge, 3, 52–3, 81, 129–30, 167; at London Bridge in afternoon, 13–14, 15, 81–5, 130–1, 133–4, 167–9; allegedly hands over Manfred, 20–1, 131–3, 134–7, 170–1, 200–1; familiarity with Dalston Junction Station, 51, 147–8, 171,

# Index.

180–2; whereabouts uncertain, 197–8; as murderer, 50–3; returns to London Bridge after murder, 171–2; at London Bridge in evening, 15, 85–7, 172, 196–7; travels to Brighton, 56, 137, 172, 173; at Brighton, 137–40, 172–5; checks in at Findlay's Hotel, 21, 105, 173, 197; disposes of parcel at Brighton Station, 6, 30, 52, 194–5; weekend with Lucas, 3–4, 16, 104–6, 165, 174; returns to London, 4, 16–17, 104, 140; keeps up deception, 175–6; writes testimonial letter for Nellie Gentle, 5, 75–6, 176–7, 211; attends teaching appointments as usual, 4, 7, 15, 141–3, 177; composure, 51, 177; reads newspaper accounts of murder in Dalston, 7, 142–3, 177–9, 202; unaccounted hours, 53; goes to sister's house in Croydon, 8, 109, 110, 143–4, 179, 203–4, 223; concocts story about Browning women, 8; fails to provide full details about the Brownings, 20, 179–80, 204–5; first statement to police, 8, 111, 112, 204–5; arrested and charged at Dalston Police Station, 8–9, 111, 113; picked out in identification parade, 15, 80, 87, 94–6, 98, 107, 112–14; committal hearings (*see* committal hearings); at inquest into death of Manfred, 9–10; hostile reception outside coroner's court, 11, 217; views Manfred at mortuary, 10, 113, 217; charged with wilful murder, 9; Old Bailey trial (*see* trial)

**After the trial:** date fixed for execution, 28; waxwork at Madame Tussaud's, 32; first petition for reprieve rejected, 33; Mutton's Restaurant alibi, 40–2, 51, 232; new witness evidence, 42–4, 45, 56–7, 229–31; mysterious letter, 235–8; second petition for reprieve rejected, 44, 240; last hours, 47; confession, 48, 49, 53; executed, 46–8; post mortem and burial, 49; press reaction to execution, 49, 251; financial situation, 35–8, 54; on her mental and moral condition, 34, 244; motive for murder, 23, 28–9, 32, 35–8, 188, 189, 221, 239; as child murderer, 54; perceived heartlessness, 55–6

Masset, Manfred Louis: birth, 1; placed under care of Nellie Gentle, 2, 73, 118, 144–5; circumcised, 5n, 73; visited by mother, 2, 73–4, 77, 119–20, 124, 126, 128, 152; illness and operations, 77, 119; and playmates, 152–5, 183–5; temperament, 119; talks in common unrefined way, 20, 121–2; dislike of trains, 125; frets at leaving Norrises, 128, 162; final parting from Nellie, 3, 74–5; travels with mother to London Bridge, 3, 52–3, 81, 129–30, 167; appearance and clothes worn by, 5, 6, 75; last seen at London Bridge Station, 13–14, 15, 81–5, 133–4, 168–9; allegedly handed-over to Browning women, 20–1, 131–3, 134–7, 170–1, 200–1; body discovered, 4, 16, 99–101, 191; murder scene, 4, 17, 114–15; description circulated to press, 5; post mortem, 17–18, 115–16; time of death, 18, 114, 116–17, 191–2; body identified at mortuary, 5, 13, 43, 76, 214–15; body viewed by mother, 10, 113, 217; inquest into death, 9–11, 217

Masset, Mathilde (Louise's sister) *see* Simes, Mathilde

Mathews, Charles, 22; prosecution counsel, 11; opening speech, 12, 69–72; examinations: Ellen Reece, 83–7, 97–9; Nellie Gentle, 185–6; cross-examinations: Dr Fennell, 117; Louise Masset, 144–80; requests recall of Nellie Gentle, 183–5; closing speech, 23, 24–5, 26, 187–8; criticised, 232

McIlroy's drapery shop, Stoke Newington, 13, 79–80, 163–4, 222

Metcalfe, Frederick Kynaston, 47, 48, 49

Millie (Manfred's playmate) *see* Browning, Millie

Milman, Colonel Everard (Governor of Newgate Prison), 47, 48, 237

Mooney, Ernest Hopkins, 13; evidence at trial, 80–1

*Morning Leader*, 42

*Morning Post*, 10

mortuary *see* Hackney mortuary

mourning dress, 58, 96

Muir, Richard, 11, 216

Murdoch, Charles, 36–7, 57, 225n, 235

Mutton, Vincent, 40, 41, 45

Mutton's Restaurant, Brighton, 21, 40–2, 45, 137–8, 173, 232

Newgate Prison, 46–8, 49, 237

Newton, Arthur: represents Louise at inquest, 10, 11; apprised of the name Browning, 20,

256

# Index.

180; submits first petition (30 December 1899), 33, 37, 213–25; and Hughes-Ellis evidence, 43; and Mutton's Restaurant alibi, 42; presents Mme Téry's petition (4 January 1900), 38–9; and Mary Teahan's disclosure, 57; interviews Manfred's father in France, 246–7, 248; forwards relatives' petition to the Home Office (8 January 1900), 33, 239, 241; possibly fabricates evidence in Masset case, 38, 248n; misconduct as solicitor, 38; notified of Home Secretary's final decision, 44, 240; campaigning strategy faulted, 58

Norris, Mrs Sarah (*formerly* Gentle; Nellie's mother), 2–3, 74, 162, 164, 176, 211

North London Police Court: committal hearings, 9, 10, 88–9, 144, 157, 215–20, 221–3; application from Nellie Gentle, 32–3, 227–8

*Northampton Mercury,* 24–5

Nursey, Detective Sergeant Richard: parcel clue, 6, 106–7; keeps watch on 29 Bethune Road, 7, 107, 108; interviews Ellen Reece, 92–4, 98, 107; evidence at trial, 106–8; investigates mysterious letter, 236

Old Bailey, 11, 14, 19 *see also* trial
Osborne House, 39

*Pall Mall Gazette,* 1, 9, 31
parcel clue *see* brown paper parcel
Patmore, PC James: evidence at trial, 102
petitions for reprieve: Newton's petition (30 December 1899), 33, 37, 213–25; petition from France (January 4 1900), 38–9, 231; relatives' petition (8 January 1900), 33–5, 37–8, 44, 239–49
Philip Lane, Tottenham, 121, 154
police court *see* North London Police Court

Ramsay, Mr Alexander, 48, 53, 239
Rattenbury, Alma, 4n
Reece, Ellen: as witness, 14–15, 50, 133–4, 168–9, 172, 196–7; interviewed by police, 92–4, 98, 107; picks out Louise in identification parade, 15, 87, 94–6, 98, 107, 112–14; evidence at police court, 88–9, 217–20; evidence at trial, 83–99
Reffell, Elizabeth Rebecca (Louise's mother) *see* Armstrong, Elizabeth
Riall, Alice, 21, 51, 197; evidence at trial, 105–6
Ridley, Sir Matthew White (Home Secretary), 36, 44, 45–6, 49

Scott, Dr James, 48, 49, 239
shawl, 13, 55, 79–81, 163–4, 193–4, 221–3
Simes, George (Louise's brother-in-law): Louise calls on in distressed state, 8, 109, 110, 143–4, 179, 203–4, 223; pursued and questioned by police, 7–8, 109; advises Louise to remain silent when charged, 113, 204; tries to keep family names out of court proceedings, 9, 54; evidence at trial, 109–11; demands return of Manfred's belongings from Nellie Gentle, 32; petitions for reprieve, 33, 242
Simes, Mathilde (*née* Masset; Louise's sister), 7, 33, 242
Skeet, Ann, 6; evidence at trial, 106
Smith, Bovill William, 11
Sommer, Celestina, 37n
Sonnenthal, Alice, 36, 142–3, 146, 159, 177, 181; evidence at trial, 108
Standing, Joseph, 4, 236; evidence at trial, 100–1
Stoke Newington, 1
Stoner, George, 4n
Streeter, Henry James, 40–1
Stretton Road, Croydon, 7–8, 179
Swaker, Kate: evidence at trial, 82

Taylor, David, 44, 45
Taylorson, Frederick, 38, 41–2
Teahan, Mary: finds body of Manfred, 4, 16; statement to police, 16; sighting of two women at Dalston Junction, 45, 56–7, 229; evidence at trial, 99–100; disclosure ignored at trial, 45, 57, 59; as witness, 178, 191; Home Office enquiry into new evidence, 57–9
Téry, Madame Andrée, 38–9, 231
*Times, The,* 30–1, 32, 69–72, 187–90
Tottenham Green, 2, 20, 73, 77, 113, 119–20, 152, 184–6
toy scales, 3, 12, 21, 52, 75, 76, 106, 139, 164, 169–70, 216
trial: bench and legal teams, 11; public interest and attendance, 11, 14, 17, 19; atmosphere in court, 19; arraignment and plea, 11, 69; Louise's appearance and demeanour in court, 11–12, 14, 19–20, 22,

# Index.

24, 56; opening speech for the prosecution, 12, 69–72; first day, 69–82; second day, 83–108; third day, 109–32; fourth day, 133–86; fifth day, 187–207; Louise Masset gives evidence, 118–83; closing speech for the prosecution, 23, 24–5, 26, 187–8; closing speech for the defence, 23–4, 25, 26, 188–90; judge's summing-up, 25–7, 190–206; further questions from jury disallowed, 27, 206; verdict and sentence, 27, 206–7; Louise's reaction to sentence, 27–8; court reports, 14, 16, 17, 19, 23–8; press coverage in aftermath, 28–32; public response to trial, 232–3; criticism of trial judge, 224

Tussaud, Madame (waxworks), 32

Victoria, Queen, 1, 39, 56

Warbrick, William, 48
*Weekly News, The*, 48
Westcott, William (coroner), 217
*Western Mail*, 11–12
Weston, Superintendent Frederick, 236
Whittle, John: evidence at trial, 112
Willis, Henry: evidence at trial, 112
*Worcestershire Chronicle*, 25–6
Worley, Georgina, 13–14, 51, 130, 167; evidence at trial, 81–2
Wyeth, Daniel, 33, 243–4
Wyeth, Elizabeth, 33, 243

# NOTABLE BRITISH TRIALS SERIES.

| Trial | Date of Trial(s) | Editor(s) | Volume No. |
|---|---|---|---|
| Mary Queen of Scots | 1586 | A. Francis Steuart | 30 |
| Guy Fawkes | 1605-1606 | Donald Carswell | 61 |
| King Charles I | 1649 | J. G. Muddiman | 43 |
| The Bloody Assizes | 1685 | J. G. Muddiman | 48 |
| Captain Kidd | 1701 | Graham Brooks | 51 |
| Jack Sheppard | 1724 | Horace Bleackley | 59 |
| Captain Porteous | 1736 | William Roughead | 9 |
| The Annesley Case | 1743 | Andrew Lang | 16 |
| Lord Lovat | 1747 | David N. Mackay | 14 |
| Mary Blandy | 1752 | William Roughead | 22 |
| James Stewart | 1752 | David N. Mackay | 6 |
| Eugene Aram | 1759 | Eric R. Watson | 19 |
| Katherine Nairn | 1765 | William Roughead | 38 |
| The Douglas Cause | 1761-1769 | A. Francis Steuart | 8 |
| Duchess of Kingston | 1776 | Lewis Melville | 42 |
| Deacon Brodie | 1788 | William Roughead | 5 |
| The 'Bounty' Mutineers | 1792 | Owen Rutter | 55 |
| Abraham Thornton | 1817 | Sir John Hall, Bt. | 37 |
| Henry Fauntleroy | 1824 | Horace Bleackley | 34 |
| Thurtell and Hunt | 1824 | Eric R. Watson | 26 |
| Burke and Hare | 1828 | William Roughead | 27 |
| James Blomfield Rush | 1849 | W. Teignmouth Shore | 45 |
| William Palmer | 1856 | Eric R. Watson | 15 |
| Madeleine Smith | 1857 | A. Duncan Smith (first edition) | |
| | | F. Tennyson Jesse (second edition) | 1 |
| Dr Smethurst | 1859 | L. A. Parry | 53 |
| Mrs M'Lachlan | 1862 | William Roughead | 12 |
| Franz Müller | 1864 | H. B. Irving | 13 |
| Dr Pritchard | 1865 | William Roughead | 3 |
| The Wainwrights | 1875 | H. B. Irving | 25 |
| The Stauntons | 1877 | J. B. Atlay | 11 |
| Eugène Marie Chantrelle | 1878 | A. Duncan Smith | 4 |
| Kate Webster | 1879 | Elliott O'Donnell | 35 |

# Notable British Trials Series.

| | | | |
|---|---|---|---|
| City of Glasgow Bank Directors | 1879 | William Wallace | 2 |
| Charles Peace | 1879 | W. Teignmouth Shore | 39 |
| Dr Lamson | 1882 | H. L. Adam | 18 |
| Adelaide Bartlett | 1886 | Sir John Hall, Bt. | 41 |
| Israel Lipski* | 1887 | M. W. Oldridge | 84 |
| Mrs Maybrick | 1889 | H. B. Irving | 17 |
| John Watson Laurie | 1889 | William Roughead | 57 |
| The Baccarat Case | 1891 | W. Teignmouth Shore | 56 |
| Thomas Neill Cream | 1892 | W. Teignmouth Shore | 31 |
| Alfred John Monson | 1893 | J. W. More | 7 |
| Oscar Wilde | 1895 | H. Montgomery Hyde | 70 |
| Louise Masset* | 1899 | Kate Clarke | 85 |
| William Gardiner | 1903 | William Henderson | 63 |
| George Chapman | 1903 | H. L. Adam | 50 |
| Samuel Herbert Dougal | 1903 | F. Tennyson Jesse | 44 |
| The 'Veronica' Mutineers | 1903 | Prof. G. W. Keeton and John Cameron | 76 |
| Adolf Beck | 1904 | Eric R. Watson | 33 |
| Robert Wood | 1907 | Basil Hogarth | 65 |
| Oscar Slater | 1909-1928 | William Roughead | 10 |
| Hawley Harvey Crippen | 1910 | Filson Young | 24 |
| John Alexander Dickman | 1910 | S. O. Rowan-Hamilton | 21 |
| Steinie Morrison | 1911 | H. Fletcher Moulton | 28 |
| The Seddons | 1912 | Filson Young | 20 |
| George Joseph Smith | 1915 | Eric R. Watson | 29 |
| Sir Roger Casement | 1916 | George H. Knott (first and second editions) | |
| | | H. Montgomery Hyde (third edition) | 23 |
| Harold Greenwood | 1920 | Winifred Duke | 52 |
| Field and Gray | 1920 | Winifred Duke | 67 |
| Bywaters and Thompson | 1922 | Filson Young | 32 |
| Ronald True | 1922 | Donald Carswell | 36 |
| Herbert Rowse Armstrong | 1922 | Filson Young | 40 |
| Jean Pierre Vaquier | 1924 | R. H. Blundell | 47 |
| John Donald Merrett | 1927 | William Roughead | 46 |
| Browne and Kennedy | 1927 | W. Teignmouth Shore | 49 |
| Benjamin Knowles | 1928 | Albert Lieck | 60 |
| Sidney Harry Fox | 1930 | F. Tennyson Jesse | 62 |
| Alfred Arthur Rouse | 1931 | Helena Normanton | 54 |

# Notable British Trials Series.

| | | | |
|---|---|---|---|
| The Royal Mail Case | 1931 | Collin Brooks | 58 |
| Jeannie Donald | 1934 | J. G. Wilson | 79 |
| Rattenbury and Stoner | 1935 | F. Tennyson Jesse | 64 |
| Buck Ruxton | 1936 | Prof. H. Wilson | 66 |
| Frederick Nodder | 1937 | Winifred Duke | 72 |
| Patrick Carraher | 1938-1946 | George Blake | 73 |
| Peter Barnes and Others | 1939 | Letitia Fairfield | 77 |
| August Sangret | 1943 | MacDonald Critchley | 83 |
| William Joyce | 1945 | J. W. Hall | 68 |
| Neville George Cleveley Heath | 1946 | MacDonald Critchley | 75 |
| Ley and Smith | 1947 | F. Tennyson Jesse | 69 |
| James Camb | 1948 | G. Clark | 71 |
| Peter Griffiths | 1948 | George Godwin | 74 |
| John George Haigh | 1949 | Lord Dunboyne | 78 |
| Evans and Christie | 1950 & 1953 | F. Tennyson Jesse | 82 |
| John Thomas Straffen | 1952 | Letitia Fairfield and Eric P. Fullbrook | 80 |
| Craig and Bentley | 1952 | H. Montgomery Hyde | 81 |

\* New series.

In preparation:
No. 86: Percy Lefroy Mapleton (ed. Adam Wood)
No. 87: John Selby Watson (ed. Molly Whittington-Egan)

www.ingramcontent.com/pod-product-compliance
Lightning Source LLC
Chambersburg PA
CBHW051039160426
43193CB00010B/1006